In this rigorously researched book, based on 600 detailed interviews with women and some men across India's metros, social scientist Deepa Narayan identifies seven key habits that dominate women's everyday lives, despite their education, success, financial status and family background.

Shocking, troubling and revolutionary, *Chup* will hold a mirror to yourself – and you may not like what you see.

A Note on the Author

Dr Deepa Narayan is an international poverty, gender and development adviser who has worked at the World Bank, the United Nations and in the non-governmental sector. She was senior adviser in the Poverty Reduction and Economic Management group of the World Bank from 2003 to 2008. Her groundbreaking *Voices of the Poor* studies brought together the experiences of 60,000 poor women and men from 60 countries to re-examine our core assumptions about the experience of poverty. In 2011, *Foreign Policy* magazine named Dr Narayan one of 100 most influential global thinkers. *India Today* named Dr Narayan one of India's 35 Great Thinkers. She has authored or co-authored seventeen books.

Chup

Breaking the Silence About India's Women

Deepa Narayan

JUGGERNAUT BOOKS
KS House, 118 Shahpur Jat, New Delhi 110049, India

First published in hardback by Juggernaut Books 2018
Published in paperback 2019

10 9 8 7 6 5 4 3 2 1

The views and opinions expressed in this book are the author's own. The facts contained herein were reported to be true as on the date of publication by the author to the publishers of the book, and the publishers are not in any way liable for their accuracy or veracity.

ISBN 9788193876725

Typeset in Adobe Caslon Pro by Manmohan Kumar, New Delhi

Printed at Manipal Technologies Limited Manipal

To my father, Surendra Narayan, who passed away just before this book was published. And who said to me so many times, 'In my next life I want to be born a woman,' to make up for taking his privileges as a man for granted.

And to Jyoti Singh and all women who pay the price for being women and still don't keep *chup*.

Contents

Author's Note

I did not set out to do research or to write a book. Having written seventeen books on poverty policies and poor people's empowerment published by the World Bank and academic presses, I had decided not to write any more. But this book forced itself upon me. It emerged from my determination not to be complacent after the rape of Jyoti Singh, or Nirbhaya. The brutality of the rape, the public outrage, the non-stop news coverage and the fact that it happened in my Delhi shook me, like millions of others, to the core. The public debate focused on law and order and the police and to a much lesser extent on the issue of culture.

As a trained social scientist I decided to turn to the cultural question. But culture is a big idea. What is it about a culture that can explain both rape and everyday sexism? The question began to obsess me. I was invited to give talks on poverty and development in Delhi, and I said I would go if I could explore the gender question. As I talked to young women and men at the renowned St Stephen's College in Delhi one afternoon, I was startled by what I heard. One young woman said her seven-year-old niece, who loves chocolates, gave her only piece of chocolate, without being asked, to her nine-year-old cousin brother when he demanded more than his share. The reverse never happened. Nor was it expected. The definitions of a woman given by some of the brightest male and female students dripped with words like 'nice, caring, compromising'.

After what I heard from women and men at St Stephen's, I went to Gargi College, Lady Shri Ram College and Amity University. And then one more college. And so it continued. I could not stop. I also met women and men in their homes, in cafes, in universities, in malls, in offices, in airports and in parks. I met women, men and children living mostly in Delhi, but also in Bengaluru, Mumbai and Ahmedabad. I was surprised by what I heard from women who were competent, educated, gender aware and often fighting for gender rights. Often men seemed less conservative, until the discussion turned to what a couple should do after the birth of children. I met young people in slums. I met Indian students and women of Indian origin in Seattle, Cambridge, Massachusetts, and New York. Sometimes it seemed that only their clothes had changed.

What I heard women saying was disturbing. Over and over I would shake my head in disbelief that yet another smart and smartly dressed woman, an artist, a business manager, a financial analyst, a professor, a dentist, an engineer, a lawyer, a researcher, a scientist, a teacher, an educated stay-at-home mom was so unsure of herself. Or that she sounded, after the obligatory gender equality claims and sometimes passionate lecture, like her mother would have sounded thirty or forty years ago.

As unexpected inner realities unfolded, I became aware that I had taken on too much. I decided to focus on trying to make sense of women's complex lives, and I stopped interviewing men after fifty in-depth interviews to give me a comparison. This was a difficult decision. We do need a book on men, on their inner lives, thoughts, confusions, hesitations and burdens.

I also decided to focus on younger women, between the ages of 17 and 35, because every time I spoke to someone or saw a discussion on television, people asserted that young women today are 'modern' and are very different from the past generations. I did not want my findings to be dismissed because the women I interviewed belonged to an older generation. Of course there have been changes. But the outer changes may have just camouflaged what has not changed. Sex ratios at birth or child sex ratios have worsened since Independence even as incomes have gone up. Female fetuses and girls 0–6 years old are still being killed or dying in large numbers.

It became obvious that I needed a team. I developed an interview guide using a methodology similar to the approach I followed in conducting the *Voices of the Poor* study, which involved 60,000 people in sixty countries, while I was at the World Bank in Washington, DC. I wasn't interested in abstractions or in how women and men *should* behave, but how women and men actually behave in their everyday life. And so I used open-ended questions that do not suggest any answers. Such research does not yield numbers or percentages, but throws up patterns of behaviour and beliefs that you did not know existed. Only very occasionally did I count the number of times something was mentioned. In this more open-ended context the researcher becomes a deep, empathetic, non-judgemental listener.

I trained six women from the middle and upper classes living in different parts of Delhi, and they conducted interviews in different geographic areas based on a simple sampling plan to contact women who fit certain age and income demographic criteria. In all, we conducted 600 interviews with women, men and schoolchildren in Delhi and some other metros. I have changed names and occasionally key identifying details to protect the women who trusted us enough to speak to us.

I ended up with approximately 8000 pages of notes from interviews with highly educated women in the cities. I took an inductive approach, letting the data speak to me, reading and rereading interviews and systematically aggregating data into larger and larger analytical groupings. I also used text analysis and searched for keywords. It takes time and patience to detect patterns. I trained new researchers who had not done any of the interviews to analyse them, to search and categorize the same data independently so as to minimize interpretation errors. This took another half-year.

As I analysed the interviews and read and reread them, the power of cultural habits, emotions and morality over education and the rational intellect pierced through the reams of documentation. There is a wide gap between our intellectual beliefs and our actual behaviour. This book is about the power of everyday culture over the intellect. It is about the all-pervasive cultural indoctrination that starts with childhood and prepares women to be deleted and then enrols women to delete themselves as well as other women, all without their conscious awareness.

The old explanation for gender inequality is patriarchy. This concept serves to highlight systemic bias against women, but it has been so overused it has become flaccid – it merely stops conversation and therefore action. In addition it blames men, without whose participation change in gender relations cannot happen. We need new ideas.

There was much I did not know when I started this inquiry. I had not foreseen the deep emotional impact the interviews would have on my team and me. It was cumulative. It crept up on us. Young women doing the interviews started telling me that listening to women's stories was stirring up trouble in their own psyches. Nor had I foreseen the torrent of emotions talking would release in women being interviewed. I had been afraid women would have no patience for the interviews, but instead they started thanking us for letting them talk about issues they had kept bottled up. It was like witnessing the breaking of dams. In the absence of any judgement, the interview process became a safe emotional space. My researchers wrote their own stories. Some continued over several months. I offered support based on my experience in leading groups in emotional literacy. Mostly I just listened. It started affecting me as well, stirring up my memories.

I scoured the extensive research literature from India and the USA, some of which is referenced at the end of the book. Despite many good departments of psychology, social sciences and management in India, most of the behavioural studies on gender differences are from the USA; the few published behavioural studies on women and men in the middle and upper classes in India focus on buying behaviour. It is clear that the behaviours of educated American women are very similar to those of educated Indian women in cities, a remarkable fact given the different histories of the countries. Government National Family Health Surveys, census data, crime statistics and surveys by non-governmental organizations provide most of the Indian statistics used in this book.

My approach to reporting on research in this book is not academic. Rather I tell stories that reveal patterns. I focus on the everyday behavioural details in the hope that both women and men will be able to see themselves and hear their own voices or the voices of their families and colleagues.

A word about the definition of the middle class, although we could argue about it forever. Everyone in India likes to label themselves middle class even when they go on foreign holidays every year! In this book, I define the middle class as families earning 12–19 lakh rupees a year. I consider families earning 20 lakh rupees and more a year upper class. I focus on the educated middle- and upper-class people because these are the groups that can bring about change. I hope reading this book will change you, just as working on this book for the past several years has forced me to change.

Many men have asked me if this book is just for women. No. Since this book is primarily about *cultural systems*, it is as much for men as it is for women – the same cultural system that creates women also creates men, and intertwines their lives. We need to become cultural detectives. We need to share our dilemmas with other cultural creatures rather than hide alone or pretend not to see. We can be more creative collectively. We are after all in the land of jugaad. We need to invent new ways to change the unequal cultural world that resides inside and outside each one of us.

1

Introduction

The Making of a Woman

Meera, 25, sits across from me, leaning forward, in a meeting room at Harvard University, USA. She looks striking, in a black kurta, silver jewellery, a tribal shawl and with kajol lining her dark eyes. But she shares her life hesitantly, pausing to breathe, trying, as she says, 'not to cry'.

'I remember that deep sense of choking. In my family, as a child, I learned to observe too much, silent, listening. My mother is a good listener; not my father – he is very dogmatic, always strong opinions. My father is a liberal in his thoughts, "you are free to choose anything, it is your life" but "being a doctor is desirable". He is a doctor. There is a big disparity between how he thinks and how he lives. I wanted to study psychology, but it was forbidden. I went to medical school . . . it was my father's dream . . . It's very embarrassing . . . I ran away from medical college after three weeks. I was seventeen. I left all my things in the hostel. I felt. . . I had no other way . . . I was dying. I took a bus and then a train for two days and nights and landed in Chennai to go to college to study psychology – I got admission. . . but I had no place to stay. It was already evening, I had very little money, I saw these women at the bus stop, it was at Marina Beach. I started talking with them; baaton baaton mein, *by and by, I told them I was hungry. They gave me a beedi to smoke. I had no place to stay. I did not want them to know I was vulnerable, so I said I am on this research project and want to live with*

you to understand your ways. The women agreed on the condition that I would look after their children when they went out at night for dhandha, *sex work. They would pay me. I lived with them.'*

Meera is a Delhi girl. She grew up in Saket, New Delhi, with her dadi, chacha, bua and parents in a middle-class family that prospered with the opening up of the Indian economy.

But Meera also lived in a slum community with sex workers under a broken bridge for over a month before her many relatives arrived with the police. I ask her if she felt safe with the sex workers in the slum. She says, 'Most safe. The most secure I have ever felt. In my family we lived together but there was a rule of silence. Nothing was ever said. It was so hypocritical; we never were a family, just individuals living together. I grew up thinking unless my father sanctions my existence, I am not alive. I was always waiting for validation. If he said you are fine, I would be fine.'

Her existence was his reflection.

* * *

India is in the middle of an independence movement. For women. As the country marches forward with high economic growth rates, millions of women in the cities have come out of their homes. They go to colleges, universities, IITs and IIMs. They can be seen on the streets, in buses, metros, offices, malls, movie halls, coffee shops, pubs and in Parliament. They drive scooters, cars, airplanes and fighter jets. They are employed in large numbers. They are government officials, entrepreneurs, scientists and wrestlers. We thought that when women became educated, they would be valued, free and unafraid. They are not. We thought they would speak up. They don't. We thought that when women earn their own money, violence against them would stop. It has not. We thought that when laws change, and women have rights to property and maintenance after a divorce, they would become independent and safe. Women are still not safe.

While it is deeply satisfying to focus on the outer independence movement of women – we can count the changes – this approach is also deeply flawed. It is misleading and, worse, it is diversionary. Just because women are visible, it does not mean that they are not invisible at the same time. This focus on visible external change assumes that the cultural ideology that kept women invisible, and even denied women life itself, has evaporated. This assumption is wrong.

We are all cultural creatures. We are born naked. Our cultures sculpt us into becoming Indian or Sri Lankan or English or American. Living with our families in particular homes and in particular neighbourhoods, we absorb through osmosis our values, behaviours and characteristic ways of being and thinking. We inhale the dos and we exhale the don'ts. We absorb these cultural values early, unknowingly. They seep into our body, our mind, our morality and our spirit. They are our foundation. Our belonging. Our core. Our culture. Our compass.

And this invisible cultural compass leads to camouflage, contradictions, condemnation and even death. We worship goddesses, but we murder unborn girls by the hundreds of thousands. Our cultural compass is inside us and we take it everywhere we go, even when we leave India. The moral compass that guides us, usually without our awareness, can be distilled into our response to one core cultural question: *What does it mean to you to be a good woman or a good man?* The strength of this seemingly simple question is that it pushes people into going beyond 'enlightened', politically correct answers.

I asked this question for three years. After meeting students at the elite St Stephen's College, I asked this question of 600 women and men, young and old mostly in Delhi but also in Mumbai, Bengaluru and Ahmedabad. Again and again I was surprised by what I heard. I started asking women and men to write down their answers so it could not possibly be an issue of hearing wrong or misinterpretation. I thought maybe the next generation had changed. I spoke to younger and younger children. In many ways they were little echoes of their elders. I met young women and men from Greater Kailash, Moti Bagh, Khan Market, Aurangzeb Road, Rohini, Punjabi Bagh, Noida, Gurgaon and Ram Das Colony, the home of those accused of Nirbhaya's brutal gang rape in December 2012 in New Delhi. I could hardly see any links between what women said and their education, their wealth or where they lived.

In early February 2013, while New Delhi was in turmoil awaiting justice for Nirbhaya, two Supreme Court justices also in New Delhi ruled that killing a boy is worse than killing a girl. It was a small news item in the *Times of India*. Justices P. Sathasivam and J.S. Khehar, in a ruling that justified the death penalty for a man in the killing of a seven-year-old boy, wrote, 'The parents of the deceased had four children – three daughters and one son. Kidnapping the only male child was to induce maximum fear in the mind of his parents. Agony for parents for the loss of their male child, who would have carried further the family lineage, and is expected to see them through their old age, is unfathomable . . .' Higher valuation of boys, or one could say devaluation of girls, has been decreed by the Supreme Court of India.

This deeper cultural story touches all of us without our conscious knowledge, from Supreme Court judges to the local policeman to the male or female CEO, to each father and mother and son and daughter. The same culture that leads to violence against women also leads to fewer women in technology and leadership positions. It leads to talented young women being locked up at home for their own safety. It leads to educated women saying they are afraid to speak up. It leads to the seemingly harmless behaviour of women waiting for men to speak first while they listen. It leads to women feeling a bolt of raw fear when they see a group of men walking towards them.

A life lived in fear is an abbreviated life. It is a feeble life. Meera's story is in some ways extreme so we can see the fear patterning clearly. But fear and the search for physical and psychological safety – where women feel free to express themselves without fear of being laughed at, humiliated, demeaned, followed, threatened, punished, cut off, stalked, trolled or raped – shape the lives of many women.

Fear traumatizes. Fear truncates. Fear drains life. Women's fears keep society stable. It serves society but it costs women.

The statistics on acceptability of wife-beating have not changed dramatically. Even in Kerala, the state with the highest literacy rate in India, large numbers of women experience both physical and sexual violence. Clearly, education and income are important in their own right, but are not enough to change the cultural arithmetic that reduces women from a plus to a minus, to less than zero. This is not just an Indian problem, it is a universal problem. The World Health Organization (WHO) estimates that one in three women in the world experiences violence in her life, usually from an intimate male partner. Sexual violence and harassment are also widespread problems in the rich countries of the West including the USA, the UK and Sweden as evidenced in the #MeToo movement.

Based on the thousands of hours of listening to girls, boys, women and men, I offer one unifying idea that helps make sense of the hundreds of definitions of a good girl or a good woman and a good boy or a good man, our cultural and moral compass.

Our culture *trains women not to exist.*

Being a woman is itself taboo. Not allowed. Invisibility is just one manifestation of this cultural training. One way of ensuring that women do not exist is to kill them. A safer and less crude way is to train women to disappear. This helps explain the hundreds of ordinary, everyday behaviours, proverbs and admonishments that are part of a cultural morass that sucks us all in to perpetuate a culture of non-existence for women. The idea that women should simply not exist explains the deep and persistent inequality between women and men despite laws, education and wealth across many cultures. I focus on India, but the behavioural research reported in this book seems to indicate that the same forces are at work in the USA.

The culture of non-existence is kept in place generation after generation because nobody talks about it. It is a nameless cultural secret. It is so unpalatable that it is disguised and buried in the cultural morass; otherwise women would surely object. Instead what we see is hundreds of cultural practices that we learn so naturally growing up that hundreds of young women say, 'Ma'am, this is normal.' Why is it normal for young girls not to tell anyone that they have been sexually molested or for a girl not to be kick-ass strong or for a woman not to share her opinions in front of men?

The culture of non-existence gets locked into clusters of behaviours that women and men absorb through training. In isolation, these behaviours seem harmless, inoffensive, sweet and even morally virtuous. But in combination they destroy, they kill softly. These clusters of behaviours observed and repeated become the *habits* that define a good woman and a good man. I deliberately use the word habits, because habits are learned and can be changed. The focus on habits also makes the big idea of culture manageable. But these habits acquire great power because they become entangled with our notions of goodness. They become moral habits. Parents everywhere teach their girls and boys good habits, to make them good women and good men. Habits make our behaviour run on autopilot. Habits beat rationality. They become shortcuts to decision-making.

Drawing on the details of the lives of women and men I interviewed, each over several hours, I found that girls are trained in seven cultural habits of non-existence. These are deny the body; be quiet; please others; deny your sexuality; isolate yourself; have no individual identity; and be dependent. It is deep training in these habits that makes so many women feminists in belief but not in behaviour. Feminists with bad habits.

These habits are not personal. But each woman thinks she is alone, she is the only one, and so she hides. When ten women are apologetic it may be personal. But when hundreds and thousands of women are constantly afraid and apologetic, it is no longer personal. It is systemic. It has to do with the lack of power of a group that is not supposed to exist. When women can't speak up, blame themselves, despair and collapse and repeat the behaviour the next time, it serves cultural expectations. *An unequal culture survives on collapsed women.* It is political strategy. This collective problem cannot be solved through the escapes of individual women. It takes collective action, working together to change unequal cultural, economic and political systems.

In writing about these habits, I describe patterns of behaviour and tendencies. I do not constantly qualify, but please know that I do not mean 'every woman in New Delhi, Bengaluru, Mumbai or Ahmedabad' or 'all Indian women' or 'all men' all the time. It is cumbersome to constantly qualify. Readers will have to decide what patterns apply to them or women in their circles. Sometimes the patterns emerge more strongly at home and at other times in offices and sometimes most unexpectedly and occasionally not at all.

Many of the behaviours I write about have been portrayed in essays, in poems, in novels and most recently in films ranging from *Secret Superstar* to *Lipstick under My Burkha*. There are also inspiring books on divas and other women leaders who have won many awards. This book is different. In my book I take apart women's everyday behaviours that do not always make women look good. My reason is simple. Unless we understand the grip these behaviours have on us, we cannot change despite our intellectual beliefs. And our world will not change.

This book is about us. It is about women in the middle and upper classes. We need to talk about ourselves and not just 'them', those poor, uneducated and unfortunate women out there. We need to break our silence about our own lives. But silence too has cultural meaning.

Is silence a virtue or is silence betrayal?

I was taught that silence is a virtue. Silence is polite. Silence is good. Silence is spiritual. But there comes a time in one's life and in the life of a society when silence becomes betrayal. A betrayal of goodness. A betrayal of decency. It is time to end this silent betrayal now.

2

Body

Women Don't Have Bodies, *Besharam*

This is a glimpse into my family.

When I was a little girl, we never spoke about bodies, our bodies. There were eight of us in our middle-class family who lived together, five children, my parents and my grandfather. I didn't even get as far as seeing my mother's legs. They were always covered. We were always covered. I never saw my own body. When my sisters and I, all living in the same room, changed clothes, we would go into the tiny, bare, not-so-nice socialist bathroom or make the others leave the room, or, if someone refused, we would make them turn away with a promise not to look. Nahin dekho. *I never looked. I had trained myself early not to see.* Mat dekho, *don't look, was a frequent refrain.*

There was no touch in our family. No touching even when my two sisters and I slept in the same big double bed, which was two beds joined together. If we accidentally touched or brushed against each other in bed, we would groan, ooof oh, hato na, *move, and push the other away. I was 11 years old.*

Very simply, my body was not part of my life. I had been trained at a young age to forget my body. I left my body. And I kept moving, into twenty-seven homes, on many continents. I wanted to be a woman at ease with herself, at ease within her skin, at ease with her body, but ease evaded me, except in moments of total defiance. My body was there because it was attached to my head. I wasn't attached to it. And I was proud of my detachment. It was Indian and spiritually superior to be detached.

* * *

Years later, I wondered if women's relationships with their bodies had changed and whether society's views about women's bodies had changed. I found that despite brave words and dramatic external changes – more legs, more butts, more cleavage, more dresses, more beauty parlours, more gyms and more skimpily dressed women at parties, on billboards, television and in the films – women's fundamental relationship with their bodies has not changed over the decades. It is still as if 'it', the body, does not exist.

The Early Training: Deny That Girls Have Bodies

> *But we never spoke about it [the body] in our family.*
> Akansha, 24

No human can exist without a body. No girl can exist without a body. But when the central goal of raising girls is to ensure that they do not exist, there is a fundamental problem with having a body. Bodies, by their sheer physicality, become inconvenient evidence of women's existence. As in any good murder mystery, the central question becomes, what to do with the body? How to make the body disappear?

It emerges that many women, even the most educated, are uncomfortable with their bodies. Many say, 'I don't think of myself as a woman.' This dismissal of being a woman when discussing their physical bodies is problematic. It means that women have bought into the cultural denial that they have bodies. It is a reflection of three pervasive cultural practices that are so central in women's lives that they are rarely questioned. These are silence about the body, disguise the body and distance yourself from the body. These behaviours become normalized as values and habits. As many young women put it, 'Ma'am, it is my personality.' What they really mean is that denial of their body is a key part of their character as good women.

Don't talk about it

The collective pretence that good girls do not have bodies in the face of constant, contrary physical evidence is a huge cultural feat. The silence around a girl's body starts soon after birth. It is the physicality of the genitals that determines the midwife's cry announcing the birth of a boy or a girl. A baby penis is welcomed with relief and joy and a baby vagina, especially if it is after a few baby vaginas, is greeted with fear, despair, disappointment, anger, hate and blame. After this initial burst of nudity at birth, the body is covered by silence.

Secrets can only remain secret when nobody talks about them. A collective agreement between 1.3 billion people about girls' bodies is held in silence. If girls do not have bodies, terrible things can't happen to them, and if they do happen, they cannot be acknowledged. Don't see. Don't speak. Don't hear. The worst consequence is the silence around molestation and rape.

Sexual violence was only one of the fifty topics I discussed with women. But it became the most talked-about topic. I asked women about 'eve-teasing', a uniquely Indian phrase that camouflages an ugly reality. The phrase itself reflects the denial that women have bodies and insinuates that women are to blame. Eve, after all, is the original temptress who led to the fall of man in the Judaeo-Christian tradition.

The word 'teasing' in 'eve-teasing' makes the act of molestation acceptable. The common expression used for 'teasing' in Hindi is *chhera-chheri*, a word that women use to describe boys' general behaviour within the acceptable range. Many women said, '*Chhera-chheri toh chalti hi hai*, teasing happens,' implying its acceptance and normality and making the act of molestation sound like casual fun. Boys tease, after all, that is their nature, boys will be boys. The word is not abusing, baiting, exploiting, hating, harassing or molesting. And the name is not Sita, Indira or Radha. The name is Eve. And she is foreign. The name Eve helps create distance from our daily, immediate Indian context. I have not yet met an Indian woman named Eve. But somehow, we have adopted Eve and she is now well known all over India, even in small towns, even among non-English speakers.

I asked women if they had been subject to 'eve-teasing' or had ever been molested. A torrent of experiences and feelings, despair, anger, shame, fear, confusion and helplessness poured out. Girls and women are teased, touched, groped, followed, chased, squeezed, spanked, stopped, surrounded, stalked, caressed, rubbed by naked male organs, and hit on the breasts by men riding away on bicycles, rickshaws, scooters, motorcycles and cars. Men in cars have hunted lone women down. It is a daily guerrilla war out there. Ritu, 25, a graphic artist, talks about her daily torture getting in and out of a crowded metro with men 'touching wherever a male hand can reach'.

There are no national accounts of the trauma on women caused by the day-to-day harassment. The need to be always ready to fight or flee means that women's bodies are invaded by potent stress chemicals most of the time. Many women just freeze. For women, it is like living in a country in a constant state of high alert against terrorist attacks, when the signal is always red. This fear is suppressed. Unknowingly, women experience symptoms of post-traumatic stress disorder (PTSD).

Anushka, 25, who works in a large accounting firm, says, 'I used to come home from work at eight-thirty at night. I used to get in the metro and the majority of people around me were men. After a point you are in a situation where you are being touched from all sides and you can't do anything. I used to cry a lot about it.' Like animals in laboratory experiments that are unable to escape mild electric shocks and stop trying to escape and just lie there even when the shocks have stopped. Psychologists call this 'learned helplessness'. Abhisa, 24, who recently completed her MBA, says, 'Most times I ignore it. Let them talk, let them look.' Teertha, 22, who came to Delhi from Visakhapatnam to complete her BEd degree, says that she has experienced eve-teasing so many times in Delhi that in her mind it has become 'insignificant'. Afraid of provoking aggression, she silently pays the price of being a woman. She copes by detaching from her body and wiping it out of her mind.

Sirija, 23, a dancer from a family where both parents are in the art and design world, is a veteran of riding

Delhi metro, describes another experience that cuts across generations. 'Yesterday I was in the metro so I was sitting *bahut adjust karke*,' meaning she was sitting with a really contracted body trying to occupy as little physical space as possible. 'This guy was sitting next to me, his hands were folded so that his one hand was near my right thigh. So after a point I started giving him bodily reactions that I knew he was trying to touch me.' This trying-to-be-subtle technique involves pulling your body in even tighter for a moment and then releasing it quickly so it pushes the man's legs a bit. Men of course sit with legs spread out. But subtlety does not work. It is mostly ineffectual in bringing about any change in the aggressor's posture but it is an important part of the micro-signalling that women use. Women are often afraid to move away; they are afraid to offend the offender. They are afraid the aggression might escalate. And worse, they start to doubt and question their own senses. Sirija then says, 'I couldn't understand, is this really happening?' Sleeping men or men pretending to be sleeping on buses, trains and planes while touching inappropriately also contribute to women doubting themselves. Women freeze, wait, do nothing or scream when it is over. There is a delayed reaction.

Sheer rage provokes some women to fight back. Rekha, 28, who works as a domestic maid, is usually mild-mannered and quiet. One day, when she was on her evening walk in a local park, a man kept passing her and hitting her with his elbow. She asked him to walk *aaram se*, take it easy, but he continued harassing her. '*Toh maine uski pitayi kari, thappad mara aur collar se pakar ke bahar le gayi.* So I beat him up, I slapped him on the face and then caught him by the collar and dragged him out of the park. After that day he did not return to the park.' Her anger radicalized her.

Other young women also kick, bite, hit, yell and curse when faced with the endless 'eve-teasing', really sexual harassment. But this has consequences. Even as they speak up or hit out, there is fear, a bigger fear, of even greater retaliation, of being stalked further. Priya, 23, is a social science researcher. Vigilance is her constant companion on the streets of Delhi. She is always on alert. 'Men try and touch the breast, the butt or whatever they can. So I have to be very careful of these men and keep my eyes open. If you are not very cautious you become a target.' She has foiled many would-be molesters. 'Once when I was in my first year of college I went to Chandni Chowk to do some shopping and I spotted a man who wanted to touch me, I could tell. He tried several times but I was cautious,' meaning she dodged him like a skilled boxer. 'The next time he came near me I gave him a tight kick and everyone clapped. That was fun. But now you cannot even think of doing such a thing as men have gone mad in India. They decide to take revenge and the next thing we hear is acid attack. Either they will rape you, or kill you or throw acid on your face. So girls have to be very cautious.'

When women under high threat decide to take action, it has to be calculated and strategic, all in a flash of a moment. Many feel angry with themselves for not reacting fast enough. Others quickly calculate the odds of winning. Sanchita, 26, rides her scooter to work every day. One day, as she was returning home to Gurgaon, she realized that she was being stalked. 'These two guys on a bike had been following me and kept harassing me. I knew that my parents were close by, so I was confident. So I stopped. When they stopped I switched on my camera, I asked them what was their deal and they started abusing me. One of them realized I had a video camera on, so he rode off. I screamed and screamed. Soon there was a huge crowd. They beat the shit out of the other guy, took his mobile phone and licence and, by the end of it, he was calling me didi. But earlier, when he did not know about the camera, he had said, "Ya, I harassed you, what will you do?"'

Even temples are not safe for girls during crowded puja times. Anu, 24, says she is now vigilant even in places of prayer. Recalling an incident when she was eight or nine, she said, 'I had gone to the temple with my mom and aunties. A guy touched me on my breasts, he was caressing them and I didn't understand what was happening. And he kept doing it until my mother saw and then he ran away. That day my mom taught me about good touch and bad touch. Now that I know what was happening I feel disgusted.'

This predatory behaviour has also spread to some schools. Little girls trust teachers, a trust abused by some. Sweta, 24, who is slight in build and works in the financial sector describes an incident with her dance teacher. She was in class 4 and excited to learn to dance. 'He called me to his room. The whole room was curtained and the doors were closed. He told me to stand up against the wall, to stand on my toes and said, "*Aao tumko dance sikhaunga*, come, I will teach you to dance." And then he came closer and rubbed his body against mine. I felt a little dizzy but thank God the bell rang then and I ran away.'

Others speak about male yoga teachers who touch them inappropriately 'here and there' and swimming coaches who put their hands down their swimsuits and stroke their vaginas. Girls just glare at their teachers hoping that would get them to stop. Mostly, though, their response is to run away and avoid these classes. They don't tell anyone. They are silenced by the chains of their family's silence. Many mothers tell or hint to their daughters, 'You imagined it, it was an accident, he didn't mean it, don't make so much of it.' Others remain silent, communicating to their girls, 'Please don't make trouble, there is nothing that can be done, forget it.' Girls retreat into themselves in confusion, feeling ashamed of themselves and suspecting that there is something wrong with them and their bodies.

At a three-day civil society workshop on gender conversations in Bengaluru that I participated in, it emerged that every woman present between the ages of 18 and 35, across social classes, had been molested, and two had been repeatedly raped. When asked 'If you have ever been sexually molested, please stand up,' every woman stood up, looking straight ahead. Everyone silently said, 'me too'. The workshop included women and men primarily from Karnataka, some of whom came from villages and small towns and spoke only Kannada while others were multilingual and spoke English. Some were from Delhi. Yet this sexual harassment has become a given, an unasked-for cruel rite of passage to a scarred womanhood. Not one woman had reported anything to her parents due to lack of trust, shame and fear that she would be blamed and not believed. Girls sensed that their lives would become even more difficult. Just about every woman I have spoken to since has been sexually harassed or inappropriately touched or both. By the time they are in their fifties and the attention of men has shifted to younger women, mothers, battle-weary, hardened and feeling helpless, often say to their daughters, '*Yeh to hota hi hai, sab ko, kya karein,* this happens to everyone, get used to it, what to do?' But the fear of men and the trauma linger.

Half the children in India are exposed to some form of sexual abuse, and 20 per cent to extreme forms, according to surveys cited by the Government of India. Another survey establishes that 42 per cent of Indian girls have gone through sexual trauma before the end of their teenage years, some before they are ten. This means that almost every other girl has been sexually abused.

Harassers, molesters and rapists have little fear of being exposed or punished. Even at work. Namu, 32, works for a large private corporation in Gurgaon and wanted to apply for a job announced in an internal vacancy list. She went to the recruiting office. 'The man said to me, "Your best efforts and charm will not work here, because if you want the position, you need to get laid." I wanted to hit him with his laptop.' But she said nothing and pretended as if he had said nothing wrong. She came home and told her husband, who is the legal counsel in the human resources department in another large firm. 'He said, "This is part of life, office politics – go for a better option." I left my job.'

Even when rapists videotape the rape, they assume that the woman's fear of exposure is so deep that they will be protected despite visual evidence of their involvement.

Sushma Swaraj, currently the country's foreign minister and a competent and forceful woman, reflected this mindset when she spoke in Parliament after the Delhi gang rape of December 2012. 'When a woman gets murdered, she gets killed once,' she said. 'But when she gets raped, she dies again and again . . . If this girl survives, she will be a *zinda laash*, living corpse, for the rest of her life.' In effect, once raped, a girl has no value to anyone. Her life is over. No wonder women keep quiet, are made to keep quiet, move away or commit suicide instead of reporting their rapes. It takes great courage to go public about rape.

Rani, 25, has a master's degree from Jawaharlal Nehru University. Rape was the first thing she spoke about in response to our question on what it means to be a woman. She immediately started speaking about her rape in a flat, robotic monotone. 'It was the day before my thirteenth birthday and I was coming back home after inviting a few friends for my birthday the next day. I was wearing a black *sharara* sort of thing because *Kabhi Khushi Kabhie Gham*, the movie, had just come out and these things were a fad at that time. I was climbing the stairs to my home and saw a man climbing down, so I moved to the left to give him space to exit. But he didn't leave. Instead, he jumped on me. I hit my head on the wall. The next thing I knew I was in this checkpost where the guards usually sit; he had taken me there. I was in a state of shock for the longest time and I couldn't even scream, but when I did a housemaid working in our building heard me. I remember the scene very clearly, it was like in one of the movies, a small, dark room, a flickering bulb, a man in his late twenties on top of me. He was big, with a moustache.'

Rani said, 'Nobody cared about me. Everyone, my parents, the neighbours and the police, only wanted me to answer questions about my virginity.' She continued, 'Nobody came to my birthday the next day. The police ate my cake and I hated that. I hated them, bloody male chauvinists; instead of telling my parents to take action, they discouraged them. "Don't do it," they said. "*Aapki beti hai, naam kharab hoga, jaane do*. It's your daughter, her name will be spoiled, let him go." I guess somewhere my parents also thought like that. Since then I've stopped celebrating birthdays.'

At 13, Rani felt excluded from life. 'I felt I didn't belong. I stopped caring. My hatred for mankind increased. I suffered from insomnia for the longest time; I thought the man would come back and kill my parents.' Instead of parents protecting children, girls learn that they must protect their parents from shame and dishonour. There is a deadly reverse. Completely alone, girls are racked by fear, guilt and shame.

Rape becomes synonymous with shame because rape involves a girl's unacknowledged body and, worse, its sexual parts. We are taught that rape is about sex. Rape is about force, control, power, anger, rage, violence, hate and cruelty. It is about dehumanizing girls and women. In the 2012 December gang rape, six men took turns raping and assaulting Nirbhaya in a moving bus. '*Mar do sali ko*, kill the bitch,' they kept saying. They were even more enraged when she screamed and fought back. They used iron rods to penetrate her vagina, uterus and intestines. Rape is a criminal act of violence.

Disguise the body

Since it is impossible to get rid of a living girl's body, girls are trained to do the next best thing, to disguise it. There are three ways of approximating invisibility: looking down or hanging one's head; contracting and hunching; and wearing loose, sedate clothing. These practices are meant to delude women into thinking that if they somehow become invisible to men, they will be safe from their unasked-for aggression. Induced invisibility says, 'I am good. I am powerless. I am no threat to you. And therefore I am safe from you and you are safe from me.' It is the cultural equivalent of walking around with a white flag of surrender and asking for protection.

Hang your head and look down

A woman's stance takes on moral overtones. In old Hindi films, the heroine, the good woman, always looked down and lowered her eyes coyly. The image lingers in our collective psyche. It's an important part of training to be a good woman. When you look down, you don't see. Looking down is a socially sanctioned way of signalling that a woman is withdrawing, even when she is physically present; within our cultural context we are taught to think of it as charming modesty. It is part of the arsenal of cultural habits that make women disappear. It creates a virtual invisibility without a purdah or a ghoongat, when the sari or dupatta covers the face. But hanging one's head also results in an inability to see. The world shrinks.

While looking up conveys power, looking men in the eye can also be misunderstood as an invitation of interest.

It can be risky. Manju, 38, is tiny but has a strategy to warn men off even while looking them in the eye. 'I never look down and I always walk very confidently like a goonda because I don't want men to think I am easy prey. I always look into people's eyes and talk straight with them. My cousins think I am rude.'

Getting the position of the eyes right when with men is a finely honed art. Meenu, 23, from the lower middle class, says, 'Within the family we maintain eye contact, but if someone from outside comes we talk without looking at them. It is wrong to talk to men while looking them in the eyes, things always go wrong.' Morality is expressed through the position of the eyes.

In the higher middle and upper classes, where women know that they should not look down, women's early training results in the phenomenon of darting eyes, eyes moving quickly hither and thither and not focusing on anything for very long. Leena, 19, a student of political science, says, 'I look here and there. I can't look into somebody's eyes too long, I get self-conscious, I am not confident. I don't know why.'

Shrink your body

Women are great interpreters of the body language of power because they are trained to be experts in the opposite, how to convey no power, no presence. Nobody was hesitant or confused while describing the stance of a confident woman: 'she walks straight; she holds her head high, her neck straight, chin slightly tilted up; she does not hunch; her shoulders are open and pushed back; her arms are swinging, not held close or wrapped around her body; there is an expression on her face that says "I am here".'

Teaching young girls bodily positions of power is dangerous precisely because it teaches them presence. The cultural goal is the opposite, to diminish their presence, to train them in habits to leave their bodies. Jaya's mother teaches Jaya, 24, to walk so lightly that no one will know she is present. She wants her 24-year-old to stop pounding the earth when she walks and constantly reprimands her. '*Dhabad-dhabad karke mat chala kar*,' she says.

Amy Cuddy, a professor at Harvard University and researcher on power positions of the body, shows that even two minutes of power posing, standing in the V-position with arms held high and legs apart, changes testosterone and cortisone levels in the blood and hence boosts confidence, presence, sense of power and chances of success in life. Some young women from the middle classes go to classes for personality development where they are taught how to walk, how to hold their heads high the old-fashioned way by balancing books on the head and how to maintain eye contact. They are taught to focus on the point between the eyes and not on the eyes. This, of course, cleverly achieves both cultural appropriateness and the stance of self-confidence.

In a totally different context, in villages in Uttar Pradesh, poor women's self-help groups begin very simply by changing how women hold their bodies, asking them to stand with heads held high and look at each other when talking. To be seen and see others. Slowly the bodies of these skinny women open up, straighten up, expand and take up space. And with their bodies, so do their voices.

Most educated women in cities, even those wearing halter tops, do not want to know about their body contraction, rounded backs and hunched shoulders. A few talk about trying to change. Gauri, 25, with an MBA in finance, says, 'Yes, I walk with my head up, but I am very conscious of my weight and keep my shoulders constricted but I don't realize it. I guess it's more out of habit. I stopped wearing my favourite kurta because it highlighted my boobs; that made me uncomfortable because people would stare at them and I don't like that. I just hate my weight.' Payal, 23, tries to unlearn her hunched posture by enrolling in a personality development course, but her mother continues to undo her dangerous, straightened-out posture. Payal says, 'I generally walk straight now. But sometimes my mother asks me to walk "posturing down" so that my breast area is not the area of focus of strangers. And I have to obey her.' Contract and shrink your body and do not draw attention to it. Be a moral woman.

Jasbeer, 33, is a tall, stately woman from a well-off family. She says, 'Whenever my shoulders get tense because of the rigidity of my surroundings [meaning staring men], I consciously relax them. Too much straight looks vulgar to me. I have seen women who stand so straight that the first thing you notice about them is their breasts.' Vulgar is bad. How straight to stand becomes a morally delicate business.

Wear clothes that cover you up

If you don't want to be molested, cover yourself, women are told over and over again. Not surprisingly, women's clothing itself becomes moral or immoral. Decent or indecent. Clothes become causative agents, imbued with an independent life.

Let's consider a sari, that quintessential piece of Indian clothing for women, and its history as a lived experience in my family across four generations. Who do you think revealed the most skin, shape and bodily curves, my grandmother, my mother, me or my daughter? It was my grandmother. She lived in the holy city of Varanasi.

When we were little, every summer holiday we went to Varanasi to visit my grandparents. Every morning at five, my Naniji walked all fifteen of us – cousins, uncles, aunts – through the galis of Varanasi to Gangaji at the Dashashwamedh ghat to swim. I don't know what your grandmother wore when you were young. My grandma always wore cotton saris but she never wore a blouse. Nor did she wear a petticoat. She wore no underwear. It was normal. She was huge, like a grandma out of a storybook. We adored her. She walked through the streets wearing a cotton sari wrapped around her body. There was nothing on her body to constrict or tie her down. You could see her body outlined. That is how she dressed at home as well.

Only relatively recently have women started layering up their breasts and bottoms with underwear. My grandmother, if she were alive today, would laugh if I told her that we now believe that clothes cause women to be molested. The wrong-headedness of this idea becomes crystal clear when we learn of the violent rapes of toddlers and terrible gang rapes of girls between two and fourteen years, wearing traditional clothes like salwar kurtas. Clearly, the issue is not clothes but out-of-control men who are raging against female bodies that society pretends don't exist.

Despite public protests by women claiming the right to dress as they please, many young women have become more conservative in their clothes. Many are no longer as sure as they once were that it is not clothes that spell trouble. Priya, the social scientist, says, 'I also think women should be careful in their clothing selection. Guys tend to eve-tease more if they see us exposing . . . but it's not like we will never be teased by guys if we are dressed properly.' Tamanna, 23, who likes modern dancing classes, has stopped wearing shorts. The strongest voice dismissing the idea of clothes as causing molestation is Shiela, 33, a domestic maid with no formal education. She says, '*Arrey didi*, you will get molested anyway. It's not as if nobody is going to tease you when you wear a sari. Recently, when I was in an auto, policemen came to check and then one of them pressed my breasts so badly it hurt. I could not do anything, fearing they may [falsely] arrest my husband.'

Distance yourself from your body

Women learn to distance themselves from their bodies to feel safe, even when they may dress their bodies well. Taking no chances, middle-class Indian culture supports this distancing by discouraging movement. Movement frees the body. The power of the body awakens. It results in an invitation to reside in the body. To occupy it. It discourages the distancing, the dissociation and the disembodiment.

But as a culture, we prefer being stationary. Please do not disturb us while we sit. Given a choice, most of us would prefer to sit around, drink tea and eat samosas. We Indians associate physical activity with poverty. While we sit around on our sofas or beds, half the work of servants in Indian homes seems to be '*Zara phone utha do, zara pani de do, zara akhbar sahib ko de do*, get me the phone, fetch me a glass of water, go and give the newspaper to sahib.'

This lack of vigorous physical activity among the educated classes, along with being taught to move daintily and not to bang one's feet on the floor, *dhabad-dhabad*, collapses the body inwards. Physical constraints become mental constraints. Girls begin to think they are not strong; they cannot be strong. This feeds their sense of timidity, helplessness and dependence, the sense that they need protection.

There is one acceptable exception to being sedentary for girls and unmarried women in middle-class homes, apart from housework – dance. In Varanasi, my nineteen- and twenty-year-old aunts had a Kathak dance guru to whom they were devoted. Both became very skilled Kathak dancers. The rest of the time they were confined to the home, talking to neighbours through open windows. Neither ever performed outside. But the joy and the freedom they experienced were obvious even to us as kids when they occasionally took us to their guruji's home. One of my aunts was quite hunched but straightened up when she danced, twirling twenty-four times at high speed, her spirit transported elsewhere. Her face glowed. There was no dance for my aunts after marriage.

Movement frees the body and cuts through layers of defence. Recognition of this has led to a variety of body- and movement-based therapeutic techniques. Another physical activity that has opened up for women is going to the gym, as the beauty ideal has shifted to slim heroines who dominate the Indian screen today. Feeding the dreams of aspirational India, neighbourhood gyms have sprouted up everywhere to slim women down. In fact the word 'gym' has become a verb. Women go gymming. Yoga is hardly mentioned except in wealthy households, where families sometimes have private yoga gurus come to the home.

But despite the draw of dance and the incursion of gyms, our cultural attachment to women being inactive outside of housework remains unshaken. Only two women spoke about the importance of sports in their lives and no woman belonged to a sports team. But the men were often part of sports teams and informal groups. This reflects a culture in which every patch of open ground in the cities is claimed by boys playing cricket, while girls are nowhere in sight. This absence, too, feeds their invisibility. No girl mentioned a female sports hero or aspired to become one herself.

Team sports teach boys that they can be strong and coach them in the 'give-and-take' skills needed in working together. Girls miss out. *Chak De India!*, the Shah Rukh Khan movie in which his character coaches a dysfunctional girls' hockey team, shows that it is only when girls are able to override their differences that they come together as a team. The recent celebration of the women's cricket team reaching the World Cup finals will over time contribute to the breakdown of cultural resistance in the middle classes.

A regular physical routine, going to the gym, running, swimming, kabbadi, boxing, wrestling, volleyball, soccer, football, rugby, cricket, turns out to be what Charles

Duhigg calls a keystone habit, a habit which leads to purposefully initiating other actions that can change one's life. It awakens the latent power of the body. Jalia, 13, who knows all the rules of good girlhood, says, 'I like to wear clothes like boys, I am a tomboy and my parents don't say anything. Learning karate makes me strong. I can do anything. I can fight better than all the girls and also better than boys. I want to overcome boys in fighting.' Sports awaken power in the self. Clearly, then, it is dangerous to get middle-class girls involved in active sports – it could upset the balance of Indian society.

The act of a young girl kicking a football is subversive. It quietly breaks all cultural taboos about what girls are allowed to do because by puberty the tracks laid down for young girls have become narrow gauge. Whether it is kicking a football or wrestling, like Olympic medal winner Sakshi Malik or Commonwealth gold medallist Geeta Phogat, whose feat is now known to millions through the movie *Dangal*, participation and excellence in sports break open the narrow, scripted, predetermined life of girls.

Participation in vigorous sports is an inoculation against a society that prepares girls and women to disappear. Research evidence is so clear. If there is any magic pill, it is this. Girls who are involved in sweaty sports study longer hours; they get better grades; they have more self-confidence; they are less dependent on how boys treat them; they have better body image; they believe in themselves; they have better health; they are more likely to use contraceptives and delay having sex; they have larger social networks; and they learn teamwork. Participation in sports may be the most subversive and the most culturally appropriate system to crack the cultural design of denying girls their bodies, and therefore their lives.

But if they are not allowed to have strong bodies, girls have only one safe place left to go to. Indian culture pushes girls out of their dangerous bodies and into their heads. Heads are relatively safe. There is no immediate danger of sex. Girls are now valued for their brainpower and moneymaking power. The head is a safer place to dwell in.

Education for middle-class girls has finally exploded. It is the best thing to keep a girl occupied till she gets married. All parents want their girls to enter a good English-medium school, college, technical or managerial institute. Studying becomes a drill. Indian parents may not be as fierce as the tiger moms of China but they are certainly relentless, expecting their girls to study hard till the day they 'settle down', meaning when they have a well-paying job that ends with a good marriage.

Sending girls to school is good. But the cultural framing around restricting girls is so strong that schools and colleges have become new forms of imprisonment for girls, partly because of cruel parental pressure to perform and partly because schools and colleges don't teach girls to learn, to question or be curious. Unrelenting pressure to do well in examinations and forget everything else turns girls into dead heads even when they excel in examinations.

So living in their heads and going to school are acceptable but having an independent mind is not. Neeru, 21, studying computer science against her wishes, says in despair, 'Everyone is studying, going to coaching classes every day; it is as if there is nothing else.'

* * *

A good girl is body-less. Therefore, the logic goes, a good girl or woman cannot get molested or raped. Therefore the entire culture turns against a woman who speaks up or fights back, because it shakes the foundation of the edifice that props up male power through female disembodiment. Perhaps it will change when women stand together to break the silence. The denial of girls' and women's bodies is still so respectable in our culture, and runs so deep, that it is difficult to dismantle. It is this denial that makes it so problematic to have a woman's body.

Ruchika, 36, says, 'I feel like taking it off, the body, just like you do with saris.'

Consequences: Society Owns Women's Bodies

> *Being a good woman means you are alive because we want you to be alive and you need to take permission even if you want to breathe.* Mandi, 38

The problem for women is this: If your body does not exist, how can you own it? The cultural denial that women have bodies is held in place by millions of mothers, fathers, sisters, brothers, aunts, uncles, friends, teachers, colleagues and leaders. It fits our rich Vedantic philosophy that holds that nothing material is real.

Why is this denial of women's bodies so foundational? The explanation is simple. No society can survive without a woman's womb to create new life. This creative sexual power is so important that it cannot be left in the hands of 'innocent girls and weak women'. Society steps in to take control of women's bodies.

Not allowed to own their own bodies, women cannot exist. Women stop breathing, afraid. Afraid to live. Afraid they may die. When women do not reside in their bodies they become unsure, ungrounded and afraid. This serves the culture well. Trained to be afraid of their own bodies, women surrender to the cultural forces around them. It is natural. They don't want to create a disturbance. It might cause a tsunami.

Every time a girl or boy criticizes a woman's body, a woman's body is violated. Every time a mother tells her daughter to be careful about what she wears or how she walks or that she should stay at home after dark, she is contributing to it. Every time a girl hunches her shoulders to hide her curves she is living out the unspoken cultural war against her powerful body. Every time a father refuses to let a girl play cricket or football or learn martial arts, he contributes to the war against girls' bodies. Every time a girl's morality is judged by the clothes she wears, the unseen war is waged. But it is when the cultural practices become elevated to the status of moral rightness that the war dangerously becomes a 'just' war.

Society dumps an undeclared war on women's bodies. It becomes a free-for-all. Within this societal context of war, the daily harassment of women's bodies in public or in private spaces becomes unremarkable. Normal. But the body remembers and carries every trauma in itself. It keeps score. More evidence pours in every day. Our guts may be the more important brain. Trained to be afraid of their bodies, women too become perpetrators of a war against women, a war against each other.

Society succeeds in being firmly in charge of women's bodies through the persistence of six cultural practices that become habits.

Demean and discount your own body

Cultures attack women's bodies by training women to criticize, belittle, hate, demean, despair over and devalue their bodies and treat them as defective. Women give long lists of body parts that need replacement. This makes societal takeover easier. I, too, would disown something so broken with relief. Of the hundreds of women interviewed, only one woman yelled with joy, 'I love my body,' and another burst into a love song.

The training in rejection starts early. Dipali, 11, from Modern School, says, 'My bad parts are my stomach, feet and teeth.' Smridhi, 13, says, 'My worst parts are my tummy and my thighs.' Saanvi, 19, an attractive woman studying sociology in Delhi University, was detached. The only positive thing she could say about her body was a reported comment made by a boy she did not know, when she was 15. She says, 'In school one time, I was really thin and a boy told a friend that I have a nice figure, so that I really liked, *ki usne aisa socha*, that he thought like this.' Her sense of her own body is totally a reflection of other people's judgements.

Alka, 30, who would be classified as a 'beauty', feels so traumatized by her bodily imperfections that she has gone into depression. She has completely rejected her body and so has no place to relax. Very early, she learned that beauty must be perfect, but she has stretch marks. She says, 'I will never have a boyfriend because I have stretch marks. Even if I have a boyfriend, oh shit, he will make fun of me.'

When a woman rejects her own body, she has nowhere to live. Her entire existence is built on a shaky foundation. She concludes she is the problem. This serves society's goals. Insecure women do not take up space. They do not demand change.

Everyone else owns a piece of your body

When women's bodies are owned communally, every aunty, uncle, friend and loafer on the street offers comments freely without being asked, always in judgement. It becomes a right, a habit. No one is spared. Justice Leila Seth, India's first woman high court chief justice, played a key role in the Justice Verma Committee to reform rape laws in 2013. When I met her four years ago we chatted about her life's work on justice and later I asked about her early experiences as a girl. When I probed her relationship with her body she suddenly shared a comment made by her older brother that she remembered over 65 years later. 'I was 17 and very shy, short and thin. My older brother was tall, confident, and went out with well-dressed, shapely women. I remember he was standing there, ready to go out for the evening with a woman in a chiffon sari. He said, looking down at me, "Flat in the front and flat in the back".' And she repeated, 'Flat in the front and flat in the back.' Deeply affected at 17, Justice Leila Seth said she lost confidence in herself as a woman and focused on earning a living. Her confidence was built back later by a loving husband who supported her in every possible way throughout her life.

It doesn't matter if you are smart or skinny or fat or short or tall or fair and lovely. Just being born into a woman's body brings its own troubles. Sheetal, 39, grew up in a protected middle-class family and became an international fashion model. I met Sheetal having a hearty breakfast at Elsewhere, an eco-lodge in north Goa. As we chatted, Sheetal said, 'Other women are angry because of your good looks. They are suspicious. Aunties who don't even know me constantly make personal negative comments. They will say, "You have put on weight, you look tired." Why do people have to make personal comments? I don't go up to them and say, "You are fat."'

There are two societal curses about looks, being dark, 'wheat-complexioned', or 'healthy', meaning not thin as a stick. There are flourishing fairness and weight management industries in India pitched at young women. Parents say, '*Tumhari shaadi nahin hogi*, you will never get married.' The focus on looks has a superficial layer that is talked about openly in terms of marriageability. But it also has a deeper layer. The bride hunting and the groom hunting are about gene hunting, about babies, about wombs. Actually the whole fuss is about getting the best womb and gene set for the family, to ensure that the next generation is 'beautiful, fair, slender, and smart'. I have heard 'aunties' discuss choice of girls based on bodily features, especially the size of hips, as they believe wide hips are an indication of the woman being healthily fertile.

With so much emphasis on physical looks, particularly the 'right' weight, to get married, no wonder some girls seek revenge by putting on weight after marriage when 'aunties' gurgle in delight and smirk and go 'wink wink, now you are joining us and having babies'. Young girls graduate very quickly to the status of 'healthy aunties' after the birth of their first or second or third child. This also leads to being 'de-sexed' and not having dangerous bodies. Women's bodies have already served their societal purpose.

Purity and family izzat are more important than you

The societal takeover of women's bodies makes purity of a girl's body the ultimate prize. Rape, then, is the worst violation of this purity. It is the ultimate destroyer of a family's izzat and honour. Unfortunately it also hides molestation within family circles. One of India's stenchiest secrets is the molestation and rape of little girls and young women within extended family circles by trusted others. This involves grandfathers, sometimes fathers, and cousins, uncles, and so-called uncles, male friends of the family that children are told to address as such.

When young girls cannot speak up about being molested by strangers, how can they be expected to speak up against the very people who are so important in their lives and whom they are trained to respect? The statistics are chilling.

In 2014, based on official criminal statistics, 95.5 per cent of rapists in India were known to the victim. The victims were young. Overall, 86 per cent of rapists were close family members. In Delhi, in 2014, of the 1704 rape cases recorded by the police, roughly 80 per cent of the rapes involved family or friends; 13 per cent involved fathers, uncles, cousins, brothers, stepfathers and in-laws. This is only for reported crime. Remember that not a single woman in our study reported any of the multiple sexual crimes perpetrated against them to the police.

Meetu, 35, is petite and has big eyes. Her father was in the army. At our very first meeting, Meetu spoke about several rapes. The first time, she was 4. 'My mother and some aunties were sitting outside in the colony and all the children were playing nearby. This one uncle comes and takes us inside his house saying he will give us toffees and chocolates. The only thing I remember is that I was with him under the *razai*, quilt, and I don't remember what happened.' She never told anyone.

Lovely, 37, comes from an upper-class family and now lives in Gurgaon with her 13-year-old son. She is still upset that her parents did not protect her from a series of marauding relatives. There were many incidents of naked touch. As she speaks she also recalls that once when they were coming back from Ludhiana to Delhi, her mamaji, mother's brother, 'insisted that we all come one by one, and lie down with him to give him a parting hug . . . It occurred to me later that this was also perverted.' She never told anyone; she says simply, 'The culture of sharing this at home was not there.'

Maya, 24, who is a marketing specialist, speaks about being molested within the family first when she was 6 years old. 'My foofaji, father's sister's husband, he used to touch me when I was alone, I felt something different. I was lying down under a blanket, I could feel him touching my bum. I felt a little hesitant, I ran towards the balcony, my brother was playing outside and I screamed, calling my brother, bhaiya, bhaiya. So first Foofaji came after me, but then he figured out that something is going to go wrong, so he went inside. And last year I told my mother this thing. She said, "*Haan woh toh aise hee hain. Aisa hota hai families me ladkiyon ke saath*. Yes, he is like that. In families this happens to girls." She didn't react so much. It was a normal thing.'

I heard story after story of harassment, molestation and rape within the family being denied, or tolerated or explained away. Occasionally the rape involved fathers. Sudha, 21, lives in Bengaluru and was repeatedly raped by her father since she was 12. Her mother slept next to her father but never 'woke up' or said anything.

When mothers and fathers look the other way, when they pretend they don't know, when they do not believe their children's stories, even on the rare occasion when children speak up or persistently say they don't want to go to a particular relative's home and yet are forced to go, mothers betray their young children to protect themselves. Children feel abandoned, helpless, alone, isolated and depressed, and lose trust in adults. This of course affects their later relationships.

Families, rather than film stars, may be India's most diligent image-makers. Laalita, 30, is currently completing her PhD in New York and working part-time at the United Nations. She was almost raped by her local guardian, whom she called Chacha, while studying at a renowned engineering college where her brother also studied. She was 17. 'One evening he picked me up, we then went to my brother's dorm. My brother was not there, so I went with Chacha alone. I did not like the idea at first but I was too scared to say no. At night after dinner when I was sleeping, I woke up and he was lying on top of me. I felt so grossed out by myself at that moment but I still could not express my anger at him. I felt so scared. I pushed him away and went to another room. In the morning he acted like nothing wrong had happened, he dropped me back to the hostel. I felt so disgusted. I too pretended – I did not tell anyone because I thought it would bring harmful consequences to me. After a year, a guy friend whom I told insisted that I tell my parents. My mother said, "Don't tell anyone because it will only bring a bad name to the family." My dad said, "We cannot tell, otherwise Chachiji [his wife] will leave him." I was so angry that my father wouldn't do anything. So I told my brother. He got very angry, but in the wrong way – he got angry with me. So my mother called me and said why did you tell your brother, *woh bahut pareshan ho gaya*, he is very upset. He wants to commit suicide.' He stopped speaking to his sister.

Laalita still has to face the almost-rapist in her own home, 13 years later, when she returns from New York. Her father, an educator, pulled strings to get him a prestigious job as a department head at the university. 'So now he keeps visiting the house and my father says, "Why don't you go to Chacha's?" I wonder if my father even remembers it?'

It is in the silence on rape that four powerful cultural agreements come together: denial that women have bodies; control of women's bodies, particularly by men in society; denial that women's bodies are sexually desirable; and the upholding of purity and family izzat. It is these cultural agreements that transfer all the burden, pain and horror of sexual violence to girls and women.

Be afraid of your bodies

How can it then be a surprise that women feel fear, a sense that their bodies expose them to danger? Society uses fear, the most powerful tool at its disposal, to get women to surrender to its authority and control. It breeds fear. Fearful women are easy to control. When women live in fear, they listen and they obey. Fear is reinforced by women's daily reality. In a 2015 study, women considered commuting to work the most dangerous activity and their biggest daily fear. Only 12 per cent feel safe in public transportation. Physiologically this means many women are constantly in survival mode. How can they thrive?

After the Nirbhaya rape, the focus rightly was on the safety of women and many safety apps have been developed. And the media played and continues to play an enormous role in breaking the silence on rape. But one perverse effect of the increasing media reports of many other horrendous rapes has been more fear, reducing women's freedom even more. Nina, 19, is a student at Miranda House. When asked to say the first three words that come to her mind about being a woman, she says, 'Careful, not independent, and rape. So many rapes happen all the time, you have to be careful. Always eve-teasing, rape. Jailed at home, you are not allowed to go out of the home at night because it is unsafe.'

Steal women's freedom

Fearful women want protection. The protection offered by society comes at a very high price for women, their freedom. The current assumption is that society cannot be made safe for over 600 million girls and women, but women should be made safe for society by keeping them locked up at home as much as possible, by restricting their movement, by regulating their clothes and by isolating them from the world of men as much as possible. Disguised as women's safety, all approaches that restrict women contribute to their non-existence and are actually about men and men's control over society, so that men don't have to bother to learn self-control or respect for women.

Neeta, 25, leads a restricted life, even though she is studying for an MBA. Since the Nirbhaya gang rape, her freedom has been drastically curtailed in the name of safety, and she has stopped being herself because of 'safety issues'. She knows Delhi is unsafe. She doesn't blame her parents, who say they are holding her back for her own good, and try to 'console her'. All parental behaviour is explained with a click of the tongue and a pained expression, 'This is for your own good,' or 'This hurts me more than it hurts you.' Neeta has contracted her dreams. She now says, 'I wish I could get just two months of my own life before marriage, like in *Dilwale Dulhaniya Le Jayenge* [an iconic movie]. *Masti karni hai.* Just want to have some fun.'

The culture of 'protect women by locking them up' runs so deep that it is reflected in the rules of places of higher learning, including in Delhi University. When women at St Stephen's protested the locks on their hostels, a male faculty member said, 'If the girls' blocks are open, we'll have to open a maternity ward.' Unlike boys, girls cannot leave hostels in the evenings to even go to the library that stays open till midnight. *Pinjra Tod*, a student-led 'Break the

Cage' protest movement at Delhi University, finally filed a complaint with the Delhi Commission of Women, which has in turn issued notice to all 23 registered universities in Delhi asking for explanations on the treatment of women in their hostels. Historian Uma Chakravarti summarizes the situation. 'We [the university] have to stop acting like a transit between fathers and husbands.'

Society has declared to women but not to men that they can be physically safe only if it curtails their freedoms, if they stay close to authority figures, and if they live their lives jailed. If they want society's protection, they have to do what they are told. If something awful happens to them, they are told it is their fault, not a failure of the protectors.

You women are the problem

After the brutal gang rape of a pub employee by six men in Gurgaon in 2014, the police proposed a blanket curfew on working women after 8 p.m., under which no woman would be allowed out of the house without prior permission from the government labour department. The proposed ban was revoked after a public outcry. The police said they could not provide security for girls and women because the ones who are out, especially at night and especially in bars, invite rape. Women should stay at home if they want to be safe.

A strategy supposedly designed to protect women is in reality designed to protect men who presumably don't want to control their lust or rage. One such proposal to protect women, made by former Haryana chief minister Om Prakash Chautala, involved lowering the minimum age for marriage of girls to below eighteen.

Fortunately, the Supreme Court of India recently ruled that sex with girls under eighteen years of age even when married constitutes rape. Another proposal, again made by powerful men, involves marrying the rape victim to the rapist. The first channels men's lust to teenage girls through the sanctity of marriage and the second protects the rapist from criminal charges. In the twisted cultural logic, the 'generous rapist' has extended his protection to the victim whom nobody will now want to marry. Or it can even be seen as just punishment for the rapist, who is punished by being forced to marry a 'soiled' woman. It is he who is making the sacrifice.

An International Centre for Research on Women (ICRW) survey in Delhi found that 51 per cent of men acknowledge that they had sexually harassed or violated girls and women in public spaces in Delhi. But the majority of the men took absolutely no responsibility for their behaviour. Over 75 per cent of the men said that 'women provoke men by the way they dress' and 40 per cent said that 'if a woman is teased it is usually her own fault' and women going out at night deserve to be sexually harassed. A *Hindustan Times* survey found that only 6 per cent of women bother to report harassment to the police while 16 per cent said they were afraid of the police.

We think of society as enlarging women's freedom by protecting them. But society works precisely in the opposite direction – it restricts their freedom. And even then, women are still not safe. As Satish, 52, who works in a government bank says, '*Rape ka koi fixed time nahin hai*, for rape there is no fixed time. Always be alert.'

This too is normal.

Reflections

When a culture is based on the denial of women's bodies, and the actions intended to help women are based on this denial, women pay a huge price. Delhi and many parts of India are filling up with highly educated women surrendering their freedom to fear. Just to stay safe. Just to survive.

Is this the destiny of women in the twenty-first century?

We must see how much we are creatures of our culture. Unless we can see and label the dull, old knots of early cultural conditioning, we cannot become who we want to be, we cannot protect our girls, and we cannot change society so that girls can claim their own bodies and be considered moral. Our societal stance must change. Men must change. And so must women. It requires cultural acceptance that girls have bodies and that nobody but girls own their own bodies. It requires a collective redefinition of acceptable behaviour by men towards women and their bodies. Punishment of a few men will send important signals, but without a sustained public conversation, the underlying cultural position that women do not exist will not break.

We need to break the silence against sexual harassers through public campaigns. But we should do it in such a way as to educate men about behaviours that violate women; otherwise the response is defensive and even more aggressive. One common response among educated men is, 'OK, if I can be accused of sexual molestation, I will not hire a woman or sit next to a woman on a plane or anywhere. I will avoid all women.' This is petulance based on fear. We are asking for a big fundamental cultural change. Let's make it easier for men to change, by educating them about specific behaviours that are not acceptable. Without sarcasm. We need facilitated conversations among men and between women and men, from Bollywood to groupings of friends and colleagues. After all, it is our collective cultural silence that has made unacceptable behaviour seem acceptable.

Changes in laws and the beliefs of police and law providers and their quick implementation are critical. These need to be accompanied by peer training and massive public campaigns, including campaigns to call out sexual abusers within extended family circles and the so-called uncles in the immediate neighbourhood. This will both reduce such behaviour and give courage to silent observers as well as to parents and children to raise their voices rather than acquiescing in silence. Otherwise we risk trauma in yet another generation of girls and young women.

Any public policy measure should be judged by whether it restricts women or it enlarges their freedom. And this too must be accompanied by a public campaign and training that focus on specific behavioural change needed among men without shaming them, so men become allies in spreading change. There will never be enough policemen to protect over 600 million girls and women. The world will only be safe for girls and women when each girl, each woman, each boy and each man watches for and speaks out against harassment, abuse and violations of women's freedom.

All children have a natural curiosity about bodies. Both in families and in schools, girls and boys need to learn about their own bodies and the bodies of the other sex from a very early age, in age-appropriate ways. Education and discussion about bodies through movement, song and the creative arts are particularly effective in teaching children and teenagers pride and respect for their own bodies. Boys particularly need to learn that a girl's body belongs only to her, and nobody else. It is not a plaything available to any boy or man. Adults will have to unlearn their prejudices and shame when talking about bodies to children and youth.

Girls must occupy their bodies. When bodies are occupied, girls exist. And fear evaporates. Regular physical sports, any physically demanding sport, are transformative for girls. Girls become physically strong and if this is combined with self-defence strategies they can fight back if threatened. The few physically strong women we talked to are from families that had only girls. Such girls were raised more like boys and not treated as fragile and dainty creatures without bodies.

Change can be a difficult and lonely process when faced alone. But together we can generate new learning, new compassion and new forms of collective action to change ourselves and the cultural climate that governs our lives, from families to colleges, offices, entertainment, markets, politics, politicians and the law and order providers.

Can you imagine a woman who is unafraid of her body? A woman who is physically strong; who does not wear clothes like a shield; who accepts, loves and takes care of her body for herself; who befriends her body rather than criticizes, cuts and judges her body, and appreciates her body without shame, guilt or apology?

This must be the new normal for women of the twenty-first century.

3

Voice

Shut Up and Shut Down, *Chup*

Meera was 17 when she ran away from medical college. Like so many other women, she was raised by loving parents to become body-less and voice-less.

'When I lived in the slum with the sex workers . . . I felt safe. There is so much violence, so much threat to life, and illness, there is no hygiene, sanitation, etiquette, all that is missing and yet in that sense of vulnerability there is a sense of . . . spokenness. Yes, that is what it is, they would talk about everything.

'That is what changed me . . . They are all such loud women, there is nothing hidden in this community, there is nothing shunned. If you want to swear at someone, you swear. If you want to express your anger, you express your anger. If you want to maro a thappad, *a slap on the face, you slap. And you patch up. Being explicit with your emotions was so liberating! As in, my God, there is nothing stopping you from expressing who you are. There is no permanence to these emotions, it makes life easier. It keeps the chest light, I think. I would see these women crying and laughing and yelling and shouting and beating and being beaten up . . . They are so good. They are not* besharam, *shameless. They have a sense of self-respect. They didn't have that delicacy of talk, this was very liberating for me, so liberating for me from that sense of choking. I wanted to talk. They talk and fix their terms with their clients, they are able to express what they think and feel. Despite the brutal realities I saw every day, especially with HIV-afflicted women, and during menstruation and*

pregnancy, they still had to go for dhandha. *It was terrible to witness, this eight-month pregnant woman . . . but within their community they are free. And I felt most at home there. That alone was enough.'*

When her family arrived with the police to drag her back home, she resisted physically and refused to leave till she had quietly negotiated with her mother to stay on in Chennai to go to college. She found her voice.

***

When the central goal of raising girls is to make them invisible, see-through and non-existent, then ensuring that girls do not have a voice and cannot make a disturbance becomes a matter of some urgency. Once parents are assured that their newborn baby girl has a functioning sound system, they teach her not to make a sound. Not to be noisy. And once parents are assured that their little girl has no speech defects, she is taught not to speak.

The task is to subvert nature. Biologically, girls are equipped to start speaking earlier than boys and as a result have a greater vocabulary at 16 months. But they become less able to speak as they grow older. Most women we interviewed were not aware that they had been systematically trained not to speak. But as we spoke, their stories and the pain from their inability to speak up came tumbling out.

The Early Training: How to Get Girls to Shut Up

> *Mom always said* kam bolo, dheere bolo, *speak less, speak softly.* Namini, 21

When little girls are told over and over again by their mothers and fathers, the very people they love the most, not to speak up, they stop. The most common term associated with speaking up is its opposite, chup or *chup kar* or the polite form, *chup karo* or *chup raho*. It means shut up or be quiet. Chup is such a commonly used Hindi word that it has now become an English word, and has been added to the Oxford English Dictionary.

Don't speak, speak softly

Priyanka, 22, has an MSc degree and remembers how her mother trained her to become silent. She says, 'When I used to go to my friends' homes I was already a quiet girl, but they were the opposite so my mom was, like, not liking their nature. She said you should be a bit sober.' 'Sober' is a very Indian usage to indicate someone who is quiet, serious, unsmiling, walking a straight path and not getting into trouble. A sober girl is a safe girl, a marriageable, moral girl, whose very invisibility makes her culturally desirable.

When girls persist in speaking, qualifiers are brought in. Girls are told, if you must speak, speak softly. Loudness among girls evokes great agitation in mothers. It is forbidden. Loudness breaks the cultural agreement to train good girls to become invisible, not to exist. The agreement itself is never spoken about. It too is silent. It is treated as harmless training for politeness. Girls must stand behind a curtain of politeness and silence.

Shefali, 15, who goes to the elite Modern School in New Delhi, says, 'When I speak loudly, my mother does not like it. She says I should speak softly.' Metali,

21, who works in the stock exchange and lives at home, says she was constantly told that her voice is too loud. Both mothers' instructions were almost identical, '*Kam bolna chahiye, dheere bolo, apne aap ko itna loud mat karo,* you should speak less, speak softly, don't make yourself so loud.'

Girls who speak loudly are scolded and punished. The desire for adult approval leads girls to lower their voices and give up the hope that they will be heard. Menka, 24, a writer and trainer of young women in self-expression through dance and movement, says, 'My parents often snapped at me when I was 5–7 years old for speaking too loudly. This did two things to me: I stopped trying so hard to get my parents to listen; and I lowered my voice. I wish I hadn't . . . I was different then and comfortable being loud.'

The culturally preferred word to persuade girls not to speak is to label them *bevakoof*, fools. Sonal, 24, from a well-off family, recalls a childhood in which she was frequently called a fool. 'Once my grandfather introduced me to his friends saying, "*Yeh bevakoof hai*. She is a fool." I was 11, I felt very bad, so I told my mom and she said he meant it in a joking way.' Most mothers automatically support the 'other' and discount their girl's concerns.

Keeping quiet is one part of a complex of behaviours to make girls fit in. This closing of the mouth starts very innocently but goes devastatingly deep when it is reinforced in schools. Girls give up their voice to belong. Aasha, 21, learned very early at home a lesson later reinforced in nursery school that to be noisy, playful, to be heard and be seen leads to punishment. 'I remember I was in nursery school. I was punished because I was doing *masti* with my friends. When we got punished I still remember the thought that I asked myself, "Why did I do this even though I knew it was wrong?"' As a four-year-old, Aasha had already learned that to make a noise is wrong. It is bad. It is better to be quiet.

It is a short step from keeping quiet to becoming invisible. Rina, 40, from a wealthy home, says she learned to become invisible in school. 'I was non-existent in school, so that is why I could not speak up. I would shiver with fear.' Schools may teach girls to read and write, but not to speak their minds. So if a girl can't speak and be noisy, what should she do? It is obvious. Girls should become listeners.

Listen and follow

In a conversation, the spotlight is on the speaker. Girls are taught that they do not need to be in the spotlight, that it is better for them to remain invisible, as listeners. This learning is mostly a silent transmission. Mothers are a girl's first role model. Young women like Jivika, 24, frequently told me, 'My mother is a good listener. I get it from her.' Some said it in a different way. Shuchi, 30, an educator, said with a giggle, 'My mother remains mum rather than make it chaotic. I also prefer to remain mum.' Silent mothers, silent daughters. Over time, listening and not reacting becomes the default position, the factory setting.

'Keep quiet, listen, *udne ki koshish na karo*, don't try to fly, don't stick out,' is what Neeti, 25, who has a BTech degree and works at Accenture, repeatedly heard her mother say. Appeals to modesty, a prized virtue in girls, reinforce the modest act of listening rather than the brazen act of speaking. Listeners are polite; they follow the conversation. They do not step out of the shadows into the spotlight. Packaged as modesty, invisibility is made palatable.

Modesty alone is not enough. Girls are also expected to be perfect. Perfection as a goal kills everyday speech. Telling modest girls to be perfect has the effect of putting their mouths on lockdown because it takes a long time to formulate the perfect thought and say the perfect thing at the perfect time while your mouth is swashing in waves of fear.

As if seeking perfection is not enough, perfect timing is made more complicated by the need for permission. Trishna, 32, who teaches in Delhi University, says, 'Dad always used to say girls should talk only when asked to do so.'

This focus on listening and waiting trains girls to become more comfortable following rather than initiating. In fact, mothers tell their daughters to be followers, to just follow, like little ducklings, and not speak. Deepti, 33, a stay-at-home-mother with a master's degree in economics, summarized it as, 'A good woman is like her mother, she follows everyone.' Follow father, follow husband, follow society and follow boss. To follow you don't need to say much. Ancestral sediments slowly choke the throats of girls. Wait for others to say something first. *Pehele aap*.

Lose your opinions

When girls are expected to only listen and follow, having opinions seems pointless. Unnecessary. Having an opinion is actually egoistic, it is an expression of the self. It indicates fearlessness in drawing attention to that self. Mariam, 21, was trained by her mother to 'never talk about myself'. Breaking it goes against the cultural indoctrination of girls not to exist. It makes sense then that most writers of opinion columns are male.

Men are expected to have loud and firm opinions, but women are not. Girls learn this very early at home by watching their parents. They also learn who has more power. Namrata, 30, who has a postgraduate degree, says, 'Papa never gave value to my mother. He respected her but never asked for her opinion. He might consult her about social situations but never on any other matters.' Himanshi, 21, who describes herself as 'big on fitness', says she feels hurt when she sees her mother keep quiet or change her opinion in front of her father. 'I don't like it when she sometimes sacrifices her opinions or needs in front of my father. If there is an issue and my father has an opinion that is A and Mom has an opinion that is B, my father won't change to B, my mother will change to A.' Himanshi does not want to be like her mother but she may be like her mother after all. Initially she said with great gusto, 'Usually I am pretty open with my opinions,' then her voice dropped as she trailed off, 'but sometimes I forgo them for the family.' And then she added almost in a whisper, 'I usually keep quiet in family affairs.'

When the goal is to raise opinion-less girls, it makes cultural sense not to ask children their opinions on simple, everyday things: What colour do you like? What dress do you want to wear? Namita, 20, says she was never given the opportunity to go through the process of thinking, deciding and expressing opinions. She says, '*Bachpan mein*, when we were children, whatever Mummy and Papa told us to do we would do, we never thought we could make any decisions. Making decisions adds to your confidence.'

In fact, many women in college say that they are still excluded from family discussions. Pooja, 18, a student at the reputed Lady Shri Ram College, says her parents have an equal relationship. 'Sometimes when Mom says something, it is final, even Dad can't change it. Sometimes it's the other way.' But she is told what many young girls are told. '*Badon ki baatein hain, tumhe kya karna hai*. This is a matter for adults, what do you have to do with it? You are young, *padhai karo*, pay attention to your studies. I was never confident about discussing anything with my parents. Even today, I think they will not understand my point of view and will scold me. I feel tense and lonely.' But her mouth stays shut.

Banning girls from participation in everyday decisions is perfect training for them to fit into the cultural role of a detached, harmony-filled, opinion-less listener. An opinion can disturb the peace. Namini, 21, who wants to start a business, says that even when she has an opinion she keeps it to herself: '*Ladai na ho jaye isliye main chup rehti hoon*, it may lead to a quarrel, so I stay quiet.' Opinion-less girls are less likely to put up a fight.

Don't argue

I heard the phrase '*ladkiyan bahas nahin kartin*', girls don't argue, ad nauseum. When having an opinion is bad, having an argument is just awful. It can lead to a *mahabharat* and the destruction of families. The capacity to argue, particularly among girls, is severely discouraged, as it can lead to possible disagreement, conflict, loss of control and independence. Non-existing selves do not argue.

The most common Hindi word for argue is *bahas*. A girl who argues is considered *bahaensi*; it is not a compliment. Arguing is also associated with being *ziddi*, stubborn, to want something your way. To be *ziddi* is the opposite of the cultural ideal of a woman who is malleable, docile and who does not have an independent mind. Ifra, 24, says quietly, 'I have a clear understanding of what is expected of me – don't shout back, don't argue, talk politely, balance your emotions, don't be too *ziddi*.'

When you are not allowed to argue, thinking slows down. It makes girls safer for society. Thinking girls are difficult to manipulate. Jaana, 25, was trained out of argumentation in a family where conflicts were 'an everyday affair'. She says, 'The first thing I used to do is always argue back, had lots of arguments, and nobody listened to anything I said to them. Ultimately I gave up and stopped talking, like I became ignorant.' She stopped thinking.

You cannot argue if you cannot think. In an argument, thinking and speaking happen in quick succession, an exhilarating experience in rapid logical thinking. But it becomes frightening because thinking is forbidden. Heena, 21, a computer science student, remembers the joy of argumentation before it became fear-laden and defined as conflict. She wistfully says, '*Woh na mind itna free ho jata hai isliye I avoid.* You know the mind, it becomes so free, that is why I avoid it.' She adds, 'It leads to deep thinking.'

When argumentation is equated with conflict, it becomes a deeply upsetting and hurtful emotional experience. Heena now uses the terms argument and conflict interchangeably. She says, 'I completely avoid arguments. *Mat karo*, don't do it, as far as possible, don't do it. *Jab pata hai zyada ladai ho jati hai*, when you know there will be a big fight, you just shut up, keep quiet.' Heena feels so anxious after any argument that first she obsesses and then takes back everything she said and tells her friends, 'I don't want to fight, so you do whatever you want, *jaane do*, let it go.' At one level 'letting it go' is maturity, but if this is the only strategy and it is used out of fear, it diminishes a girl's ability to reason and be heard. It diminishes her aliveness.

The Nobel laureate Amartya Sen makes an eloquent case for India's long history of reasoned argumentation and debate in his 2005 book, *The Argumentative Indian*. But today's parents prefer moulding their girls for survival and acceptance in society, where speaking up and arguing are still definitely not considered desirable female virtues.

Respect your elders, jawab nahin dena

Silence, however, is a female virtue. Girls are taught silence by appealing to one of the strongest values in Indian families – respect, especially for elders, particularly men. The dictionary meaning of respect is 'to regard, to honour, to esteem, to admire, to notice with special attention, to heed, to defer, to defer to their point of view, to have a high opinion of'. As a noun, respect means admiration for someone's abilities, qualities or achievements. But these definitions miss one aspect that is central to Indian thinking: status based on position in a hierarchy. This respect is expected; it is demanded. Demanding is an exercise of imposing one's will on another with the threat of punishment and withdrawal of benefits.

The word respect has been hijacked in many homes. It has come to mean fear. It means control and obedience through threats, scolding, demeaning, punishing, followed by yelling or withering silence by loved authority figures in the guise of love. Fear and respect fuse.

Aroma, 23, from the upper middle class, says that when she was a child she was so afraid of her father that she just hid. 'I had fear in my mind, sometimes I used to shiver also, there was a fear of scoldings. I wanted to talk and share but could not as there was no ease. I never even tried to initiate anything, because I had the fear that I would have to face up to his scolding, so I was better off being quiet – my parents used to ask me to shut up and sit quietly when I tried to speak up in family discussions. This was not right of them.'

This fear-filled respect is also fed by teaching girls that their primal safety depends on men. If men are needed by girls to keep them safe, it is wise not to make them angry by arguing with them. It is a much smarter strategy to be liked by them. Thirteen-year-old Anushka's mother tells her, 'Girls are the best. But only one difference is there, that she always needs the protection of her father, brother.' Smart girls like Anushka and Diksha, 14, learn that girls who are 'respectable, lovable and always caring for others' are more likely to avoid making men angry and will therefore remain protected by them. The mouth closes to become desirable, to survive, for women's protection is only guaranteed through marriage.

Girls are prepared to 'fit into' marriage, and the behavioural criteria have not changed across generations.

Tamanna, 25, who has an MBA, says, 'My mother used to say, "If you behave like this, if you say anything loudly or yell about anything, your mother-in-law will throw you out of the house, *ek din bhi nahin tikegi*, you will not last even for a day, you should be polite, *tameez se baat kar*, talk with respect."'

I asked my mother if her mother, my Nani, had given her any advice when she got married. She said, '*Ek hee cheez boli, kabhi jawab nahin dena, kisi ko bhi.* She said only one thing, never answer back, to anyone. *Jawab nahin dena.*' We too heard it constantly from our aunt who would open her bespectacled eyes wide and say in a sonorous voice meant to impress upon us the seriousness of the matter, '*Beta, ladkiyan jawab nahin detin*, darling, girls don't answer back.' We would mimic her later and die laughing. But I did still absorb this message. I just did not know it.

'*Jawab nahin dena*' is still operational and widespread; it is part of the cultural landscape. Drishya, 32, says, 'I was brought up to these words, "*Badon ko jawab nahin dena, Papa se aise baat nahin karna.* Never answer back to elders, don't talk to Papa like this, it doesn't matter if you are right or wrong. It left no room for healthy discussion and I was left sulking. Strangely my mother was worse than my father, so not raising my voice and not even voicing what is right was an integral part of my growing-up years.' Kajal, 20, already feels so smothered by the '*jawab nahin dena*' regime that she says, 'When I feel *mujhe jawab dena hai*, I must answer back, I am unable to speak up or say anything.'

Girls with strong minds and the ability to express their views openly are assigned a negative value in society, in college, at work and are the nightmare of future parents-in-law. Puneet, 27, an IT consultant, considers himself like many younger educated men as a supporter of equality with women. He says, 'I want a wife who has a mind of her own. But the problem is that my parents' ideal *bahu* does not match this picture. They do not want a strong-headed woman. Because my mom is not strong-headed so they want a woman similar to her. For example, I met a girl who is a journalist, so they didn't want me to pursue her further. They were like, "*Journalism ki ladkiyan itni bold hoti hain*. Girls in journalism are so bold. They do whatever they want to do. *Humein nahin chahiye aisi ladki*. We don't want this kind of girl."' Even though Puneet's sister is a journalist, he is searching for a girl who fits his mother's behavioural criteria of a good, marriageable woman.

Speaking up, expressing an opinion, arguing and defending oneself are considered discourteous, disrespectful and dangerous. They lead to conflict and being disliked. Girls learn that men are still kings, and if they want a fairy-tale life of getting along with them, it is best to be quiet. Their training is complete. Girls grow up and become their own self-editing, self-censoring and self-monitoring systems.

Consequences: There Is a Foot on a Woman's Throat

> *I get tired of wondering why everyone has a say but I don't, why am I always the listener and not the one talking? Why can't I start a conversation in a group? What is my opinion?*
> Navya, 24

Voice is one of the most fundamental aspects of being fully human. Voice is not just about voice. Speaking is not just about speaking. It is about thinking. It is about being heard. It is about recognition by another. It is about belonging. It is about one's very existence. Our voice is so central to our being alive that not speaking up sometimes feels like a slow death. Smriti, 19, from the upper middle class, sums this up saying, 'We try so hard to actually be quiet all the time, not ruffle things, we end up rejecting ourselves – it starts out small but snowballs into something ugly . . . I'll self-destruct.' Locked lips are not sexy. They kill the self.

Each time I interviewed a smart, competent woman, I would be startled to learn later in our conversation how little she trusted her voice. This difficulty in speaking up was so striking that I did additional interviews with highly educated Indian women aged 17 to 35 living in New Delhi, Seattle, Boston and New York. When asked to choose the most significant one of five problems I listed, just about every woman chose voice as the biggest struggle in their lives. Choked voices. Choked throats. As if a heavy foot was on their throat no matter where they lived. Education does not shred the moral belief that keeping quiet is good and speaking up is bad.

For highly educated working women aware of their human rights, it is embarrassing to acknowledge even to themselves that they are afraid to speak up. It is not becoming. Naturally, intelligent women disconnect from their fear in many ways. Riya, 32, says, 'I am not afraid of speaking up but I just don't want to speak up.' Suchi, 24, denies her fears in a different way: 'I never speak my mind . . . it's a pointless exercise. People will never listen anyway, so why bother.' Conflicted about speaking up, women begin to lose confidence in their own abilities.

Doubt yourself and hide

The early training that kills the ability of girls to articulate their thoughts later limits their sense of well-being and confidence. Constant suppression, negation and criticism, overt or subtle, sow doubts about themselves – their thoughts, their intelligence, their minds and their actions.

Smrita, 24, who appears confident in her tight jeans and fitted top, says, 'I have doubts. I constantly question myself. Am I doing the right thing? What is the right thing? But my questioning myself leads to low self-esteem. I always had low self-esteem. I don't know why. Let's blame my parents for it. Because those are the very few people you interact with while growing up. Ha ha.' She laughs off her constant self-doubt.

Reetu, 32, an analyst, describes her inner churning. 'Societal norms, fear, boundaries, rules, things we hear, being told what to do, the perception of women, I have felt defenceless, not as much in reality – when I think of my life, not in actuality – I have got what I wanted, done it, but in my mind, I am always defenceless. Chaos, a lot of roundabout thoughts, questioning, doubting, fear, anxiety.'

Nineteen-year-old Ambika's words reflect what many women say. '*Main bolun ya nahin bolun?* Should I speak or not speak? If I say something and I am wrong what will happen then? What will everyone think about me? What will everyone say about me? It is better to be quiet.'

Plagued by self-doubt, women start isolating themselves. They are aided by a culture that prefers to keep them at home for 'their own safety'. Prerna, 22, from the upper middle class, is forced to stay at home. 'But I don't have people to talk to at home. And Papa will say "*Kahin jane ki zaroorat nahin hai, ghar pe baitho*. There is no need to go anywhere, sit at home."' For a while she keeps thinking about how to get out of her house with friends, but then she gives up the fight to go out and becomes good. Her parents are relieved. Gradually hiding becomes a habit. Invisibility becomes safe. A habit.

Become invisible at work

Many women carry the habit of invisibility to work. When Neetu, 37, who works for American Express, is asked to rate her self-confidence, she says, 'I am confident when I am working in isolation, but my confidence sort of fumbles when I am in work situations, when I have to deal with people.'

This unconscious habit of hiding but not seeing it as hiding is widespread. Devika, 25, has a degree in journalism and works as a media coordinator at an educational institute. Her work philosophy reflects her early training not to speak up, not to be difficult, not to disturb others, not to make demands and generally remain invisible but respectful and loyal. She learned these lessons from her mother: 'Never be jealous of seeing someone's success in life. If you want to grab that position just work hard and have patience. No one can snatch your destiny. Whatever God has to give you he will give you at any cost. Just be nice, talk nice . . .' She adds, 'I believe in being a loyal employee. Just do your work in a fair way and you will succeed. God is tracking you.'

Devika's behaviour fits perfectly the kind of cultural expectation employers have of women, including Microsoft's CEO Satya Nadella, who grew up in Hyderabad but has lived for decades in the Seattle area of the USA. Satya Nadella is a brilliant man, but his early cultural training carves deeply his thinking about how women should behave at work. At a conference to celebrate over 8000 female engineers in Arizona, USA, Nadella was asked what advice he would give a woman on how to ask for a salary raise. He said, 'It's not really about asking for a raise, but knowing and having faith that the system will give you the right raise . . . that might be one of the "initial superpowers" that, quite frankly, women who don't ask for a raise have. It's good karma. It will come back.'

In other words, women employees in a technology world dominated by men should be quiet, work hard, be loyal and in time they will be noticed and get a salary raise if they have good karma.

Nadella quickly recanted his comments and, unlike most public figures facing public backlash, who say they were misunderstood, said he was wrong and that women should ask for a raise when they feel they deserve it. In their book *Women Don't Ask*, researchers Linda Babock and Sara Leschever report that in the USA men initiate salary negotiations four times as often as women do and women systematically ask for less. That women don't ask for raises, together with the bias against women, contributes to the great disparity between women's and men's salaries.

Bias at the workplace starts in the hiring process. Research indicates that raising awareness about bias is not enough, that it can actually increase bias. 'If everyone does it, why not me?' Only when biases are labelled undesirable do they disappear.

Akansha, 24, who works in a large accounting firm, says of her male colleagues, 'At my workplace they are all *bhaiyas*, they are crude, they are very chauvinistic in their reasoning, even if you express something that is intelligent, they always try to make fun of it so it is not taken seriously . . . so I don't express my opinions. I feel there is no point, it is brushed off . . . it is just laughed at and it is frustrating.'

Akansha's experience is reflected in research findings in the USA. Even for women CEOs, competence ratings given by male and female peers fall by 14 per cent when they speak more, while the ratings for male CEOs increase by 10 per cent! Damned if you speak and damned if you don't.

Women feel trapped. They are forgotten when they don't speak up but if they do speak up they are considered attention-grabbing and unlikeable, particularly by men. Gaurav, 26, a software developer for an IT company, says women should speak up but with his next breath he adds, 'Women are attention-seekers, which I don't like.' Similarly, Sai, 30, a man with a degree in computer science, wants women to voice their opinions and also feels 'women are fake, saying things to show off to get attention'.

Uncertain, confused, used to keeping a low profile and plagued by self-doubt, many women take refuge in over-preparing, working long hours and trying to get it perfect before they speak up or participate. But in the process, they become invisible.

I almost fired Aastha, 23, because of her unconscious habit of going-into-hiding and over-preparing. I had hired Aastha through a competitive process, involving a written task and an interview, for a two-month research project. She lived in a different city and agreed to send me brief daily notes or one-liners to keep in touch. She kept delaying sending me a note and after many polite reminders I was ready to fire her over the phone. I called and asked her why she hadn't sent me anything. For a moment there was silence. Then she said, 'Ma'am, I want it to be perfect before I send you anything, I don't want to be a failure, so I keep looking, adding and refining; I want to do my best. The money is not important to me.' Afraid of being judged poorly or 'looking stupid', Aastha over-prepares and she discounts her monetary worth to show how she cares only about her work. But without the daily brief interaction I had suggested, I had no opportunity to either guide Aastha or to get to know her in any way. She remained a stranger.

This tendency among smart women to isolate themselves and work harder results in wasted time and being overlooked for good job assignments and promotions. Researchers Bob Sullivan and Hugh Thompson call this the 'Plateau Effect': frozen women terribly afraid of failure as they attempt to win praise by trying to be perfect.

In the modern work environment, till the rules change, it is important for women to be seen to contribute, to interact with others in the workplace, to assert their presence by speaking up and being noticed. 'Lean in' is the phrase made famous by Sheryl Sandberg, COO of

Facebook, in her book by the same name. But when women are trained not to be in the spotlight, they instinctively shrink from it. Women tend to be backbenchers in conference rooms, even when there are seats at the table. I saw this constantly at World Bank meetings. Even the simple task of raising hands to draw the attention of a speaker becomes complicated. I too had a trick that allowed me to tell myself that I was bold but actually kept me safe. I would raise my hand but only when the speaker was looking elsewhere. As soon as his attention shifted to my side of the room, I would look down pretending to take notes. As soon as the danger had passed my hand would shoot up again. Many women rationalize that by not speaking up they are not dominating and generously giving others a chance to ask questions!

I wasn't pleased to find out that hand-raising is still an issue for young women when I read about the 2012 gender experiment at the Harvard Business School in Cambridge, USA. It emerged that even these women seem to lack self-confidence compared to the men in the class, and had to be trained to raise their hands confidently and keep them raised till the mostly male professors called on them to speak. The professors were videotaped to make them aware of their biases.

Respect and fear men

'Good women' defer to men. They wait. Deference to the father's authority is particularly sacred in the Indian context. Sudhir Kakar, India's most respected cultural observer, said, 'This deference later transfers to other authority figures, politicians, bosses, husbands.' Nancy,

14, is already aware of this dynamic in her behaviour. She says, 'My father is my biggest fear . . . I think a relationship with a boy is more difficult for me because I have no confidence to say anything.' Not surprisingly, when women are in a conversation with men they tend to wait and not interrupt men, whereas men interrupt women much more frequently than they interrupt other men. Women become waiters.

Geetika, 25, who is a trainer in a British language institute and is also pursuing an advanced business degree, does not speak her mind out of respect, particularly towards the men in her life. 'I had this conversation with Dad. I said for the rapist in Nirbhaya's case, why is justice delayed? Papa says, "*Yeh to aise hee hota hai*, it happens like this." I said, *Kab tak?* Till when? I felt rapists should be castrated but Papa says, "*Aise nahin hota*, it doesn't happen like this." That time I couldn't confront him and I got afraid, thinking I am saying the wrong thing.' Asserting a different opinion is perceived as disrespectful, and because there is no exchange, the conversation stops. There is no new learning. Women stop growing.

Even a woman like Garima, 31, who describes herself as fiercely independent, lives alone in Ahmedabad and travels all over the country by herself, is unable to speak up to her boyfriend because of her early training. 'There is this guilt associated with speaking up. When I speak up, it's not a fearless, rightful way of speaking up, it's like always apologetic about who I am. So you develop tactics – plead, beg, lie – maybe then they'll say yes. So the practice of speaking up became a very servile way of expressing. You are less, you are asking for too much, and the one who is granting – the one above – is huge, almost a deity figure.' Fear of her father and later of her boyfriend kept Garima's mouth locked. She finally turned to therapy for help.

Barkha, 37, works as a voice-over artist but lost her own voice to deference to men. She objected to her mother's dictate to 'follow your husband like a cow'. She hates herself for behaving like a cow despite her determination to be different. She said, 'I did it most of the time but it only made me feel I had no intelligence. I have no mind of my own and it is Vikram's mind I have to follow and whatever he says is right. I don't have an opinion and even if I have an opinion it doesn't matter. Taking permission from him for everything, believing he is the authority and I have to take permission from him. Now I feel I could have stopped this a long time ago.' But her mouth would not open. After eight years she finally walked out of this marriage.

This deference to men extends to the workplace, and plagues women. Shravanthi, 23, doesn't engage in the conversations at meetings out of deference and fear that they, the men, will look stupid. 'My thought process goes something like this at work meetings: how can that senior man say such stupid things, isn't he embarrassed? But if I point it out I will make him look bad and I can't do that.' She protects him.

Despite keeping their mouths locked, many women do advance at least to the mid-management levels. Divya, 37, has a PhD in economics and is currently director in a prestigious international agency in New York. At the end of a long conversation over lunch at an Indian restaurant in downtown Manhattan, I asked Divya about her biggest problem as a woman. She said without hesitation, speaking up. 'I was taught to be obedient, so in my professional life I am not very good at speaking up.'

Divya is competent and has won a string of awards. But she does not approach her boss to sort out delays in clearances; instead she waits for her boss to call her. She is afraid of interrupting his work, and in the process delays her own projects. She considers initiating contact to solve problems to achieve common goals as 'pushy, a confrontation'. 'With my Indian upbringing, I remain quiet, being polite. I don't like to confront, I believe in peace.' And Divya is not alone. Research shows that when women are in the minority at work, which becomes even more common at senior levels, they find it difficult to speak up. Early orders to be respectful keep competent women silent.

Let argumentation, reasoning and debate die

How can women who have been told to shut up, to have no opinion, who have been scolded, shamed, told they are stupid and no good and locked up at home, be expected to discuss, debate and argue? It is like expecting the sun to rise at night. Women's training distorts the very meaning of argumentation – it becomes synonymous with fighting, yelling, anger, hurting and the end of relationships and jobs.

Argumentation is the use of reasoning to persuade others of an idea, action or theory. It is an act of communication that involves going to and fro, changing and adapting how and what one says to persuade the other. It involves thinking, talking and listening rapidly in real time. It involves questioning. The essence of argumentation is making a claim and using reasoning to support that claim. Since women are taught not to talk or form opinions, it is difficult for them to practise reasoning to support their claims.

Shivani, 28, from the upper middle class, is one of a handful of women who said she learned the art of reasoning from her dad. She said, 'For issues that matter and deserve my energy I argue. My dad does it with me, he asks me to justify my point, to give a reason. If my boss wants me to do a task and it's ridiculous then I ask for a reason. I love the word justification. *Aisa kyun karna hai, aisa kyun ho raha hai?* Why should we do this, why is it happening like this?'

A woman who argues breaks the core rules about womanly goodness and this distresses many but particularly her trainers, her parents. In Suneha's middle-class family, arguments were labelled 'nagging' by her mother, an educator. Her mother's constant refrain was, 'You don't need to nag out in front of others.' Suneha, now 30, says, 'I hate such things, nagging.' Women who argue are called loud, crazy, nags, nasty, scolds, shrill or hysterical. Men who argue are called leaders!

The language of war and weapons is frequently used when talking about women who argue. Shuchi, 30, was trained not to argue by her mother constantly saying, '*Zaruri nahin hai ki har baat pe talwaar leke khada hua jaaye*. It not necessary that every time something is said, you have to take out your sword and stand . . . if you can, ignore, don't argue, *jaane do*, just leave it.' Chanda, also 30, has a habit of answering back even for small things, like the volume of the TV. She says, 'My mom calls me Jhansi ki Rani, your sword is always ready.' It is not yet a compliment. When women become quiet, they are, with relief, called mature. They have finally grown up.

If everything about women's voice training could be wrapped up in one sentence, it would be this: only bad women argue. Just as women's clothes become labelled as moral or immoral to keep women in line, a woman who questions is not just impolite and stubborn, but is also vulgar and immoral. A woman who argues is not a woman, but untethered, wild, aggressive, angry, loose, a 'bitch' and a 'whore' out to make war. Meera found her voice by living with 'whores'.

Afraid of being misclassified, women argue cautiously and only when they are more than a hundred per cent sure of their facts. Nikita, 24, with a graduate degree in finance from the USA, says, 'If I am not sure of something I won't say it.' Swati, 25, an engineer, sums it up saying, 'Women are more afraid of everything – men are very confident, *chahe unhe kuch bhi na pata ho*, even when they know nothing.' Research from the USA shows that she is right. Men systematically overestimate their abilities and what they know and women underestimate their knowledge and abilities. Research also indicates that to succeed confidence matters more than competence and that women are more afraid of failure.

Women make it even harder for themselves by framing an argument as winning or losing, with everybody else cast as hanging judges. It becomes a psychic nightmare. Every time you open your mouth there is the risk of 'losing'. For Sangeeta, 38, who heads an advertising business in Gurgaon, speaking and judgement go together. She has only one framework. When others speak, she judges them as right or wrong, and when she speaks, she assumes others do the same to her. Suhana, 33, a medical supplies entrepreneur in Mumbai, doesn't speak up in any discussion 'because I think people will judge me'.

Unexpressed, women ruminate, loop over the same thing multiple times, and further lose their confidence by keeping themselves stuck in the past instead of moving forward and taking action. Divya, 37, says, 'At work I am on guard, I think too much. I go crazy speculating about things. If someone says something, I think, what did they say, what do they mean? It may be a casual comment, but I keep going deeper and deeper, stuck in my head and discussing the same thing over and over again. Maybe I said something wrong. What did I say? Both my mother and husband tell me, you are sitting here, but you are not with us, you are thinking.'

Used to swallowing their words and unpractised in the give and take of jostling for position, women take arguments very personally and brood on them long after the arguments are over. Sanchita, 26, observes, 'Men fart it out, women carry it on forever, just in general, including me. Men will fight it out and go and have a Pepsi together afterwards.' Men stereotype women's tendency to repeat grievances as, '*uski sui attak gai*, her needle got stuck.' Shashank, 31, a male director at Morgan Stanley, says, 'For me when a topic is finished, the topic is finished. *Khatam*. If it is with another guy, it will never crop up again. With a woman, an argument may have happened three to six months ago and they bring it up again, it is still there. Women don't forget, never.' He starts laughing.

Research from the USA shows that men shrug off non-events while women ruminate and personalize small things and conclude something is wrong with them. Then it is difficult to let go. They blame themselves. The assumption is, 'it's me, I am the problem'. Of course it gets intensely personal. Women also report feeling more affected by criticism and losing arguments.

Don't be emotional

Although women commonly claim to be more emotional and more emotionally sensitive, they also block their emotions, including anger. This reflects the early training of conflict as something bad to be avoided. Such women become afraid of raised voices. They not only hush themselves, they hush others. The pressure to be perfect, polite peacemakers robs women of the ability to express their emotions in appropriate ways. Women can become walking oversensitive stereotypes. They have meltdowns, they dismiss the problem as not important, they withdraw and they shut down as they try not to be 'too emotional'. These are learned behaviours, a consequence of societal training, of unexpressed words and feelings, and not genetic endowments of women.

While many women are proud of their ability to feel and express their emotions more easily than men, many still feel crushed by men's negative stereotypes of women's emotionality. Women say they are so afraid of being labelled 'drama queen' by men that they tiptoe around, not saying what they feel. Tripti, 17, still in high school, tries to act carefree, as she is convinced that behind her back men are saying, '*Woh kitna natak kar rahi thi yaar*, she is so dramatic . . . so we have to pretend to be easy-going.'

Stuffed feelings are always in danger of leaking out at the most inopportune moments. For Rohini, 24, with a degree in business management, emotional containment is tough. 'I can't hide emotions, I can't control myself when I say things . . . And if I try to do so, I become depressed. I say a few words, and then cry . . . I have the urge to talk to anybody about anything.' Noni, 33, lives in fear of her own emotions. 'A lot of times I ignore myself, I keep my words inside, I do not express myself properly. One reason is that I am emotionally sensitive. Weak – I don't like saying emotionally weak. Physically, I am strong, but when I have to emotionally contain myself, I get afraid too much, I cry.'

Told a hundred times to bottle up their emotions and not argue, women report feeling choked and unable to breathe. Not surprisingly, they sometimes burst into tears – tears of anger, tears of unspoken words, tears of words that refuse to leave the mouth. Sirija, 23, who comes from an artistic, liberal upper-middle-class family, says, 'I know I have a lot of anger inside which I have not really expressed and I know for a fact it is filling up . . . I don't like the restlessness.'

Unfortunately, the outpouring of unexpressed emotions during aborted arguments makes both women and men conclude that women are more illogical. It results in the kind of view held by Arunima, 25, who works in HR in the personnel division, that 'men are more logic-driven than women'. Arunima has misidentified the problem. The problem is not lack of logic but the unexpressed emotions that derail the rational mind and logic. For many women, an argument is like being in a tiny boat in a storm – there is only one goal, to get out of the storm.

Often young men said women don't have logical minds. Raju, 27, a physiotherapist, broke up with his girlfriend because 'She couldn't follow logic and she wouldn't speak up. I know she was upset but she would say nothing. So it dwindled into chit-chat and then we broke up, it was not interesting.' Neither women nor men made any connections between women's behaviours and their early training to fit cultural definitions of moral goodness.

Trained not to argue, women also find themselves defenceless and exposed. Nandita, 50, says, 'We are expected to remain mum . . . even if someone is doing wrong to us. You have to live with *atyachar*, brutality, atrocity, torture, it becomes part of your personality. You don't have the courage to clarify and speak up when *jhoothe ilzaam lagaaye*, you are accused wrongly. If someone snatches your things, you can't speak up and say *yeh meri hai*, this is mine.' Women are often afraid to speak up even when they are inappropriately touched. Death by goodness.

Become silent and boringly safe

In trying to be good, having faint opinions and unable to make their case, women become uninteresting conversational companions. Their world narrows down. Saurabh, 24, says, 'The only concern my mother has is about food, have you eaten, why have you not eaten, what did you have for lunch, what do you want to eat now, did you like it?' He doesn't mean to discount his mother; he is merely reflecting a common reality.

Many smart young men criticize educated women for being boring, not speaking up and for not engaging in intelligent discussion. Like women, men are also blind to the long training that stifles women's intelligence. Navjeet, 33, has a MBA and is a successful photographer. He is a warm, kind man and very concerned about gender inequality. But in talking about his parents, he praises his father as the only one who can engage in conversation, logic and debate about anything. He says, 'My father's range was huge, from finance to religion to relatives, he would always say that a discussion always leads to something better, we would really be shouting at each other, have a lot of debates.' His mother did not debate. Navjeet labelled his mother, whom he loved dearly, as 'superstitious'.

Navjeet then praises his mother as the 'shock absorber' in his family, the social glue. As a shock absorber, his mother by definition could not engage in debate. Shock absorbers by mandate and function don't initiate, interrupt or disrupt. They absorb the jolts. They don't create the jolts. It is then no surprise that women don't do well in conversations, meetings or heated arguments, whether at work or at home. They remain silent. They absorb the tension.

Expressing his irritation, Navjeet says, 'Young women seem so ignorant and lack confidence to speak out. Women are also too submissive at times, they should speak back, you have the right to express everything, why is that right not exercised?' For people groomed into positions of power and privilege, it is difficult to see their own power or to understand why the less powerful act in the way they do. To them, it makes no sense.

Men have very important roles in bringing about change. Self-awareness is important but by itself it does not change behaviour. Men have to stop keeping silent and must interrupt when they see bad behaviour or bias, and signal that it is uncool, unacceptable.

Both women and men must change. Who should change first? How do we change?

Reflections

The foot on a woman's throat is not her own. Her voice is not her own. It belongs to society. It is her mother's voice. It is her father's voice. It is her teacher's voice. It is her brother's, her sister's, her husband's, her friend's, her employer's, it is the shopkeeper's voice. Over time, though, it does become her own voice. The cultural machinery to create invisible women who do not exist and who cannot speak, let alone create a racket, is functioning well.

Silence steals women. Silence ghosts women. Silence kills women.

Yet, every woman thinks she is alone; she is the only one. Everyone pretends. It is freeing to know that this fear of speaking up is not personal. Fear is the outcome of deliberate training by cultural, social, educational and political systems passed down generation after generation. It permeates all our systems, from home to the office. These systems of silencing women must change. Stop punishing girls and women for speaking up. Instead, coach women in groups to discuss, to debate and to negotiate. Make it normal. Listen. Coach the men particularly to listen. In the public sphere, do not allow male-only or male-dominated boards, committees, conferences, conclaves, panels, houses of parliament and summits. Change the formal and informal rules that enable participation. Educate both men and women to participate in new ways, with each other.

Despite their training to delete themselves, there are many women who find their voice. Some simply start speaking up and don't give up; some prepare beforehand; some find their voice in college through sports, theatre, dance, debating clubs or dialogues; some through therapy and alternative therapies; some through supportive boyfriends and husbands; some through spirituality. A few find their voice through the appreciation of kind bosses, though I found this to be rarer than the intervention of gurus or God. Some find their voice at work. Some find their voice after horrendous personal tragedies. Some find their voice at 20. Some find their voice at 60. And some, like Meera, only after dangerous, disruptive action that no young woman should have to go through.

Don't be Chup. Speak up. Again and again.

4

Pleasing

Just Slide, Squeeze, Shrink, *Adjust Kar Lo*

Poonam, 54, is a senior United Nations official. She joined the elite Indian Administrative Service as a 23-year-old.

'No, no, I am not afraid. I think I wanted to be thought of as a nice person . . . not someone with a bichhoo *[scorpion] in her mouth that comes out suddenly, so I didn't speak up. Like you know that aggressive Punjabi woman, I didn't want that to happen. I think it was all these things – what will so-and-so think, how they won't see it from my point of view and thinking that the whole relationship will fail. So many fears, imagined or real, who knows . . . I just want to please, please, please. I have never been able to communicate or talk openly and clearly with people who matter to me, who I love, my family and friends, about what I want. I would get small small ideas from outside like keep your own account – but I was so scared to say it. Even today. Slowly I am changing with little little things. What TV show to watch, what food to eat.*

'At home, I was trying to be a good wife and a good daughter-in-law. We did not discuss any problems we had. We never had enough money. Even the SBI [State Bank of India] fellow would feel so sorry for us IAS officers because at the end of each month I would take a loan of Rs 2000. He would call me and tell me about small loan schemes. Everyone thought I am in the government, so full of money. I felt exploited financially, emotionally, physically, space-wise. Not appreciated. It was a very authoritarian household. Sometimes

there was nothing for me to eat. I don't blame them. I feel the mistake is mine. I never sat them down and said calmly, listen, we have to talk. Maybe I started compartmentalizing and shutting myself off because I was not happy.

'In my own life I have seen two selves, one body, doing different 12-hour shifts. One at home and one outside the home. One very insecure person at home unable to express herself. And the other person in the office a straight talker that everyone trusts, with no fears or insecurities. In one body; in one life. In 24 hours. Every 24 hours for 30 years and nothing changed or seeped through from one life to the other. I hadn't realized I did this till now. I am telling you, in the office I don't care what people think of me. I am just honestly dealing with everything. In the office every issue is discussed. My mother never worked, so in the office I had no role model. But in the household, I did not have the guts to say what I was actually thinking. I paid a high price for being a pleaser. Bad relationships. So if I were to write my autobiography I would say if you are fearful and keep quiet, don't be; it just ruins relationships. If you are afraid of looking like a bad woman, it will happen anyway. Because sooner or later the bubble will burst.'

And a scorpion will jump out.

* * *

'Adjustable girls' are desirable, good girls. The English word 'adjust' is used so often in raising good girls that it has become a Hindi word. Adjustable girls automatically change their bodies and behaviour to please others; they fit in anywhere and obligingly slip, slide, squeeze and shrink into the tiniest physical and psychological spaces. *Beta, thoda adjust kar lo*, darling, adjust a little. You learn it when sitting in a car, legs tightly squeezed together, while the men sit back with their legs apart; you learn it when you can't wear tight clothes, pants or dresses in front of disapproving visiting relatives; you learn it when you are not allowed to speak back to that idiot of an uncle who calls you dark, fat, hairy or stupid and pities you; you learn it when you are scolded for being upset about anything; you learn it as you watch your brother get the bigger chocolate or go to a better school or college and you pretend it does not hurt; you learn it when you are left at home but the boys go out; you learn it when your mother does nothing when your father is rude to her, scolds her, demeans her or hits her. As many mothers say to their daughters, *Apne aap ko thoda adjust kar lo*, you adjust yourself. This is a deceptively benign way, bit by bit, to start erasing any signs of an independent self in girls. It teaches girls to discount themselves and makes girls available at a permanent discount in the world. In marriage it is reflected in dowries and at work in lower salaries.

Having a self becomes confused with being selfish. Being selfish of course is bad for nice and caring girls. Having a self is made shameful by associating it with being 'difficult, demanding, aggressive, nasty, bitchy, stubborn, opinionated and bad'. Rashi, 25, who spoke in a soft voice, put it this way. 'I was taught to learn to adjust, not be too demanding, whenever I started crying over something I wanted, then Mom always used to say, *beta, thoda adjust karna padta hai*, darling, you have to adjust a little.'

Learning to delay gratification and to exercise self-control is good, but not when it is only and always the responsibility of the girl. When their young daughters ask why they should adjust, mothers feel helpless and say, '*Arrey bhai, ladies ko karna padta hai*, ladies just have to do it.'

Girls learn to shrink themselves to take up as little space as possible. Women gave many examples of learning to adjust, including how to sit in the iconic Ambassador car. Himani, 24, says, 'If I talk about childhood, in the old days, we had only one car, *usi mein*, in that only, we all used to all go. So I was like creating spaces for others, *khud thoda adjust kar ke baithke*, I would adjust myself and sit and I used to feel so proud about it that I am doing something good for others and got appreciated by my parents too.'

Parents now avoid the word sacrifice but the end result is the same. Dismissing the examples of 'Sati–Savitri', the devoted and loyal wife, held up to be the model of women's selfless sacrifice in previous generations, many educated women deny sacrificing, but it dribbles out in different ways.

Dipali, 25, a financial planner, says forcefully, 'Nobody has told me to sacrifice. I hate sacrificing. I was told by my father to be more adjusting, compromising.' Adjusting behaviour is tied to family honour and then it becomes even more difficult to break. After all, why would you want to dishonour the family? *Thoda adjust kar lo* is the Indian way of creating what psychologists call 'a compulsive people-pleaser', particularly among women. Pleasing others and making others happy is part of the delight of belonging to a family or a circle of friends. But compulsive pleasers always put the needs of others first while ignoring their own needs. It becomes a life-draining habit. Surviving on approval, fear becomes the first lining in the body. Poonam, the United Nations official, names the fears which ran her life: 'Fear of displeasing loved ones, fear of rejection, fear of being left by my husband, fear of being judged and fear of never being good enough, never measuring up.' Acting 'goody-goody', she lives in fear, guilt and resentment.

Everyone of course likes a pleasing woman who is so 'nice' and who makes life so easy. Because pleasing is so rewarding initially, it is difficult for us to see its dark contribution to women's joylessness. Buried in a mound of sweetness, the compulsion to constantly please others is the perfect ploy to further kill the self after the body is denied and the voice has been silenced. Do not exist. Focus only on others. Covered in sugar and everything nice, pleasing others allows women to go down smiling. Women become pleasing drones.

Khushi, 30, a lecturer at Delhi University, summarizes this: 'Women smile to please. Men smile when pleased.'

The Early Training: How to Please and Serve Others

> *I have been taught girls should always wear a smile on their face*. Preeti, 24

Good girls are trained early to be loving and nice and to please others. I heard the same thing over and over in the definitions of a 'good girl' from middle-class and elite schools in Delhi. Swati, 14, from Model School, defines a good girl as 'being loving and everyone's favourite'. Everyone's favourite is never a threat. Girls are trained to please by becoming non-aggressive and therefore non-threatening, especially to boys and men. Baani, 14, from Delhi Public School, says her goal as a good girl is 'to take care of everyone'.

Take care of others

The internalized rule to always take care of others locks a girl into ignoring her own self, her own needs and wants. Slowly it becomes a deeply ingrained habit. Nishita, 19, from a well-off family, describes herself as a 'blender'. She says, 'I was trained like that as a child. You basically blend yourself into the other person's energies so much because you just want their happiness and that is what I wanted to do. I asked myself, why are you on this earth? My answer, to make people happy.'

The purpose of her life and others' happiness become interlocked. This in itself is not bad but when this is only an obligation for girls, it creates unequal relationships. Blenders get absorbed into the needs of others and do not have a strong self. And there is pressure to do it perfectly.

Aiming for a perfect score each time makes pleasing behaviour even more exhausting. For Namrata, 30, a stay-at-home mother with an MCom degree, this means, 'To always satisfy others and give them no opportunity to complain. And pleasers can never complain about the constant demands.' Ishita, 28, says, 'You never complain, never, never. No cribbing, do everything. With grace, poise, intelligence and lots of selfless love.' Complaints about serving others are not only considered ungracious, but a complaining pleaser is culturally dangerous. A complainer signals the possibility of defiance, rebellion or stoppage of service. Pleasing is in essence training to forget yourself, because if you have your own needs and preferences, it interferes with the total focus on serving others.

In this cultural context the goal is to prevent girls from developing preferences in the first place. One way is to train girls to never ask directly for anything they want, not even for the littlest things they may love. Ginny, 25, with a degree in finance, learned this lesson early. 'I used to love Coca-Cola as a five-year-old so when asked, what do you want, I used to ask for it everywhere I went, until my parents told me not to. They said what will people think, *kitni besharam hai*, she is so shameless.' Ginny's parents were just training her in society's rules. Their teaching is not about good manners, Coca-Cola being good or bad nor about how many Coca-Colas she drinks. Ginny is being shamed into not asking for what she wants. She is being taught that her preferences are not important but shameful and that it is better to let others make decisions for her, including what she should drink. These little suppressions of the self result in an undifferentiated self and signal the making of a pleaser. A good, moral girl.

When a girl's life goal is to serve others, it helps not to have a strong, differentiated self, not to have well-defined preferences and strong likes and dislikes. When you don't have preferences, it is easy to go with other people's preferences. A girl who is continually erased can adapt anywhere; it makes adjustment easier.

Smile, please

The ultimate signal of being nice and safe is a smile. We are taught the minutiae of how to smile, when to smile and how much to smile. Nishi, 20, a student of history, says, 'My parents teach me everything, including how to stand, and a smile matters. *Thoda smile achha karo, kam karo*, make your smile nicer, a little less – they teach me these small small things.' Netra, 28, who works for the *Hindustan Times*, says 'A girl should smile, smile, smile.'

Women distinguish between an innocent smile, a shrewd smile, a sensible smile, a gentle smile, a confident smile and a sexy smile. For Rani, 20, it has to be a 'smile with a pure heart'. Most importantly girls are taught to smile, so others, especially men, feel good about themselves. Amisha, 18, whose father is in the army, says, 'My father shows me a lot of love and care. He says if I do not see you smiling, I do not feel good.' So she smiles. A smile becomes an obligation.

A compulsory smile is the cover behind which girls are trained to hide their feelings and problems. Woman after woman said they are trained 'to smile even in the worst of situations and not make demands or disturb the happiness of others'. Reva, 20, from a business family says, 'My papa always said, "Even if you are in difficulty and suffering and if you are still able to keep others happy, then only will you also feel happy." *Agar main pareshan hoon*, even if I am worried and in great difficulty, even then I answer with a smile on my face. I feel just because I face all these problems why should I worry the other person. Nobody should be in worry because of me.' It isn't enough to smile at others when you are happy. The real test is, can you smile even when you are unhappy and suffering. This suppression of feelings and hiding of problems isolate a girl from others, and eat away at her own mind and aliveness.

As important as it may be to smile through everything, it is still possible for girls to over-smile. Tina, 25, who loves design, is a smile expert. She says, '*Bahut over-smile nahin karna chahiye*, you shouldn't over-smile. Just a normal smile, looking at you people should know *senses mein hai*, you are in your senses, and you are not going to smile just at anybody. I have seen in the movies that if a girl smiles at a boy, he feels that she is impressed with him. I have observed this also. Once we were in a mall roaming with friends and then waiting to see a movie and we were laughing so much (not smiling), there was a group of boys who observed us and got so much guts that one of them came to us and said we are doing research to see if girls can lift [pick up] boys. Because of our attitude of happiness they started acting familiar. Over-smiling is not good.'

Over-smiling crosses the boundary from the innocuous pleasing of a good girl to a bad girl with a loose character, because it signals that a girl exists. A girl with a self can destabilize the existing social order. Therefore, there is a smile scale that rates girls from good to bad.

But don't laugh

Laughter, as Tina cautions, is a totally different matter. *Hasee Toh Phasee*, she who laughs is trapped, the title of a popular Bollywood movie, captures this piece of cultural knowledge: When you laugh you are present. Laughter is not just the next level up from smiling. It falls into a different species. Laughter implies that the focus on the other is forgotten, if even for a moment. It draws attention to the self. Joy is bursting within you which means you must exist. It violates the rule of non-existence.

Laughter of girls therefore makes mothers nervous. Not surprisingly, then, mothers have clear rules about laughter. Akshita, 16, from Modern School, says, 'It is amazing to be happy but when I laugh very loudly my mom says, "What are you doing?" My mom doesn't like it.'

Sarina, 24, who has a serious demeanour, says her mother often tells her '*Dhang se haso*, laugh properly or don't laugh. I was told not to laugh too much or show too much excitement in front of guests. It was considered ill-mannered.' Shefali, 30, says, 'When we were young we were not allowed to laugh in front of men,' and then laughs very loudly. Laughter is dangerous because it means that the training to erase girls has not been completely effective. Laughter beckons, and so the laughter of young girls in front of men is even more strictly regulated to protect them from male attention.

If laughing is inappropriate, loud laughter drives mothers crazy. Laughter, especially unrestrained laughter, indicates moments of sheer happiness. This contradicts the training of good girls to put others' happiness before their own. Loud laughter can be rebellious, either way it indicates the presence of a strong, independent self. Mothers insist that girls press the mute button. *Dheere haso*. Laugh softly.

Unrestrained laughter is so tainted with whiffs of immorality that restraint is still modelled by the most famous Bollywood actresses. At a Filmfare award night event screened on television, every major female superstar from Deepika Padukone to the young Alia Bhatt bent her whole body forward, head towards the lap, and covered her mouth with her hands while laughing, so that her face was almost hidden. None of the male stars did so – they laughed heartily with their heads thrown back a little and mouths wide open.

New research shows that laughter across species indicates play, it bonds us to each other and it activates the dopamine or reward centre of the brain; laughter is a joyous high. In the service of pleasing others, joy is banned, even though no one says this aloud. Society just makes the expression of laughter rude, unsafe and a bit immoral.

Consequences: The Eraser – The Woman Who Smiles, Speaks and Lives for Others

I never say what I feel but what others want to hear.
Niti, 25

Teaching girls to please others relentlessly is teaching girls to erase themselves. A woman becomes an eraser. She fits in anywhere and everywhere, erasing herself and camouflaging like a chameleon. Over time a woman becomes a master eraser. By erasing herself, she upholds society, she upholds her family, she upholds her husband and she upholds her children. Darsha, 25, proudly describes herself as 'Highly elastic. The core of who I am has been overlapped with what others want me to be.' She waits to receive signals from others and then changes to win their approval.

A woman becomes an approval-seeking missile. She tries to get the approval of everyone – mother, father, brother, doctors, lawyers, neighbours, cheaters, exploiters, aggressors, abusers, strangers, society, husband, mother-in-law, father-in-law, bosses, colleagues and friends. She lives and breathes on approval. She develops finely tuned antennae for approval and becomes deathly afraid to offend. Like Kaveri, 23, an engineer, who constantly scans her world to ensure she is likeable. She is only reassured when she 'sees a general liking for myself in other people'. Abhisha, 20, who is in the final year of a BCom honours degree goes further: she is compulsive about making herself lovable all the time. 'My strength is to easily draw people towards me, I am so lovable and friendly.' The compulsive need to be liked all the time signals the presence of an erased woman. A compulsive pleaser is a sacrificed woman who lives a partial or compartmentalized life. It signals the victory of her trainers.

The training to compulsively please is not erased by education and employment because pleasing is framed and internalized as a high virtue. Women are proud to claim they are giving, adjusting, elastic, compromising, adaptable, flexible, likeable, lovable, non-complaining and non-aggressive. How can you object to this behaviour? It is so 'nice'. What is wrong with this behaviour is that it forces women to erase themselves, and erased women are at the mercy of others. What is dangerous is that such behaviour is considered 'natural' and an 'inherent quality' only for women. What is even more dangerous is that no woman or man identifies unstoppable pleasing behaviour as leading to partial death, to creating a woman fuelled by fear, a woman who lives on the fumes of approval.

A seemingly confident woman with advanced degrees, Richa, 25, talks openly about her constant fear of displeasing. 'I am afraid all the time of being the real me, all the time the fear of having to explain myself as to why I am the way I am. It is not easy for me. I think a hundred times before I talk about what I want or need or even before I crack a joke unless that joke has been laughed at before. I have that uncontrollable desire to be liked. I do and say things just because I know that the other person who I am with will like what I said. I am still afraid to be who I really want to be at all times.' Although men too can be pleasers, no man I met expressed such agony about pleasing. Persistent pleasing behaviour slowly eats away at women's lives. It keeps them half-alive and half-dead.

Don't have any preferences: Kuch bhi

For adjustable girls, it is truly ideal not to have preferences – it makes life unruffled. Flat. It makes it easier to blend in, to be liked. If you really don't care whether the wall is painted blue, white or yellow, or whether you eat chaat or a dosa, or whether your husband controls your money and gives you a little or nothing, it is easier to avoid strong emotions, conflict and any possibility of rejection. It is easier all around when women just stop thinking.

The most common phrase well-adjusted women use when asked what they want is *kuch bhi*, anything, or I don't mind. Do you want to go for a movie? I don't mind. Should we go out to eat? I don't mind. Where do you want to go? Anywhere, you decide.

It used to drive me crazy when I'd ask my mother during visits home, what do you want to do tonight?

Kuch bhi. Or which restaurant do you want to go to? *Koi bhi*. Any. But now after a lifetime, I understand why, so I ask her in a different way. I play a binary game, I give her two choices at a time. Do you want to go to Sagar or Kwality? Do you want to go to the Gymkhana Club or Habitat? I watch her face very carefully as she sometimes likes neither. Then she keeps quiet for longer. So I back off and start with general categories. Do you want to eat Indian or Italian? It is a game to see if I can ferret out her preferences. My mother loves going out. It would be so much simpler if she would just say, 'Take me here today.' But that is a rare day. It would violate her deep training about being good and moral by not having and certainly not expressing preferences.

Really well-adjusted women are so well trained that they applaud their preference-free state. Tanya, 17, says, 'I am not a very particular person on many things. I hardly dislike anything. I am not very fussy about food. I usually agree with what everyone likes.' Srija, 23, is happy with herself because she thinks she has wiped out her preferences. 'Yes, I think so, I am a very easy person, you can please me very easily. If I am with another person, I try to take the safer option.'

It is difficult for an intelligent human being to erase herself completely. Surbhi, 25, is so afraid of having a preference that she explains most things about herself as temporary. 'I like things very momentarily. I do not have a permanent liking for anything.' She drifts. Kavi, 33, who has realized with some alarm that she still has some preferences, adopts a strategy of non-disclosure. She says, 'I do not disclose my likes and dislikes to everyone.'

The high goal to be preference-free is so virtuous that some women, like Diya, 30, are still struggling to reach it. 'I am working on getting out of this like and dislike thing. It shouldn't matter to me.' Diya feels guilty all the time. She says, 'I live in a state of agitation.' Pleasing slowly erodes a woman's sense of self. It does not lead to salvation, but to pretence.

Pretend nothing hurts, hide your emotions

Emotional suppression is a requirement across many habits. When the purpose of life becomes pleasing others, pleasers are forced to pretend. They pretend to be loving; they pretend to be happy; they pretend to never feel hurt; they pretend that nothing affects them. Pleasers, in effect, become pretenders. Shaloo, 44, the principal of a school, describes herself as jolly but she says keeping her emotions 'under wraps' drains her life energy. 'As a woman I think about being a pretender. Keep pretending; other than that, I think nothing is challenging.' Loveleen, 36, who describes herself as an emotional creature, is proud of her ability to pretend. She says, 'Even if I am hurt, people will not know from my demeanour. I take pride in that.'

Not allowed to express their full range of emotions, women find it difficult after a while to even identify their own emotions. Women, the supposed emotional experts, become emotionally illiterate. They take refuge in thinking. Pallavi, 25, says, 'Mostly I am just thinking, not feeling. Even if it's extremely sad or happy, after a while you are just thinking, so it is difficult to say if I am a happy person or a sad person. I guess I am just a person. I guess I am happy-ish. Mostly I am just blah.' Thinking is safe, but emotions are not, so women flatten out their 'unruly' emotionality. Like a reversed pressure cooker, their steam under pressure implodes, burning, scalding and ripping from the inside.

The clamping down on everyday feelings depresses the mind and carves fissures into the body. Science has now established the power of emotions and the strong mind–body connection. Aneeta, 27, says, 'I develop toxins by keeping things inside me. I develop stress and acne.' Depression rates are 50 per cent higher for women than for men in India. Mithali, 25, went into severe clinical depression after she broke up with her boyfriend at 21, she lost 25 kilos and came close to committing suicide. She quit her job, quit all her friends, quit talking, she quit her life. She stayed in her room and her loving family pretended nothing was wrong through it all. She received no professional help. She slowly clawed back to life after discovering guided meditation and 'love yourself' videos on YouTube that she watched day and night month after month. YouTube saved her life.

Burying their emotional life and posing as ever-flowing fountains of love, women start to lose intimacy even with those they adore. Sonia, 31, says she does not share her tears with anyone, not even her sister. She cried for days alone when she broke up with her boyfriend but she faked it to appear happy all the time. Some women avoid attachment as an emotional control strategy. Niti, 25, says, 'My biggest fear is to bond with people at the emotional level. I hate attachments.' In fact, women start judging their emotions negatively. Rima, 33, calls herself foolish, an emotional fool, because of her 'emotional sensitivity'. Yet it is this emotional intelligence that is fundamental to human happiness, to making decisions, to building community and for successful leadership. Just about every quality associated with women becomes discounted and somehow made wrong or a sign of weakness.

Can't make decisions, stay confused

It is human nature to want to be liked and approved of by others. But the extreme training women receive in pleasing, in being likeable all the time, makes the brain like a tightly packed ball of Maggi noodles – it is impossible to disentangle and to figure out what you want as distinct from what other people want.

Clear thinking becomes difficult. When I asked women if it was easy to make decisions, the majority said no. One after another, even women with post-graduate degrees said they feel very confused when it comes to making decisions. Not being allowed to develop preferences and being scolded or rejected for stating preferences flood the intellectual process of decision-making with fear – fear of disapproval, fear of rejection and fear of abandonment because of choices made. Fear of displeasing men becomes particularly ingrained. I, too, discovered this about myself, much to my annoyance.

I love road trips. A few years ago, my husband and I decided to do a road trip down the West Coast of the USA and across the south to New Orleans and back to Washington, DC. I suggested we take turns in picking hotels for the night. He would take five minutes. When it was my turn, I would take hours, reading the guidebook and the free motel guides advertising discounts. I could not make a decision. And then I would badger him with questions, trying to get him to decide for me. A very patient man, he was surprised, and one evening he pointed out that it was my turn. I persisted and he finally said, 'Motel 6', the cheapest place to crash for the night. I felt completely deflated. I enjoy luxury but when I spend the money, it makes me feel guilty. I had wanted him to choose some place nice, overlooking the ocean, so that I could enjoy a luxurious place without anxiety. I didn't know I was anxious; after all, it was such a simple decision, and we were on holiday. Once he said Motel 6, I was automatically locked into the decision, a sucker for approval. It never occurred to me that I still had a choice. Feeling acute disappointment, I went to check us in. For me the evening was already spoiled and I was angry with him.

Unbelievable, I know, but wait, there is more. I was quite hungry and wanted to go out for dinner. I asked him, 'Do you want to go out for dinner?' He said, 'No.' I was furious and could have kicked the stupid microwave with the Styrofoam cups that faced me while he went to sleep. I didn't kick nor did I say a word. Twice in a row, I could not get clear about what I wanted, I could not make a decision and tried indirectly to manipulate my partner to choose what I would choose. And when I failed, I was furious with him, I blamed him. I was afraid to take responsibility for my simple choice.

Unfortunately I have a lot of company. Tara, 24, is a computer engineer with Andersen Consulting. She says, 'I am confused. I think a lot and many things keep going around in my mind, I am so stressed, I have so many responsibilities. Adit, my boyfriend, is helping me out, to calm me down, and tells me that these are my priorities, this is my first, second and third priority, but with all these things going on in my mind, I get fever.'

And it is not just about big decisions. Tara, like many others, finds it problematic to make tiny decisions every day. 'It's really difficult for me to decide about small things, like what to eat and what to wear. I am extremely confused about things in my life.' So like many others, she takes the easy way out and lets others decide for her. It is much safer. Letting others make the decision, however, is neither a capacity-builder nor a confidence booster; it increases dependence and it becomes harder to make subsequent decisions. Soon women give up trying to make decisions. Dependent on others, women start blaming everyone else for what is happening in their lives. It is easier than taking action and responsibility for your action.

Avoid taking action

Unpractised in decision-making and afraid of disapproval and failure, taking initiative becomes a frightening task. Women with partial selves freeze. Many men we spoke to commented on women's learned behaviour not to take action. Dhruv, 35, who runs a wildlife ecotourism company, says that what frustrates him most about women is 'There is less of action and more of thinking . . . in a woman's head there are too many things going on at one point . . . It is better to put something in action, too much staying in the head slows you down.' He defines himself as a man of action. Aakash, 22, an

IT student, says, '*Sochti bahut hain, har cheez ke bare mein*, they think too much about everything . . . and they always want the man to take the initiative . . . *unko strong, independent hona chahiye*, they should be strong and independent, but they are very dependent on other people for things.'

Women too are soaked in stereotypes, unspoken and spoken. Action is so associated with men and inaction is such a strong, unspoken expectation of women that Sangeeta, 38, who is an entrepreneur, says, 'Masculinity is cut-throat, like a knife's edge; feminine is grace, charm, even if you are supposed to pick anything from the floor, it will be very gracefully done. I don't like the Nike [ad] as the phrase is very masculine – Just do it. There has to be a way to do it.'

One sure way of not giving offence is by not doing anything at all. Many young women develop a habit of 'not doing much'. Deepika, 24, says, 'I need a lot of push and encouragement to take the first step in anything. I don't like initiating, I feel like *pata nahin*, don't know, what will happen.'

Appu, 25, explains her behaviour thus. 'Sometimes I initiate action and sometimes I have to be pushed into doing it, which I don't mind.' She and her friends scold each other into doing things, without which she said she would mostly just stay in bed at home, since it is easier. Such young women are unlikely to challenge the world or act to help themselves. Each woman thinks these traits are her own. They don't realize they are the result of long training in habits that combine not-taking-initiative-behaviours with beliefs about what is good, normal and moral for a woman.

It is not surprising then that when some women do try to initiate action a negative culture comes down hard to break them. Aaliya, 22, who is in the fashion industry, holds her breath, her lips tighten and her face visibly clouds over when asked about initiative. She says, 'We are strong but not perceived as strong. For example, if I want to start something and I feel strongly about it, Papa and Mummy will always say, no, this is not good and you can't do it and they break your confidence.' When the mantra at home is don't do this, you will fail, don't try this, you will never learn it, don't do this, you will get sick, some girls fight back, but at some level the messages get absorbed.

Compromise your career, it is not important

For the middle classes, going to college is no longer a choice. Women grow up on some variation of '*padh likh ke kuch ban jao phir jo chahe karna*', first study and become someone and then later you do what you want. Although this is progress, women bring the same habit of erasing the self to please others to a new realm. Combined with not knowing or fighting for what they want, girls are sucked into a vortex of love and pleasing parents.

Women give up their choices of colleges, what to study, whether to work, where to work, how much to work and when to quit to parental and parent-in-law manoeuvring, all in the name of love.

For Jiya, 25, as for many others, it's all about parental choice and control. 'It was always like *jo family bolegi*, whatever the family says. Study in case you ever need it in the future. I did an MBA but I thought, why did I do this, I should have done fashion design, my mind is more creative in design – I did it because *Papa ne bola*, Papa said it. I also studied Chinese on the side, not my interest but Papa needed help in the business, so I can converse in Chinese now.' Papa's word is final.

The key criterion parents use to guide their daughters' choices is the hope of easy 'adjustment' in marriage. Education is important but careers are not. Parents fear careers are likely to 'make a girl too independent'. In other words, it strengthens a woman's sense of self. To reduce this risk, the most repeated mantra to girls is, 'Don't become career-minded, nobody will marry you.' Jaya, 24, who works in a bank, says, 'My mom often tells me, being a girl, your life will get screwed if you focus too much on career. A woman's life is mostly about bringing up a family and being a good family member. Sacrifice. I guess I sacrificed my dream because my parents taught me to choose a job that gives you stability, a nine-to-five job. Take a job and get settled as fast as you can and let us find a match for you. A guy who is dating will find a girl who is career-oriented and independent attractive . . . but when he looks for a wife . . . he asks, can you cook? Can you wash clothes? Can you manage a child's potty? So respect goes out and responsibility comes in.'

Women feel the need to 'find the balance between family and job'. But not a single man talked about balance. They did, however, expect women to 'adjust', particularly after having babies. Anoop, 32, a lawyer who supports women's rights and works with women lawyers, says with a tight jaw, 'It is only reasonable that they stay at home.' But half an hour earlier Anoop had been waxing poetic about equality and how difficult it is for women to leave everything they know after marriage to start a new life while men just continue their lives in a familiar home. Many intellectually free men still want women to be the primary 'adjuster'.

Adjusting is actually training to let go of power. Ambition and careers for women signal power and therefore are circled in red. Recent research based on graduates from top management schools in the USA shows that women, when asked to choose jobs on a ladder of power, do not choose the job at the top to avoid power and the perceived dark cloud and conflict associated with power. At home as well, if power is supposed to reside only in one, two people wanting power can signal conflict. But this is never discussed or seen clearly, only camouflaged as the adjustment needed by a woman to make a marriage work.

Supriya, 24, is no pushover but she was forced by her parents to give up her desire to work with poor people in slums, since they felt it was not respectable and it would be too demanding a thing to do after marriage. Supriya is still adrift. 'I am confused, I really don't know what to do. All the time I am questioning everything and doubting everything. After doing my MSc it took me a year to make my parents understand that I will work and I want to, but even then they did not allow me to do that and kept pushing me to do a government job. So now I am in a real dilemma about what I want, and if I want that, will people allow me to do it? I surrender myself to my masters.'

It is not in a woman's DNA to aim lower or be different, but rather their imaginations are clipped as they are reminded over and over again to be modest in their goals, aim low and to stay 'within boundaries'. *Udna nahin, zamin pe raho*, do not try to fly, stay on the ground or bad things will happen. Akshata, 23, from a well-off family, is just one example of clipped ambition. 'I was always told and taught to dream but just don't have the hope of fulfilling them.' She no longer aims high. A lifetime of modest aims has become a habit.

Neela, 44, a senior administrator, has come to terms with her clipped wings. She says, 'I want to reach a situation when I am fearless and not apologetic. But I never feel the need to break free and spread my wings.' Poonam, the senior United Nations official, could have been heading agencies, but never applied for leadership positions. It never occurred to her, or if it did, she buried such ambition. Owning her ambition is somehow morally tainted even though intellectually she knows that is not true.

The combination of clipped ambition and training not to take initiative has consequences in the economy. Few women create disruptive start-up companies. In India, in 2013, only 6 per cent of IT start-up companies were founded by women, even though equal numbers of men and women enter the IT field at the college level. In the IT sector women make up only 28 per cent of the workforce. Most do not make it past five or six years, most prefer employment to entrepreneurship and most choose jobs in the administrative or human resource sections and remain primarily at lower- or mid-managerial levels. Indian women are not alone. A global study on entrepreneurship across 67 countries finds that women entrepreneurs rate their confidence and competence as lower than that of men, have a greater fear of failure, have lower aspirations for growth and choose sectors such as retail business rather than capital-intensive manufacturing or knowledge-intensive businesses.

Don't say no, it is a bad word

In the world of pleasing no is a no-no. No is a powerful word that pleasers cannot use as it comes heavily wrapped in fear. Moral girls don't say no to others. Aamani, 30, says bluntly, 'I am afraid that the other person will get upset.' Afraid of giving offence, women do not say a clear no or even a squeaky no or even an under-the-breath no. How can they? The other may be displeased. Living in fear, women become tentative, wispy and open-ended, particularly with people they love. Saying no to their requests becomes equated with not loving them. Neha, 23, says, 'To people who are extremely close to my heart, my family and best friends, it's very difficult for me to say no. I am a very emotional person and I will suffer and give up my personal comfort for the people I love . . . My basic approach to life is that I go along with every situation.' She adjusts to everything so as not to upset anyone. The deeper reason of course is to avoid conflict. Shefali, 30, says, 'I just can't say no, *yaar*. I can't. I don't like friction and a no might lead to it.'

Women avoid even talking about conflict. They call it 'emotional drama'. Emotional drama with loved ones evokes high anxiety. Sireesha, 25, says, 'It's very difficult to say no, especially with people who are very emotional and who can't abide by that no. If I say no to them, I will have even more emotional chaos in me. They can cry, throw tantrums, create emotional drama and so on.'

Ragini, 23, is even more indirect. 'If I know that the other person's reaction is going to be an issue, if I apprehend a negative reaction, I am definitely scared to say no.' Neela, 44, despite being a senior administrator, says, 'If it means getting too uncomfortable saying no I say yes.' To console herself, she says, 'I have put something in our emotional bank, that is more important . . . it always comes back. But if I feel *yeh to galat hai*, this is wrong, then I say no openly, I have that much social skill.'

Only a few women feel their underlying fear, but they still cannot change their behaviour. Adhishree, 26, says, 'I can't say no. Papa even bought a book and gave it me, *How to Say No*, but that book did not help me. First I try and avoid saying anything and then when I cannot avoid it any more I think, somehow I will do this, find the time to do this even if it harms me, even if I lose out. For example, at the time of my internship there was a senior and he had to come to Delhi and my parents had to go to Chandigarh, and he asked if he could stay with me. I couldn't figure out *kaise mana karun*, how to say no. I kept thinking I hope he doesn't think I was making excuses. So I finally said it with great difficulty and I kept thinking I hope *bura na laga ho*, he didn't feel bad.' And she feels guilty.

It is this *others ko bura na lage*, and especially Mummy should not feel bad, that led Mansi, 32, from a wealthy family, to marry an investment banker who even before marriage had started 'misbehaving', intimidating her with cruel jibes. She tried to tell her mother but avoided conflict first with her mother, who told her to try harder to please him, and then for years with her fiancé, who became her husband. As we spoke, Mansi listed 27 situations when she could not say 'no, this behaviour is not acceptable' to avoid conflict and to continue pleasing. Here is a brief sample:

After the first year of marriage when I started making rotis for his tiffin, which wasn't easy for me since I was working as well, I asked him on the first day if he liked them since I had made it with so much love for him, he responded saying his mother's rotis were better.

I was expected to plan my routine around his. When he needed to use the bathroom, it had to be empty, and if I had to leave for work at the same time, I would have to wake up early and finish getting ready so as not to cause a change in his routine. Every morning he was in a rush. He needed his milk prepared in a particular way. If it didn't turn out like that he would throw a tantrum.

I sing well and I like to sing in the car. He always reprimanded me, even in front of my friends. Once he was going out of town and I started singing to him, 'Aaj jaane ki zid na karo' [please don't insist on leaving today]. I have received many compliments for this but he mocked me.

When we moved to a new place I bought some really pretty curtains, sheets and throw pillows and decorated our room. Not once did he appreciate it. Every night he did nothing but complain.

He criticized every gift I bought for him including a big chocolate airplane I carried for him from New York. He loves chocolates.

On his 29th birthday our relationship was quite strained. I decided to make a special effort. I sent him 29 cupcakes, a huge bouquet of flowers and 15 little gifts each with a personalized note. The 15 gifts were reminders of the times we had spent together and things we liked. In spite of all this we didn't go out for dinner. He had already celebrated the whole day with his colleagues. He only praised the bad cake his colleagues gave him.

Post-marriage, our sex life was sporadic as if we were in a long-distance relationship. After the second year we stopped having sex. I would woo him in different ways and he'd say I was fat and ugly. I even wore fancy lingerie and literally threw myself at him. He just turned around and slept. He would even tell me I had body odour, not true!

Mansi eventually found her no and left her husband. After nine years of begging, her mother finally accompanied Mansi to a lawyer's office to file for divorce, still worrying *ki uske son-in-law ko kitna bura lagega*, that her son-in-law would feel so bad. It was only when the lawyer scolded her for worrying more about her son-in-law than her own daughter that she agreed to the filing of divorce papers. For her mother, it was the breakdown of a woman's implicit moral code to always please. Mansi has gone on to build a new, fulfilling, creative life and is now trying to build her financial base.

Don't negotiate

One way to deal with unreasonable demands and avoid potential conflict is to negotiate. Trained to please, for most women the idea of negotiation belongs to a foreign land. The English word negotiate itself gets in the way. To many women, the word implies a business or businesslike relationship that feels inappropriate in the context of personal relationships. Vineeta, 50, from a well-off family, is emphatic. 'Relationships don't work on negotiations, it is not a business deal. There is never a negotiation in a relationship. It is an emotional deal, a mental deal, a physical deal. There is always understanding and acceptance. Negotiation *wahan karte hain*, it is done where there is scope for refusal or acceptance.'

In other words, negotiation is not possible in personal relationships because you can't say no; and it is not possible even in most businesses, as relationships become personal. At a recent conference in Delhi, I met an American trainer on negotiation skills who felt that her workshop for mid-career women had been a complete failure. 'The women were so uncomfortable, they did not participate, they just sat with their arms crossed in front of them.' In effect, the women were saying, 'In our culture we don't negotiate.' The idea of negotiation felt dirty and wrong. Good women don't negotiate.

Negotiation needs to be examined through the lens of the cultural definition of a good woman and reframed. The trainer should have used the Hindi word 'adjust' to introduce the concept of negotiation as a moral process to manage relationships better and uphold the moral values of women. Negotiation contradicts the idea of women as selfless creatures who only give and don't take from others. How can women negotiate when they are taught not to be clear about their wants and preferences? When girls are taught that it is wrong to ask for what you want, how can they negotiate for what they want?

Suneeta, 25, a psychology student, says, 'I don't think I negotiate, I don't know why. I have thought sometimes that I deserve this thing but after that I feel *woh boyfriend mann se kare to koi faida hai*, only if he does it with his heart is it worthwhile, why do I have to fight for it. Even at home, if I say something and I am refused, I don't negotiate, I just leave it.' *Jaane do*.

Human beings are weird. We negotiate hard to get discounts for cheap things but not for the big things in life. Naina, 26, negotiates prices daily with the *sabjiwala*, the vegetable seller, but cannot negotiate time off with her husband to attend her own sister's wedding. She knows intuitively that she has more power than the *sabjiwala* but less power than her husband.

Lacking the skills in the to and fro of any negotiation, some women make unilateral demands out of acute frustration. But they think they are negotiating. Anika, 24, has a master's degree in communications and declares herself a fearless negotiator. She lectures, 'Negotiation is the need of the hour. In today's life when ego has somehow taken over, I feel it is important to compromise. I do at times but not always. I have never negotiated. I used to negotiate in my first relationship with my ex boyfriend but after that I have become so stubborn, I stick to my point, and my anger just says everything and the other person of course is not understanding.' She is a unilateralist.

Nalini, 24, has misunderstood even more the nature of successful negotiations. She says seriously, 'Negotiation is a part of relationships. You have to negotiate every time. I told my boyfriend I will leave my job when we get married. I am not some idiot. Who can do both things, home and job, perfectly? But I keep saying this one thing. I will decide the terms of my negotiation, not him . . . I don't understand why there is so much indirect communication. Women say, *isko burra nahin lag jaaye*, this person shouldn't feel bad, that person shouldn't feel bad, but I don't think like this. I am not afraid of conflict. I say let's have it all out, *ek baar ho jaaye sab*, let's just fight it out. Be expressive. That is why I have become so retaliatory in nature . . . I will just throw my things around and all.' Retaliation and aggression may feel temporarily good, but they do not lead to fulfilled needs.

Stay unfit for leadership

While we may not have a science of leadership, we have developed a finely honed science of non-leadership. It is embodied in the training of women we have seen so far.

Train girls to feel unsafe, live in fear, stay at home, shrink, judge themselves and their bodies, make girls feel wrong, inferior, immoral and dirty; don't let girls speak, reason, question, have an opinion, argue, debate; teach them modesty, to wait and follow; make girls suppress their emotions, seek only approval, always please others perfectly, especially men, never say no, avoid conflict, never negotiate, and never initiate action, and then bundle all this behaviour and spray it with morality.

This training would make anyone unfit for leadership. No wonder only 5 per cent of CEOs of Fortune 500 companies are women. Studies show that confidence matters more than competence in influencing and selling ideas to others. And women are less likely to ask for a big job or assignment; it is risky and immodest to shine or want to shine.

Indu, 60, a graduate of Miranda House in Delhi University, just retired as chief secretary, the highest administrative post in the states and union territories of India. She looks relaxed in a blue and white salwar kurta on holiday in Goa. I ask her about her science of leadership and the first thing she talks about is the need for a woman to protect her character, even if she is a senior officer in the Government of India. 'Steer clear of men, your antenna has to be super functional to make sure you don't accidentally fall into a trap, your antenna has to be constantly up to protect yourself and your reputation. I used to be very careful, it takes time to get through complicated files with the boss – I would always leave the door open, I would deliberately ask for tea, so people could come and go to serve tea – you have to be alert and not casual like men. But on the other hand, don't have such a high and mighty attitude, you have to steer yourself through troubled waters. A certain holding back, a certain discretion in how to behave. You can't be *bindaas*, without a care, you always have to be careful, anticipate, it could happen at any time, unfortunately there is no other way. It is unwanted sexual attention.' She says if you object and it becomes known, 'they will first destroy a woman's character and then blame her, it is the surest way of not rising'.

Indu speaks about the systemic negative assessment of women who rise in leadership, even by male colleagues. 'People will always pounce on you. You make your mark through work that is fine. But if you want to catch the attention of your boss, for men who do that, they call him a sucker and leave it at that. For women, they say she is making a "line" for the boss. Men never say that a woman is a good officer and a nice person in the same breath, it is impossible, I have never heard it. There is always a "but".

For men you never go into character analysis but for women they are very, very negative. And these are fellow IAS [Indian Administrative Service] officers. A man cannot stand the rise of a female and her popularity. If you think of men, men never sit around and say their wives are great. If you praise your wife you are henpecked, other men tease the man, they say *kehana mano bibi ka*, he has to obey his wife. I have never come across any man who genuinely praises his wife.' This too is learned behaviour.

Indu is one of the few women who reached the top of her field with a brew of good performance and being a 'good woman', constantly being on alert around men, dressing conservatively, avoiding conflict and ducking low. Never sticking out. 'Even the best women will usually play second fiddle to maintain the general harmony of life with bosses, husbands and in the workplace. You keep working very hard but you don't do anything to attract too much attention to yourself, because people will pounce on you immediately and you just don't want to create controversy. A man never looks at life in this way; it is just not part of his upbringing. At work I don't like to come in the limelight, I like to work in the background. I don't like head-on controversy, I don't want to attract upheaval, I don't want to create a problem, I want *shanti*, I don't know why. You learn it from your childhood, women's likes and dislikes don't get so sharp, so it's not really a sacrifice – it's an attitude to get along from childhood on.' She says she rose to the top because of supportive male bosses.

Women leaders are judged by a different standard. Indu says, 'If it is a woman, for example, Kiran Bedi, she is a public figure, she likes to boast about her achievements of jail reform, they decry her achievements and dig into details and then criticize. Men they criticize in a general way, but if a woman speaks up at a meeting, later they will say she is aggressive – she goes around to meet people, to be noticed, some suggest she is having an affair with the boss.' Women who emerge as leaders have to navigate a cultural minefield inhabited mostly by men. Indu's comments have been backed by study after study in the USA and the UK. They are captured in the title of a bestseller, *Nice Girls Don't Get the Corner Office*, by Lois P. Frankel.

The absence of women as economic leaders in India is still stark notwithstanding some successful women, particularly in the banking sector, like Chanda Kochar, Shikha Sharmam, Renu Sud Karnad and Arundhati Bhattacharya.

It takes a strong woman, and usually a male sponsor, for a woman to emerge as a powerful leader in a man's world.

Reflections

Constantly pleasing others is a dangerous habit, precisely because it looks so innocent, nice and harmless. Pleasing teaches women to stop thinking. They don't know what they want; they become muddled and can't make decisions; they appear brainless, boring and incapable of logical argument; they forget how to take risks and initiative. They are hit by paralysis. For such women being a leader is a terrifying proposition. No wonder most women avoid it. The pleasing syndrome is a deadly disease that keeps women half-alive to keep on serving others and half-dead to serve themselves. Pleasing as a moral life principle simply means do not exist for the self, but exist only for others. Unable to live up to such high expectations, women get pickled in guilt, fear and a sense of failure.

The opposite of pleasing behaviour is not displeasing behaviour. It is not aggression. The opposite of pleasing is to have a self. A strong self that can choose when to please, when to give, when to sacrifice and when to say no at home, on the street or in the office. The opposite of a pleasing woman is a strong woman.

A strong woman wears a salwar kurta, a sari, pants or a dress. A strong woman speaks in Hindi, Punjabi, Rajasthani, Kannada or English. A strong woman is vital, joyous and alive with dreams, hopes and thoughts. A strong woman can love and care deeply for her family. A strong woman chooses marriage and family, early, late or never. A strong woman chooses to stay at home and never work outside the home or chooses a career and family passionately. A strong woman chooses to compete and excel or not. A strong woman chooses what and when to sacrifice for her family and society. A strong woman cares and pleases but also knows when to stop. A strong woman is not by definition oppositional; she chooses when to collaborate, when to oppose, when to support and when to be a solo player. A strong woman is unapologetic about her choices, yet she has the wisdom to know when she has wronged someone and the humility to say 'I am sorry' without making 'sorry' her life mantra.

5

Sexuality

Please God, Don't Give Me Those Breasts

This is me, in my pre-teen and teen years:

I wanted breasts. I wanted breasts badly. I was 12. I had noticed that boys really went after my older sister. She was 14. And she had breasts. So I concluded I needed breasts and soon. I was impatient to grow my own. From then on I kept a close eye on my older sister, hoping to learn. I thought my sister was the most beautiful, mysterious creature, who had this heavenly power to make all boys and men stop in their paths. There was something about her. I watched and tried hard to copy. It never worked for me, not even with the oddest-looking boys my age. In my wretched failure to interest boys, I concluded I did not need breasts. I rejected them in advance of their arrival.

I decided I wanted to be free like a boy. I spent most of my life in my school uniform, a thick, layered green tunic, high white blouse, banian, green and yellow tie and big green bloomers, the uniform of Bishop Cotton Girls' School in Bengaluru, where my father was posted as a government official. I somehow persuaded my mother to buy me a pair of yellow-and-black check pants. I took to hanging upside down from trees. I started playing cricket in front of the garage with my brothers.

Soon I was 13. One day my sister called me, beckoning me to our shared bedroom. As she closed the door, she had a strange expression on her face. She held out a bra. It was one of her old bras, which by now was off-colour but had clearly come from a white lineage, a sturdy, no-nonsense cotton. She said, 'Wear this. And don't try to escape. I will check every morning before you go to school.' I could have died. I felt revolted. By now I hated breasts. I was not even aware of mine so how did she know? I rushed to the toilet. I bent over and heaved. She never said a word about it again. But every morning for months, like a furtive lover, she would feel my back for the bra hook. My mother never said anything. Never was a word exchanged. Never tenderness. Never pride. Never joy. Never comfort. Never an explanation. Nothing. My sister remained her quiet emissary. One day an uncle helpfully commented on my growing underarm hair. I backed into myself. I carried the burden of my sprouting breasts and hair. Silent. Sullen. Resentful.

The fact that I had breasts got me attention in Delhi but it was not the kind I wanted. I started feeling reptilian, ugly and undesirable, except to the perverts on the streets – in Durga Puja pandals, in markets, in shops, on streets, on trains, on buses, it seemed everywhere. I felt lost, bewildered, hurt. My breasts seemed to connect directly to everything that went wrong. They ruined my life. I lost interest in my studies. I went from having a free mind to hiding even in the classroom. I became indifferent. My body tightened even more. My shoulders turned in. I was sweet 16.

* * *

From the second century BC till the eighteenth century, sacred Indian sculptures, inscriptions, paintings and poems celebrated the human body and sexual desire. The human forms of gods and goddesses are worshipped because divinity rests in these perfect bodies and their very perfection is meant to evoke the divine in human beings. In Indian thought human bodies too are abodes of the divine. Your body and my body are therefore divine. Sacred Indian texts and poems about ecstatic and divine love, particularly in the Bhakti tradition, see physical beauty and form as the way to the divine.

Goddesses were praised for the perfection of their bodies: their abundant breasts, their ample thighs and their graceful movement. And sexuality was not a taboo subject. In fact it was sacred. It was an invitation to merge with the divine. Vidya Dehejia, a renowned scholar of Indian art, says 'Unlike anywhere else in the world, pre-modern India celebrated the sensuous bodily form; singing praises to Uma's full breasts is surrender to divine love and divine beauty.' The sensuous and the sacred intermingle. Shame did not exist. In her beautiful book *The Body Adorned*, Dehejia writes about the seventh-century child-saint Sabandar, who sang sacred hymns to the Ardhanari, half-woman, half-man form of Shiva and Uma, in the temple of Pundurai, in present-day Tamil Nadu:

Fresh as newborn lotus buds
Lustrous like kongu blossoms
Honeyed like young coconuts
Golden kalashas,
Filled with the nectar of the gods
Are the breasts of resplendent Uma.
She is one half of the silvery glory
Of Shiva of Pundurai
Where rare birds roost
And fine flowers bloom
In shady groves of green

But that was then and now is now. While we continue to worship full-bodied goddesses, the connection between divinity and the body is gone. Gone is the notion of the breasts as portals to the cosmic, to divine power. Instead of being divine, women's breasts have become profane – they are leered at, commented upon, rubbed, pinched, pulled, groped, hit, bitten and cut. Emblematic of India today is the action by three young women engineering students in the city of Chennai in response to the horrors of the Nirbhaya rape. Aware that research indicates that the first body part groped by men who want to violate women is the breast, they invented breast-armour filled with electric wires to stun any gropers and would-be rapists with a 3800 kilovolt shock followed by 82 more shocks to protect their 'purity and integrity'.

This fall of a woman's body from divinity to profanity, to a thing – a bad, dirty, polluting, shameful-but-desired-by-men and yet marketable thing – is entombed in the modern-day denial that women exist and women have bodies.

The Early Training: Good Girls Are Body-less, Sex-less

A girl is always innocent and pure. Alisha, 13

If girls do not have bodies, they can have no sexual parts. If there are no sexual parts, there can be no sexuality and there is no need to teach girls or boys about sexual parts and no need for sexuality or sex education. Even today it is shocking to say aloud that women have breasts. It is shocking despite the half-nude pictures of women plastered everywhere. It is even more shocking for a girl to say aloud, 'I have my period today,' even though every woman bleeds every month for 30–40 years, starting from age 12 or younger. Girls' bodies are effectively de-sexed. Some parents go to extremes to deny their girls' sexual bodies to keep them 'safe' from boys and men. This makes the underlying impulse of denial clearer than when the denial is more subtle.

Anjali, 19, studies at Gargi College, in Delhi. She and her younger sister were raised disguised as boys but without the freedom. They were always dressed in boys' pants and shirts even as little girls. There were no frocks or dresses. A barber always cut their hair short. No hair clips or ribbons. No make-up, not even kajal. They were denied all signs of femaleness in clothes, hair, jewellery and they were kept at home as much as possible. Once, when Anjali returned home with nail polish on her nails from a friend's house, her mother hit her and the nail polish was scraped off. These restrictions continue in college. Anjali feels suffocated and slipped me a note in a college classroom requesting me to intervene.

Since a girl's body and sexuality are denied, the burgeoning physical evidence to the contrary is buried in denial and shame. Thus developing breasts, hips, body hair and menstruation happen in a barren, desolate, sombre, confusing and often fright-filled landscape.

You don't have breasts

If mothers had any control in the matter of growing breasts, they would just plonk breasts on girls the day before their marriage. The nuisance of breasts would end.

But since they can't, mothers spend the most effort on denial. As a result, girls often develop breasts without any awareness. It sounds insane but it does happen because girls learn early to distance themselves from their bodies.

Reshu, 27, is slightly built, and has a master's in science from Delhi University. She says that in her family, like in most families, 'there was no discussion about bodies at all'. So she did not notice that her breasts were growing, and she talks about them as if they were not part of her body. 'When I was in class 6, I think the breast development started but I never took notice of it. It was not an issue I think, I never got to know them, even when my breasts were fully developed.'

Such is the power of denial, you don't notice the swell of growing breasts but you notice a mosquito bite. While her growing breasts did not register on Reshu, men noticed. 'I remember an incident when I was walking on the road to my friend's house. A man on a bicycle hit my chest hard with his hand and just cycled off. That was the time I noticed that my breasts hurt really badly, that is when I realized that they were growing. Please God, don't give me those breasts.' Reshu became afraid of her breasts, never 'comfortable', always policing.

Un-parented in an environment of determined silence about bodily changes, some girls who do notice feel alarm at their growing breasts. Nisha, 37, a talented young woman who lives in Dwarka, says, 'When my breasts started to grow, I used to hate it. I started hunching and I used to wear a tight *ganji* inside and used to make it even more tight by putting safety pins all around. So that my chest looked plain.' In the absence of open conversation, breasts just become 'things' to hate.

When it is no longer possible to ignore girls' breasts, mothers shame girls through looks, glares, twitches and worried or barbed comments, asking them to disguise their breasts, make them invisible and guard them. My older sister, my mother's designated breast-guardian, reminded me several times not to walk with my then very modest breasts sticking out. I hunched over till they disappeared.

Many mothers, like my own, outsource the task of handing over first bras to young girls to older sisters and sometimes to aunts and even to fathers. Only one young woman had a positive first-bra experience. She was given a beautiful new yellow lace bra especially bought for her by her mother. It is not the quality of the bra that matters, it is the reception given to breasts that matters. Many girls unfortunately receive both bad emotional framing around breasts and bad bras.

Farida, 42, can still feel the rage of her 13-year-old self, when her mother, with a particular lack of kindness, handed her an old bra of hers. 'I don't mind telling you,' she says, 'when I was 13, I was a tall girl, 5′6″ and quite developed. Do you know what my mother did? She gave me HER bras to wear. She was a mother of FOUR children – just imagine, the bra of a mother of four children is to be worn by a 13-year-old? I feel at times mothers can be jealous of their daughters . . . and I don't know why that should be . . . why? Why your poor, helpless daughter; you have brought her into the world and she is at your mercy.'

For a young girl, then, one way to cope with troublesome body evidence is to pretend in your mind that you are a boy. It is so much safer, uncomplicated and fun with its promise of freedom. I heard this repeatedly in our interviews. Tesu, 27, who wears a loose shirt, says, 'I was generally apologetic about my sexuality, out to prove that I have no desires. I am a boy. Sexuality must be kept under wraps.'

The result is that most women we spoke to fear, reject, judge, criticize, batten down and somehow distance themselves from their breasts that are right there. When asked, women complain about their breasts – about their size, shape, strength, firmness, texture, marks and anything else you can imagine. Their negative judgements about their breasts include: 'too flabby, too huge, too small, too painful, too bulging, too dipping, too jiggling, too awkward, too uncomfortable or too shameful'.

While they may dissociate from their breasts, when they judge their breasts it is based on whether they think men will find them attractive and desirable. Piya, 17, dressed in jeans and a tight blouse, says, 'My breasts are perfect . . . I love my boobs . . . my boyfriend loves my tits, they are really firm and nice but I like to wear a padded underwire bra to enhance them and make them look sexy.' If girls do not objectify their own breasts, others do it for them.

Many women were so uncomfortable with their breasts that they did not want to talk about them at all. Shubha, 24, said sharply, 'I don't think there is any need for anyone to talk about it, I think they are fine.' Sitting with a straight face, straight body, arms crossed, she looked away. You may think it is different with younger girls in this modern age, but it isn't. When we asked girls between the ages of 13 and 19 to write about how they feel about their bodies in total privacy so as not to embarrass them, they made no mention of breasts, not one mention. It is as if breasts do not exist. The gap between what is being taught in homes and what is plastered outside the home on every bus or billboard has increased, making girls even more vulnerable.

Don't talk about 'that place down there'

Breathing in the air of their homes, little girls somehow know that nobody wants them to know about, talk about or draw attention to their private parts, even in the privacy of their homes. If girls don't have bodies, logically vaginas don't exist. It is then totally rational not to talk about them. Think about it, if you cannot talk about your body, how can you possibly talk about body parts that are involved in sex? Vaginas are to be ignored. *Baad ki bat hai, shaadi ke baad*. It is a topic for later, after marriage. In our early discussions, only one woman mentioned the vagina, and that was in reference to a performance of Eva Ensler's *Vagina Monologues* that she had attended.

So I added one question to our private one-to-one conversation with women about their bodies. I casually asked women what word they used for girls' genitals in their native tongue. Most women either giggled or looked uncomfortable. Some did not answer. Some said they had forgotten. Some suddenly looked very serious. Some averted their eyes. Some said don't ask technical questions and get into scientific matters. It turns out that the most frequently used word for women's genitals by women in Delhi is '*susu*', the same word as urine. Or *susu wali jagah*, the place of urination. Other words women used are 'pee-pee', 'that place', 'down there', 'that place down there', 'shame-shame', 'lower part' and '*nunga-punga*' (naked). Women whose mother tongue is Hindi or Punjabi are more comfortable saying the word vagina in English than the words in their native languages. It is safer saying the word in a foreign language than in the language of their own heavily shame/guilt/fear-laden native context of their childhood. This was true for women from the ages of 17 to over 65. Babies come out of the *susu wali jagah*.

When the forbidden zone is so buried in shame that it is called 'shame-shame', it is impossible to be rational and logical. When even grown women confuse the place of urination with the place where a baby comes from, it displays a dangerous ignorance about basic anatomy. Most women are not sure about this, really. Grown women continue to use the words that children use for vagina. Men, on the other hand, have a lot of words for vaginas, none of which are used in polite company or denote respect. Most are used as swear words. This is true all over the world.

No sex education for you, what is sex education?

The pretence that girls do not have bodies makes it impossible to deal with sexuality as a natural and universal human phenomenon. Babies are bundles of sensations. They receive through all their senses and are very sensitive to touch. Without touch they do not thrive, they do not even gain weight. They develop the failure-to-thrive syndrome. Babies experience great natural curiosity about their body parts including their genitals, but this makes parents very uncomfortable.

When sexual parts are deemed dangerous, any curiosity about these parts in girls becomes a source of shame for parents and generates great anxiety and guilt in girls. Mita, 30, who runs her own marketing business, talks about one such incident. 'I was four when I was with a little boy and we were both rubbing each other with our pants down. His mother saw us and she screamed. She came and told my parents. My dad tied me under the table and he showed me a big, hot spoon and said, "*Garam karchi laga denge*, we will hit you with a hot ladle, if we ever find you doing this again. That is dirty and bad." So that is the thing that stayed with me. For me sex became dirty and bad.' In school as well she picked up that sex is dirty and still cannot bring herself to engage in sex.

When parents are uncomfortable with sexuality, it leaves little girls unguided, unprotected and alone, and curiosity can tip into sexual abuse. Astha, 25, lives in West Delhi and is engaged to be married. She has experienced repeated touching by several cousins and an uncle. 'I must have been five or six. I don't know how it started. I remember the images, the places, sometimes behind the sofa and in bed if no one was at home. They would say *dikha, dikha*, show, and both would touch there . . . Mama was in the kitchen. They would stimulate my nipples sitting in their *godi* [lap] in the car and whisper rubbish. Somewhere I knew this was wrong. I was ten and there were many incidents. I said no many times. After that I said I will tell someone, then they stopped talking to me. I felt so guilty, why is this guy not talking to me, why did I say no to him? Throughout my adolescence I tried to get him to talk to me. At 22, I finally went to a counselor, the thoughts were, *maine galat kaam kiya*, I did a wrong thing. I started crying and she brought me out of that, she said you were victimized, you did nothing wrong. It took about two years for recovery. It gave me the power to confront my mother.' Astha blames her mother for not being alert and protecting her from older male cousins and uncles. She is still afraid of sex and her sexuality.

Afraid of leaving girls unprotected, some watchful parents start separating girls from boys at eight or nine and definitely at puberty. Contact with boys is viewed with great suspicion. The standard line, as Suman, 29, daughter of a professor, says, is, 'Stay away from boys, don't get too close.' This separation without explanation and lack of contact with or understanding of boys as ordinary beings also creates problems later and contributes to the mystique of 'men as gods'.

Some children do find out about sex but most girls know to keep hush about it and learn early that if they talk about it openly they will be punished. Amu, 29, who now lives in Gurgaon and is a strong feminist, says, 'When I was in school, I would talk to boys freely because boys to me weren't special creatures, they were normal human beings just like us. However, being in a convent school, I faced a lot of shaming. My teachers always thought I was "loose" and my parents were constantly worried. Once Mum had one of her kitty parties and we kids were also there. I remember saying, "What's the big deal? We are all products of sex!" I eventually forgot about it until a few days later when my mother took me aside and asked me, "Did you say something like this? Saurav went and told Reena Aunty and Reena Aunty told me." At that moment, I realized I had done something wrong. I denied it. I must have been around ten.'

We have many excuses for not teaching girls and boys about sex and for not providing sex education at home and in schools. 'Let them enjoy their childhood. Let's not spoil our children's innocence with something they cannot understand. Let's protect them from such bad things. Let's not give them ideas. It is embarrassing. *Jaldi kya hai?* What is the hurry?' These are legitimate anxieties of caring parents. But pretending that sex does not exist has serious consequences. Surveys establish that 50 per cent of children in India are exposed to some form of sexual abuse and 20 per cent to extreme forms. Fearful parents unwilling to deal with the widespread presence of sexual predators amongst us expose their uneducated and therefore unprotected children to sexual danger.

Many girls still learn the bare biological facts from friends, movies and the Internet. Parents, schools and legislators fear that once children know about sex they will become sexually active. Yet several studies from the USA show that making 'virginity pledges', for example, makes no difference to the extent of sexual activity among young people and that, contrary to fears, comprehensive education about sexuality leads to delay and less engagement in sex, with fewer partners, as well as greater use of contraceptives.

You are cursed with the period

When I asked about sex education, women spoke about their periods. In the context of denial of sex, the first conversation about sex is triggered at puberty by the arrival of the first period. Actually the first conversation, if it happens at all, is not a conversation, it is a short mix of four biological and cultural truths. Girls are told, '*Yeh toh sab ko hota hai, ab tum badi ho gai, sambhal ke rehna, ladko se door rehna*. Yes, this happens to all, now you have grown up, live carefully, stay away from boys.' Young girls draw comfort from the fact that if it happens to everyone it must be all right. When girls start bleeding, mothers sometimes thrust someone else in front of them to explain what is happening. This may be an older sister, an aunt, a bhabhi, a chachi, a mausi, a bua, a neighbour, a friend or even the father.

This behaviour fills girls with shame about their own bodies, bodies with which they have to live for the rest of their lives. How can a girl be confident and sexual as an adult if she carries deep shame about the functioning of her own body?

This messaging about shame is so strong that even mothers who are nurses react to their daughters' first period like other mothers. Geetha, 22, who is from Kerala, talks of her mother, who is a nurse and deals all day with human bodies in different states of undress but does not bring this ease home. She says, 'I used to go to Carmel Convent School and I had no idea about periods . . . no idea at all, Mother did not tell me anything, she did not know how to do it. So one night in class 6, my mom was not there, she was on a night shift. I was at home and some aunty was staying with us . . . I saw blood on the bed, I thought there must be a cut, that I hurt myself playing . . . so I didn't tell anyone and I threw my panty away, cleaned myself and went to school. I was wearing a red sweater and white skirt . . . I didn't share it with anyone in school. I realized later I was bleeding so much, I kept sitting on my chair, I put my head down . . . later I used my scarf as a pad . . . then I tied my sweater around my waist . . . then I came home.'

Her mother, when she came home, told her neighbour but could not bring herself to say anything to her daughter, hoping the school would educate her. Very few girls are told that starting periods means they could become pregnant through sex with a boy and have babies. The links are left in a fog. That would be giving girls too much information.

Some mothers get angry with girls for starting their periods, as if it is a personal flaw in character and they could have avoided or at least delayed their periods. Mothers say, *Abhi hona tha?* It had to happen now? The inconvenience is not just periods, it is the entire package of being a girl. Barkha, 37, says, 'My mother was angry when my periods started. I was 12. She said, "See I used to tell you not to eat pickles and eggs, see now what you have done?" So I asked my mom what will happen now. She said now you can deliver a baby. So it was very shameful that I could get pregnant at any time.' No details were given. Misinformation about eating particular foods as the cause of onset of periods and worse – 'now you can deliver a baby' – leads to misplaced fears and faulty conclusions for years. So deep is the information hole that menstrupedia.com, a website recently created by Aditi Gupta to educate girls about healthy periods, receives one lakh visitors a month.

Periods are not only considered shameful, they are also considered dirty. By association, vaginas too are tagged 'dirty'. Meeta, 28, works in the publishing world. For her, everything associated with her private parts became dirty. She stopped all contact with these parts, including not cleaning them even though she thought she was ultra hygienic. 'I was very particular about hygiene, about dirt, so I wouldn't touch or clean my private parts as they are dirty . . . it was all dirty . . . discharge, panties, loo. When I was eleven, I developed severe itching and my parents took me to a gynaecologist. It was the gynaecologist who taught me how to clean myself.' Meeta considers periods and other such things 'down there' dirty. She is still filled with horror about her own body.

Taboos around women's menstrual blood are particularly strong. This blood is considered dirty, impure, polluting and bad not just for the woman but for anything she touches. It is bad for anything sacred, tulsi plants, crops, puja rooms, temples, festivals and rivers. It is also bad for anyone who touches a menstruating woman. So girls are isolated in rooms without food or little food, light or human contact for three days. They are put out of sight. Society controls women's bodies and what women can do during their periods. Some people put a spin on these old cultural practices and claim they are good for women because it ensures they get rest during their most vulnerable periods. This is an even more dangerous argument, because it distorts a harmful taboo that isolates women into a form of 'caring'. It converts mistreatment into societal generosity. Why do women need to be labelled dirty, dangerous or impure or kept isolated or not given food in order to rest? Women's rest is regulated because if a woman were to decide when she wants to rest she begins to exist. Culturally that is a sign of trouble.

Almost nothing that is related to a girl's body is celebrated communally by women or by society in educated North India. It is no surprise that when asked about the heaviest burden of being a woman, most women singled out their monthly period, another cultural victory against women's bodies. Many girls call their periods 'the curse'. Periods are associated with shame, dirt, smell, pollution, inconvenience, physical pain and restrictions. To avoid restrictions, girls start hiding the fact that they are 'chumming', having their periods, from other women in the house.

Surprisingly, men are more willing to talk openly about periods than women. Perhaps not surprisingly then, sometimes it is husbands who help women break taboos, also reflected in the new movie *Padman* starring Akshay Kumar based on the life of Arunachalam Muruganantham, and his determination to create low-cost sanitary pads for menstruating women in rural areas.

Raunak, 28, from a highly educated family, grew up with menstrual taboos. She recounts her dilemma during a trip to Rishikesh, up in the hills on the banks of the sacred river Ganga. 'I was in Rishikesh and I was chumming and because of all these beliefs I thought *ki Ganga me kaise step karenge*? How will I step into the Ganga? Because the Ganga is considered holy. But then my husband told me, "Are you nuts? *Aisa kuch nahin hota*. Nothing will happen. It would not be wrong to step in the Ganga." Then I also thought *ki haan*, ah yes, it is a natural process. What is the problem? So now I don't follow all this.'

The only way you can talk about menstrual blood in polite policy circles is by focusing on economic losses. It is estimated that the economy loses $53.8 billion a year due to increased health costs, lower productivity and tourism losses due to poor sanitation and hygiene. Couching losses in dollars and cents sterilizes Indian menstrual blood from its impurities and its filth, ideas that have violated women's bodies for so long.

The silence around periods, a physical event with clear evidence, blood, an event that happens physiologically to every woman every month for decades, is another astounding example of cultural success and the power of cultural agreement among millions of people against biology and of course against girls' bodies. We all participate in this cultural silence. Person to person, generation after generation. The silence is a denial not only of basic biology, but of the health needs of girls and women.

Fathers withdraw

Puberty is the great disrupter in the lives of young girls. In an environment of denial of girls' bodies and sexuality, fathers face a particularly difficult task of navigating closeness with daughters without getting entangled in their bodies. This is more of an issue now that many fathers have moved closer to their children and do not always play the 'distant dad'. When daughters have a close relationship with fathers, who may carry them as babies, play with them and cuddle them in the early years, the abrupt withdrawal around puberty leaves girls confused and reinforces the feeling that 'something is wrong with my body'.

Girls like Chanchal, 18, who with great cheer describes herself as Daddy's girl, get lost at puberty, trying to recapture their father's attention by acting like a man.

'Dad was still encouraging but there was this blockage created that now you are a woman, he never said it directly but . . . I thought I had to be emotionless, manly, that is how males are supposed to be, being emotionless and cold, I guess. I don't know where I got this idea, so I went into this business thing – I was totally confused by what was happening.'

Navtara, 19, who lives in Ahmedabad, is even more explicit. In class 6, when her body exploded at puberty, she found herself totally alone. Nobody gave her any explanations. Her father, with whom she had been very close, withdrew. She says, 'The first male a daughter looks up to is her dad and at times it felt distant. We stopped having conversations, it all felt so distant, even when we were talking – it didn't feel the same.' Navtara rebelled against this injustice and became 'bad' in her own judgement, chasing boys, abusing alcohol and drugs, trying to get attention from her father and her uninvolved, silent mother.

Growing up in 'loving' homes that deny bodies, deny sexual zones of the body, deny sex education, categorize girls' bodies as dangerous, dirty and polluting, and expose girls to inappropriate touching or sexual abuse, makes establishing healthy sexuality a Herculean task for both adult women and men.

Consequences: Healthy Sexuality Becomes Difficult

There was this Indian girl in the UK who used to sleep around with guys casually just like men also did but all these guys used to call her a slut. They named her the

Public Ltd Company. And other girls did too. It was sick.
Nikita, 24

In a land of 1.3 billion people, one can safely assume that sex is not a new discovery. What is new is that sexual acts simulated or real are easy to watch on television, on YouTube, on WhatsApp, on porn sites and in movies. What is also new is that we now have numbers – the percentage of people engaging in sex in small towns vs. metros, in Gujarat vs. Bihar, in Jabalpur vs. Hyderabad or Delhi or Chennai – through nationwide sex surveys launched first by the magazine *India Today*. What is new is that the boyfriend phenomenon has become very common in large metros and other cities. What is new is that 30 per cent of class 10 students in some metro cities are not virgins. What is new is that despite greater sexual exploration before marriage, girls' virginity is still prized. What is new is that 30 per cent of women watch porn. And all this is happening in a context of denial of sex and sexuality at home, in schools and in colleges, the places where teens and young people spend the most time. One thing has remained the same. Parents still do not know what their girls or boys are up to sexually. Shikha, 25, and her friends laugh incredulously at their mothers who deny all sexuality. 'They have always told us, "No, we never had crushes," as if crushes were warts or head lice. My mother told me you can kiss after you are engaged but not before. I could never tell my mother I am experimenting or exploring my sexuality in a relationship.'

Despite the double standards and an overall climate of cultural inequality, many women choose to have casual sex and see sex as a part of their life. Many apps, including

Tinder, make casual sex a right swipe away. Tinder alone has grown to 14 million daily swipes in India. But what the statistics and the scorn of their mothers' denial hide is also the confusion, the pain, the misunderstanding, the exploitation and the violence generated by the cultural denial that good women have bodies. The denial of girls' bodies and the lack of training in healthy sexuality leave girls and women exposed to sexual violations within homes, in public spaces and in offices. It also makes them vulnerable to disease and afraid of or ambivalent about their own sexuality.

There is perhaps no other subject more overladen with morality, judgement and the fight for control than women's bodies and sexuality. It is widely recognized that sexuality is a normal, natural and important part of being human, and yet its expression is so controversial that when the WHO produced a paragraph-long 'working definition' of sexuality in 2006 it cautiously stated, 'It should be noted that this definition does not represent the official WHO position and should not be used or quoted as such.' When there is discomfort with sexuality, sex becomes tainted with guilt, shame, ambivalence and exploitation. It is no surprise then that many of the definitions of healthy sexuality have emerged from the field of sexual trauma, as a way to help women and men to heal from sexual abuse and to learn behaviours that lead to healthy sexuality, intimacy and sexual closeness.

Healthy sexuality is more than just sex. It involves appreciation of one's own body. Healthy sexuality involves the capacity and the right to express one's sexuality without guilt, fear or shame and without harming the other. It includes feelings, values, communication and behaviours. This is difficult when women cannot claim their bodies and when men have learned that sex with a female is their entitlement. Most sexuality researchers and therapists seem to agree that healthy sex requires five basic conditions: consent, equality, respect, trust and safety. These conditions minimize the chances that something bad will happen during the sexual experience.

One of the core themes to emerge is that even while women are aware of their sexual rights their sexuality is still dominantly about making themselves desirable to men. Women assess their body and their sexuality through a man's eye. They want to please. Navtara, 19, says, 'I sought appreciation in physical appearances . . . so if a guy was not making a move on me, I felt there is something wrong with me.'

Just about every woman intellectually acknowledges the importance of fulfilling a woman's own desire but most still consider it secondary, a lucky side effect. Radha, 32, said, 'I keep fit so that he [husband] will not get bored of me. He would lech at women with big boobs and big butts.' He, on the other hand, assumes that she will service him whenever he wants, no matter what his shape, and she obliges. The internal expectation to be desirable to men in a cultural context of denial of self, denial of body, denial of sex, fear of sex and fear of men can be nothing but confusing.

Moral dilemmas: Should I or shouldn't I? Am I good or bad?

Even when women assert that sexual desire is normal and a right, deciding to have sex evokes a resetting of their moral compass. Many young women simply said, 'Sex before marriage is bad.' Virginity is still the gold standard. In the *India Today* sex survey of 2016, 28 per cent of women said that they were not virgins before marriage. Bela, 22, who has very clear standards, says, 'I won't smoke, never eat non-veg, never drink, *haan*, yes, physical, it is there [physical exploration], but I would not lose my virginity before marriage.' Many young women want the safety of one sexual partner. Shefali, 30, now married, says, 'What is the point of giving yourself up if there is no future?' Sex before marriage is seen as a performance without good returns, without the safety of commitment, by most young women. But if a woman waits long enough, virginity may begin to feel like a burden, the subject of a Madhuri Banerjee novel, *Losing My Virginity and Other Dumb Ideas*, which details the adventures of a woman determined to lose her virginity before her thirtieth birthday.

Some young women feel uncertain and confused by their desires, choices and morals. Tamanna, 28, who teaches at Delhi University, talks about this moral dilemma. 'I carry a lot of cultural and emotional baggage around sexual expression. You form a weird split personality because your parents cannot "permit" your sexual self to exist outside of a marital relationship. It's like on an intellectual level we know we have zero to be guilty about. We deserve the freedom to express ourselves as we want. There is nothing wrong in it. And still, why do we have these emotional guilt pangs?' Sexual ambivalence reflects an inner conflict about one's decisions.

Amrita, 25, who now lives in Mumbai, is torn between the strength of her own sexuality and her internalized social morals. Intellectually Amrita fights for her rights but her sexuality is passive and enmeshed in guilt. She says, 'As a woman I am not supposed to be expressing my sexuality to the extent the man does. I hold myself back. So even if I wanted to initiate something, to express my need clearly, I wouldn't do it. So while it is OK for him to say, "let's do it", I would not. I would clam up, still do.' Then she expresses her body's longing. 'Not sure if the expression is correct but it's like a tiger tasting human blood – as long as you have not explored it, you are OK telling yourself it's OK. But when you have explored it, at times I feel very needy . . . I know my relationship was not a mistake, it was voluntary, but I don't know what it will cost me in the future, my fears and apprehensions. Knowing your emotional and intellectual self is good, but the sexual is important – how do you know your preferences? This part of me my parents don't know at all, am I betraying my parents?' Many single women even in their late twenties and early thirties said, 'My mother would kill me for sure if I told her.'

Elements of healthy sexuality

What I find striking is that while all the women we met endorse the idea of female sexual desire, some shyly and some with a broad smile, when you go beyond ticking boxes about 'Have you had Sex: Yes or No?' one or more dimensions of healthy sexuality are often missing from women's experiences. Achieving healthy sexuality based on consent, equality, respect, trust and safety in a context of moral ambivalence and secrecy is bound to be difficult.

Consent

The first element of healthy sexuality is consent, which means you can freely and comfortably choose whether or not to engage in sexual activity. It is granting permission. This assumes you are conscious and informed. Consent is widely interpreted to mean a verbal yes or no, leading to campaigns around the world of 'No means no', an acknowledgement of the sexual aggressiveness by some men and 'Yes means yes', an acknowledgement that women have the right to voluntarily express their sexual desire. The Bollywood film *Pink*, starring Amitabh Bachchan, is exactly about this. But women will have to retrain themselves to speak up in a culture that defines a good woman as a silent woman.

Many young women struggle to say a clear no to boyfriends who want more and many feel they are not heard even when they say no. Some young women feel violated and some end up having sex against their will. Kaira, 17, says, 'I am not able to say no to him.' Many more feel afraid to say a strong no, a loud no, afraid of giving offence and afraid of displeasing their boyfriends. About half fall silent and no force is involved. They simply give in. Many find it easier to go along and get it over with than to stop the guy once sexual activity has started. It is easier than saying no.

When we talk about sex, Sona, 24, who seems confident, laughs and says, 'Yes, it is a pleasurable thing, this physical intimacy. Yes, absolutely, I know what gives me pleasure. Me and my boyfriend, we try a lot of different things . . . It's completely OK to ask for it. I ask for it.' But she quietly adds that she feels guilty saying no to her boyfriend. Unlike Sona, who has had one boyfriend, Sakshi, 25, who is sexually active, says, 'I have been with a lot of men to find out what gives me pleasure and what not. Definitely. Just as a man has his needs, so does a woman. Women have the right to indulge in sexual activities just as much as a man does.' But Sakshi too has difficulty in saying no to her boyfriends and instead of speaking up she just breaks off relationships when they ask for what she doesn't want to give. Siri, 23, was initially reluctant to have sex, but she flipped over after her first experience. She says, 'What gives me pleasure is alcohol, spicy food, good sex, *bas aur kya chahiye life mein?* That's it, what else do you need in life?' Despite the facade of being carefree and in charge, Siri has so much difficulty in saying no to sexual engagement that she too leaves relationships instead of speaking up and she too has decided that for now it is simpler to live on her own.

Saying no seems so simple, it should be easy; but it isn't because it goes against the deep training of pleasing, being always agreeable, serving others, avoiding conflict, all rolled into the wrapper of being morally good. Breaking this package is a huge feat. It is a shift from an automatic yes to a deliberate, conscious no.

Equality, respect and trust

Equality in this context means that the sense of personal power is equal and neither partner dominates or intimidates. Respect means a person must have positive regard for their partner and for themselves. And trust must apply to both the physical and the emotional levels. In an unequal culture, mismatched assumptions and double standards are everywhere and leave young girls feeling used. It is a time of sexual change, but not everything has changed. The Hindustan Times-MaRS Youth survey of 2014, for example, shows that while 61 per cent of youth believe that premarital sex is no longer a taboo, 63 per cent want their partners to be virgins and in Delhi this number is even higher at 67 per cent.

Maya, 24, with a master's degree, who lives in Subhash Nagar, says, 'I had to break up with my first boyfriend because he asked for sex and I was only 19 at the time. I am not that kind of person. I was thinking love, and guys were using me for virtual sex while talking on the phone. People were like let's have chat sex, phone sex, and I was into it also, enjoying it no doubt, not realizing I was being manipulated.' Angry at the breakdown of respect and trust, she says, 'One of my friends is planning for an arranged marriage and the guy said talk to me only if you are a virgin. If a guy is dating a girl, *woh toh cheetah hai*, and if the girl does it, she is a characterless bitch? A girl with a past is a big challenge. I don't like this.' According to the *India Today* sex survey of 2015, 69 per cent of men expect their wives to be virgins and 63 per cent will not marry a woman if she has had a sexual experience. This has given rise to vagina restructuring surgeries, advertised now even in small clinics in small towns; non-virgin men have no parallel problem.

The idea that sex exists primarily to fulfil a man's needs still lurks somewhere in women's psyches, making equality, trust and self-respect difficult to achieve. Nupur, who grew up within a vigilant but otherwise remarkably regular middle-class family, has a boyfriend. At 25, she already sounds old. She says, 'I do everything to make him happy and I enjoy that. I give him pleasure but somehow I am not able to take it. The woman has to do it for the man. I feel that sex is painful for the woman. I cannot ask for this physical thing. Unsatisfied, I feel bad about myself, that I am not able to enjoy this. How can I enjoy the sexual thing? It is bad for me. Sex is bad. Sex before marriage is bad.'

Sexual inequality can also exist within the safety of a marriage. Prachi, 35, is a successful entrepreneur and paid off a big loan from her earnings on a flat in Noida that is only in her husband's name. Although she has all the words about women's rights and equality, her psyche is so deeply imprinted with inequality that her life operates around trying to make her husband sexually happy while discounting herself. She is being good. 'In sex also, I will provide it to him, like a mother, it takes the burden off me. It is his bodily requirement.' She tries to fulfil his sexual fantasies even when she finds it personally degrading. 'He would want me to do things done in the porn films . . . I would tell him let's get the basics right. It didn't happen. I thought it is OK as he loves me and sex is not that important. That's what we were taught growing up.' She continues to dismiss her own needs. She says, 'One year, I did everything. Pole dancing, wearing lingerie, he would enjoy it. One day I checked his browser history, I saw so many porn sites, I puked . . . Then again I started thinking what I can do for him. He would talk about sex with two women, threesomes and I said all right.' They went to Thailand to try. Then he wanted to go with his friends to the North-East. 'I agreed.' There is nothing healthy in this practice of sexuality for Prachi. It is neither equal nor respectful nor trustworthy and not even safe.

But it does have consent based on a morality that women should wipe themselves out.

When healthy sexuality is difficult to achieve for heterosexual women and men, the dilemmas of a young person navigating a different sexual orientation that is legally a criminal act are difficult to imagine. India's attitude towards homosexuality is gradually moving towards acceptance. This is despite the flip-flop of the courts in removing section 377 of the Indian Penal Code written by the British Raj over a century and a half ago. This act criminalizes 'carnal activities against the order of nature', a reflection of British sexual fears rather than Indian culture which at that time had a much more relaxed acceptance of the human body, fluidity of gender and sexuality in its many forms. Section 377 legalizes fear of homosexuals.

Gowri, 33, who teaches science, shares the trauma in her life created by her sexual identity as a lesbian. Her sexual being is by definition in opposition to the state that has the right to arrest her at any time, so she also tried to be with a man. She says, 'In 2005 while in my second year MA, I fell in love with my friend Meghna. I had been in a love relationship with a woman before but that girl had strongly condemned what happened between us and felt that our love and sex was a sin. Meghna did not suffer such conflicts about us and I was happy to be in love with someone who was not ashamed of our love. One day, while having dinner, my mother mentioned that now she only needed to see me find a man and she would be happy, as my brother had just gotten engaged. Eager to share my own finding of "The One" with my family, I told my mom I had found a woman . . . that was it. I was unprepared for the questions, disgust and anger that spewed out of my mother. I was shocked. My family had always been liberal. My mother is a gender-training expert and ran an NGO besides. She had friends who were gay. My father later was against it too. So I left home. It was traumatic. I knew how much they loved me. Not pleasing them was traumatic. Not having any job or income was scary too. An older queer couple gave me shelter initially. I took three part-time jobs and found a room . . . The strain with my family continues and continues . . . their love, care, and concern for me, and their inability to accept my relationship. I feel both strong and fragile. I got pain, rejection, freedom . . . the daily battle that swings.'

Lack of safety, violence

When the underlying attitudes towards women and their bodies do not change, even the burden of physically safe sex falls disproportionately on women. Consider one statistic. According to India's National Family Health Survey for 2010–11, 83 million women use the emergency pill as contraceptive compared to 16 million men using condoms, a five to one ratio.

Sexual safety is achieved when a woman feels secure and safe with her partner and safe from other unwanted consequences such as STDs, physical injury or unwanted pregnancy. Sexual violence within the intimacy of the home is a very difficult area to explore. Studies show that in highly unequal cultures when masculinity is defined as power and dominance, men feel three times more entitled to sex with their wives without consent and they punish resistance. It also found that 20 per cent of men in Delhi acknowledge that they had raped their female partner and overall 24 per cent acknowledge that they had perpetrated sexual violence against women including their wives. Women, on the other hand, tend to severely under-report sexual violence. In another study across seven states, only 7 per cent of women admitted that they had experienced sexual violence compared to 16 per cent of men who acknowledged that they had been sexually violent at home.

Researcher Aashish Gupta estimates that less than 1 per cent of sexual violence committed by husbands is reported to the police.

Unfortunately, several of the women we spoke with, young and old, unmarried and married, working and non-working, from the middle and upper classes, lived or live with sexual violence in their homes. These women did not report sexual violence to anyone because they could neither see any escape from their homes nor the possibility of change in their husbands. And they could not break their own moral code of being good.

Minni, 32, has an MA in economics and teaches at Delhi University. She is very vocal in her external world. But she says, 'I have lost all romantic notions in personal life. After marriage I gradually lost the pleasure in sex because of the trauma in my body. Mohit has become more aggressive and he is a different person after drinking.' She is still *theek hai*, all right with it, as she feels it is her duty and wonders, 'where will I go?' with the problem. Her inaction is ruled by the code that domestic problems are private problems. She has absorbed the pervasive but arbitrary public–private divide that keeps the women's world away from the scrutiny of standards of human dignity and the law. The cultural code is that outsiders do not interrupt in the private world, a code that organizations like the Indian organization Breakthrough TV are trying to change through their TV commercials. This code of the male having total authority within the family, no matter what happens, is old and deep. Manjeet, 63, has lived this code all her life out of 'goodness'. She is dressed in a simple cotton sari and describes herself as a 'God-fearing' woman who dedicated her life to raising her four children and taking care of her husband. She lives in Defence Colony in South Delhi. She says quietly, 'My husband raped me repeatedly, it stopped only when he died two years ago. He also openly went to prostitutes.' She continues to be good and now honours his image with a garland.

Sex and sexuality have become terribly mixed up with being good or being bad without any reasoned discussion. This is bad for girls, for boys, for couples, for families, for society, for public spaces, for offices and for spirituality. We must change.

Reflections

We have to make bodies sacred again. The seeds of healthy sexuality must be planted at home and tended in school through conversation and through celebrating the inevitable changes in girls' bodies. Families have failed their daughters and their sons. What is at issue is not at what age girls and boys should have sex, but how girls and boys can be prepared for a lifetime of healthy sexuality. Boys and girls have to be trained to respect and honour their own bodies and each other's bodies. India's unbalanced sex ratio, increasing inequality and habit of keeping girls at home, while young men travel in bands will make women even more vulnerable in the future, not less.

Our families are very important and still largely intact, but they are often not a safe harbour for girls nor do they provide guidance about healthy sexuality. Amu, 29, who is very smart and heads an international organization, summarizes it thus: 'My family is my greatest strength and my greatest weakness. I love them a lot. If something exciting happens in my life, I still tell Papa before I tell my husband.'

But when Amu was ostracized in a convent school and called loose for speaking to boys as a 9-year-old, her family did not stand by her; when she was 10 and said that sex is normal, she was severely reprimanded by her mother; in college, when she was raped at a party by an older man who plied her with drinks, she did not dare to speak to her family. When she was 24 and told her mother about her live-in boyfriend, her mother refused to acknowledge him. When she later married him, her mother silently showed up like a ghost the day before despite repeated pleas to come early. When she wanted an abortion she couldn't talk to her mother or anyone else about her confusion. She went to the clinic alone. When her husband's job stresses changed her sex life from exciting to nothing, Amu still had no one to guide her. She finally turned to Tinder.

But her parents love Amu. And Amu too loves her parents dearly. She still reports her joys and successes to her family first, particularly to her father. But her traumas, her failures, her deep questioning about what is right and what is wrong she keeps to herself. There is no great Indian family ready to hold her and listen with empathy and compassion, clarify assumptions and values and come up with solutions to new problems in new times. Listening deeply is not agreement. It is just listening deeply.

Is Amu's family the model of a good, loving Indian family? Good for whom and for what?

6

Isolation

I Am Alone and Afraid, Keep Women Apart, *Akeli Hoon, Darti Hoon*

The life-negating isolation for Naaz, 49, started immediately after she eloped to marry the man she loved. She was 21.

'The very next day after my marriage, he made me write a resignation letter to the bank although I kept on pleading with him. He said, "My wife will not work in a bank." He was not one who would allow any dialogue or negotiation or anything, so lamely I wrote it and we went to the bank. This was a coveted job like getting into the IAS . . . I was so completely gone in that man's control.

'He completely controlled my every breath and heartbeat, you know, I am not exaggerating when I say this – he controlled everything about me. He made me cut off my relations with all of my family and friends. No visitors were allowed. He never gave me money, not even to buy vegetables to put food on the bloody table. He would ask me "paise hai? *You have money?" I would say* haan, hain, *yes. Because I had lived in a home where I did not even ask for money from my parents, how can I ask it from a strange man? So, oh God, I did all kinds of things. I remember, when I was pregnant with Chetan, I used to walk around the whole city pretending to be fond of it, I had no money for an auto. When either of my grandmothers secretly came to visit and they wanted to give me a gift, I would say, "Give me money." I had so many pent-up feelings of anger, my whole body would shake, become stiff. It looked scary.'*

She became an actor and played the 'perfect wife' and nobody guessed that she was being beaten or that she cried endlessly, alone. She 'adjusted' to her situation.

'I justified all his behaviour, even his beating. After a while you become tolerant, not questioning, accepting everything. After all, what is the reality of a middle-class woman? There is little scope for original thinking or action. It's all been decided. If your husband is a good, loving person, then it's a bonus for you.'

She has fleeting glimpses of herself as a member of a social class. But all alone, she concludes it is her personal dysfunction. 'Alone I was always depressed, I was not . . . not looking forward to anything, sort of like jee rahe hain, *just existing. If it is morning, I'll get up, make tea, eat food. Passively existing. Whatever happens to me, I'll take it. I would get crying fits, crying uncontrollably.'*

A depressed woman is no threat. Millions of depressed, helpless, malfunctioning, even screaming and isolated women are no threat.

* * *

A particularly cruel cultural practice to perpetuate the non-existence of women is the isolation of women from others, including other women. It is easier to control women physically and mentally when they are alone rather than when they are with other women who support them. When women live in enforced isolation, they start to lose trust in their own judgements, they feel helpless and they blame themselves if anything bad happens to them. They try to adjust to a bad situation rather than to question cruelty, injustice or unfairness.

Isolation is the enforcement mechanism that classifies women's problems as personal rather than systemic and therefore political. Political problems are important and worthy of public attention but personal problems are, well, just personal and private, and not worthy of public scrutiny or public policy. Personal problems are a personal responsibility. Dysfunctional women deserve to be ignored.

Imprisonment starts early and is strongly physical; it starts with shutting the body down. Girls are shut down in a million little ways, each personalized and each seemingly harmless. *Achchi tarah baitho*, sit properly; *bahar nahin jao*, don't go out; *raat ho gai*, it is night, so you cannot go out; *dhyan do*, be aware. It is code for keep your body covered or watch how you walk, stand, sit, move or speak; to not trust anyone and be alert to dangers; *chup raho, mat bolo*, be quiet, don't speak, don't express your opinion and don't answer back. Shut bodies. Shut mouths. Shut minds. Naaz said she had eloped with a man to escape this oppression at home.

Marriage practices later guarantee that women are also physically isolated and cut off from their families, deepening their sense of aloneness. When a young bride leaves her parents' home to move to her husband's home, her entire network of support, all her family and friends, gets left behind. In the modern age, she may also leave her job behind. Marriage is a glorious moment in a girl's life that may also mark the shrinking of her world to choosing the colours of curtains and cushions. And waiting. Siya, 25, an MBA graduate from a leading business school, says, 'It is challenging being alone from 8 a.m. to 8 p.m., twelve hours every day.' Even though her mother-in-law is at home, she feels a *khalipan*, an emptiness. Women's employment has been decreasing even with increasing education of women and a growing economy.

Lonely is how Kalpana, 60, describes her life despite having a husband and raising three children. The isolation is also psychological. Women are trained not to trust, furthering their sense of isolation. Men are dangerous and women untrustworthy. Since there is no one left, this ensures aloneness. The cruelty lies in this paradox: women are trained to feel alone and isolated but their very survival depends on their being in relationships as caring relationship experts. Filled with fear, women don't trust others, so their world shrinks. Isolated from the world of information, contacts and support, women start to feel unsure and alone. They stop trusting their own capacities. So they shrink their own world.

The consequences of social isolation are grim. We all know intuitively that social connections and a sense of belonging are central to being well. We now have evidence from large cross-country surveys and research in neuroscience, the science of how the brain and nervous system work. Isolation literally beckons death. A recent study found that social isolation increases the likelihood of death by 29 per cent, loneliness increases it by 26 per cent and living alone increases it by 32 per cent, numbers as high as other better-known health risk factors.

While I was at the World Bank I researched widely the idea of social capital, the web of social connections and trust, a term popularized by the political scientist Robert Putnam. The 'World Happiness Report' of 2015 taps into decades of this research and finds that social support (whether a person can bank on someone to help), the freedom to make life decisions and generosity all contribute significantly to subjective well-being or happiness across 158 countries, both rich and poor. Think of the anxiety produced when a friend or colleague doesn't return your call or text message or when a friend 'unfriends' you on Facebook. We may not recognize it as pain, but loss of social connections is painful. Recent neuroscience research shows that the pain experienced from social isolation is very similar to the experience of physical pain; the same parts of the brain light up. Social isolation hurts. Yet women are systematically and socially isolated from everyone, including other women, their potential allies, even when they live together. In this chapter, I focus on women's relationships with women.

The Early Training: Fill Girls with Fear

> *I am full of fear. My life is so narrow and restricted that I cannot enjoy my life, I cannot take an independent step. I panic.* Shipra, 31

I call the way girls are raised 'fear training', literally, training girls to become fearful. It is training based on no and don't. No, you can't do this. No, you can't do that. Don't do this, don't do that. Don't go there. Girls get little practice in testing themselves in life; they start to live an unpractised life. The very thing girls long for, life, slowly becomes fear of life. The paradox is that, as adults, women find it hard to say no to other adults. But they have no difficulty in raining no down on their young, powerless daughters. The problem is not the occasional boundary-setting no, but the constant, unrelenting no.

A regime of noes cracks the confidence of girls. Sabina, 24, who works in an advertising agency in Mumbai, was brought up by no-saying, fear-filling parents. When she was young and even now, she says, 'I feel scared to ask, I hesitate, I don't know why, even for valid issues, like with teachers . . . Some kids are able to say what they want, whether the answer is yes or no. But me, I am stupid, I never say anything. I never ask so I never get, and then I curse myself.'

Silent fear disconnects her from others and she blames herself. In Indian culture, the fact that most fathers hold power has a big impact on their children's self-esteem. When mothers say '*Papa se pooch*', ask Papa, girls know who has the power. As power holders, fathers' criticism has a particularly harsh sting on girls. Criticism and constant fault finding are a core soul-sucking strategy of fear-training. I found women's accounts of their childhood particularly empty of praise, a pattern confirmed by Dr S. Anandalakshmy, who has been India's leading scholar in child development for over four decades. She was also my professor in college. An astute observer of families, she said, 'Yes, it's true, we don't praise easily and girls receive much less praise than boys.' Talking about her unhappiness with her father, Eshani, 27, a marketing specialist who lives in West Delhi, says in a raised voice, 'I would like him to appreciate something in me. In both my board examinations, for 10th and 12th standards in school, I got 88 per cent and 89 per cent. He would say, "*90 aana chahiye tha*, you should have got 90 per cent."' She feels crushed; no achievement of hers is ever good enough. Fault finding, with everyday ordinary things like how a girl combs her hair or how a girl stands or talks, is a strategy intended to dampen confidence.

Lack of confidence induces anxiety. Neetu, 37, a website designer, feels fear all the time except with one friend, Stuti. She says, 'They could have instilled more confidence in me as a child. It is a parental responsibility. I was loved but they could have told me that it's all right to have this dark complexion. I was treated like I was not cool enough. As long as I am in isolation, I am good.' Uncertain and insecure as a young girl, she withdrew even within her own family, resisting family pressure to attend family functions.

Fathers may 'pamper' their daughters but they still restrict them. Restrictions teach girls that they are not trusted. Speaking about her father, Sabha, 37, a struggling singer, says, 'I wish he hadn't made me realize that I am a woman and I am weaker than a man. We got freedom but there were so many boundaries. If we were given that liberty, I would have been standing somewhere in life. I had to fight with my dad for everything.'

Dimple, 25, is from a wealthy family in Sainik Farms. She looks like a model. I arrived at her home as she finished a session with her personal trainer. When I asked Dimple what hurts her the most about her father, she said unhesitatingly, 'He doesn't trust me. Always restrictions.' Now Dimple goes out when she wants, but she no longer trusts herself to make any decisions about work or boyfriends. She stays frozen in fear.

Restrictions prepare girls to be fearful even when the restrictions are removed and when they are technically free. *Bahar nahin jao*, don't go out, is perhaps the most universal restriction. Aarushi, 19, a student at Lady

Shri Ram College who fought with her parents for the freedom to go out, says, 'Now it is very difficult for me to go out. There is always fear. You know people are watching. You have to protect yourself and there is no one with you. You don't feel relaxed outside; you feel relaxed only when you are at home. I can't just go freely anywhere, even when my parents don't say come home early. Why was I born a girl? Why was I not born in place of my brother?' Her brother, who is not restricted, does not fear going out, but she is fear-filled and stays home even when she has a 'real' choice. She is overcome with anxiety. She has been perfectly trained for dependence on men. She adds, 'What I want most from a future husband is protection.'

There are more restrictive rules for girls than for dogs, cats or cows. Everyone knows these common boundaries, 'boundations'. These restrictions often continue through college and even till the day girls get married. Curfew hours range from 6 p.m. to 10.30 p.m. For Abhisha, 20, studying commerce, the curfew hour is still 6 p.m. or 6.30 p.m. She says wistfully, 'I have a lot of dreams, like sometimes to hang out with my friends, but my mother and father *allow nahin karte*, they don't allow it. Because they think it is not safe for women. I feel they won't allow me sleepovers, so I never ask, I feel anxious that they might refuse. *Hesitation hoti hai*, there is hesitation.' Once she hesitatingly asked her father permission to go somewhere and he did not allow her. She did not talk to her father for a year, but she did not defy him or fight back. She says, 'Now I have let it go. It was something small. But it affected me a lot.' She no longer even asks. Passive, she just waits for life to happen to her.

Mothers are the daily fence-keepers since they are the ones at home most of the time. Some mothers become portable fences in their zeal to protect their girls everywhere. Tanya, 17, a high school student, says she is only allowed out of her house to study. '*Har dam*, always, there is comparison with my brother, you are a girl, you stay inside. My mother accompanies me to tuition classes, she drops me to school. I feel very unhappy that she goes everywhere with me. I look around and see other girls, their mothers don't accompany them, so I also want to go alone. My school is very close by, still my mother comes every day to drop me, I am so *dukhi*, unhappy.' Her mother is just trying to be a very vigilant mother. But in doing so, she steals opportunities for Tanya to feel fearless in the world by learning simple things like finding her way to school, crossing the street, negotiating with vendors and talking to other parents, students and teachers.

Her mother is in effect teaching her that she cannot take care of herself, she needs others to protect her, but she must not trust others. Dependence without trust is a serious problem. The most powerful training in fear, however, does not involve words. It is through observation of mothers, the first models for little girls. Although most girls love their mothers, they are not blind to their mothers' confined, low-trust, fear-based lives. When asked what she learned from her mother, Ananya, 33, a lecturer at a university, says, 'Nothing *yaar*, for my mom it's only home, clothes, kitchen, routine. Her life starts and ends there, she is happy there. I didn't learn how to fight with a situation, because that is not there in my mother. She is also scared but she hides it behind irritation and I do not like that.'

Most mothers do try to hide their fears, but this is difficult to do with children whose gaze is constantly on them. Sonali, 26, a software engineer, first says how much she loves her mother and then says with a scowl, 'I have inherited not standing up for myself from my mother. She will not utter a word to others, but later she will blabber. She lacks the courage to tell anyone anything, even on the phone. I don't like this thing.'

Girls also internalize the behaviour of mothers who don't feel free to express their anger and, in their helplessness and dependence, cry instead. Komal, 30, says, 'My mother cries about the smallest things, even I do the same.' Anger is demonized and very quickly girls conclude that being angry is a character flaw, it is not 'normal'. Tanushri, 24, with a postgraduate degree, considers herself 'flawed' because of her anger issues. She says, 'I behave abnormal sometimes because of this thing. My mom tells me to do yoga.' She is working on 'ironing' it out of herself. She also isolates herself, just in case her 'emotional behaviour' – meaning anger – emerges.

The lack of permission and skills to express anger directly means the unexpressed anger can emerge indirectly in constant petty complaints, irritation, shutting down and withdrawing from others. Young men frequently describe their mothers as irritable, passive-aggressive and unable to express their anger. Neel, 22, who has just completed his commerce degree, says, 'Like my mom, she will have so much anger in her, every time you talk to her, she will be cribbing about something or the other, why can't they just relax? Is it necessary to always be so irritable?'

Carefully groomed in fear and dependence, women as a category are doomed the moment we classify these behaviours as personal faults. Women start to hide in order to hide their flaws. And if women as a group are such faulty, fearful, helpless, irritable and irritating creatures, why would any smart woman want to associate with even more of them? It would be smart to run from women and run them down. This is exactly the intent of the careful construction of a cultural design that fills girls with fear and flaws and trains them to go into hiding, to be alone. *Akeli hoon.*

Consequences: Divide and Rule, Don't Let the Women Unite

> *I have realized that every woman on earth is jealous of another. Even my closest friends, they are always jealous, not genuine with their advice, even when they are happy for you, there is comparison in their hearts. Males will never be jealous.* Monica, 29

Women should be other women's natural allies. The fact that they are not is not accidental. It is the genius of cultural design: to ensure that each woman stays alone and isolated. If women came together to stand up for each other against unfairness or misuse of power, whether in the home, offices or on the streets, it would break the cultural, social, political and economic arrangements that prop up the power and privileges of men, and the non-existence of women as full human beings.

When I asked women and men about women's relationships with women, especially after seeing them in happy groups in shopping centres, malls, cinema halls and coffee shops, I expected to hear stories of sisterhood, empathy, compassion and love. Instead, what emerged was a stream of negativity, example after example of broken trust. The more I probed, the more the pattern showed up. Women talked about women as if they are deeply flawed characters beyond correction. I did not find a single strong case of an adult woman standing up for another adult woman within her circle of family and friends who was in trouble. This was true even of women who work on issues of empowerment of poor and abused women. Women speak about empowerment but they do not embody empowerment in their own lives.

On the contrary, within their own circles, women often embody many disempowering qualities. Most books about women do not plumb the depths of the specific types of behaviours that do not make women look good. But only if we talk about what has been kept hidden, and, most importantly, understand *why* women behave in these ways, will we go beyond sloganeering and see real change. Patterns of behaviours that repeat across hundreds of individuals are not personal flaws but reflect and serve to perpetuate deep power imbalances in cultural, economic and political systems. They keep unfair systems functioning.

I found two sets of cultural strategies that prevent women from coming together to take positive collective action to change their own lives and the lives of others. The first set protects the existing cultural system by making women dependent on men and isolating women from each other, and the second set relies on women demonizing and destroying the character of other women like themselves by defining themselves as different, the exception to the rule.

Become dependent and isolated

Naaz, whose middle-class friends turned away from her when she hesitatingly tried to tell them about her terror, stayed in a bad marriage for 17 years. Naaz is an extreme case but many other highly educated, talented and high-earning women collapse into a puddle in their relationships with boyfriends or husbands in ways that make no rational sense but reflects early training to depend on men for their life.

Depend on men and be fearful

Sangeetha, 42, who is very successful in the sports world and who fearlessly approaches CEOs in boardrooms to negotiate contracts, finds that a meek self emerges when she is with men in long-term romantic relationships. She says, 'You will not recognize me, I become timid, I don't know why, but I observe it.'

Reena, 26, who is a well-paid business consultant, says, 'I know I should speak up with my boyfriend, but I can't. I don't raise issues and the whole focus shifts to him. It's fear . . . you are so afraid if you express demand, desire, you may get abandoned, so you say, *jaane do*, let it go, don't say anything.' Trained in the importance of relationships with men, even financially independent women like Sangeetha and Reena get caught in their early training of emotional dependence and meekness in the company of men. Maneesha, 26, says her passionate two-year relationship with her boyfriend 'filled my need for dependence'. Dependence in itself is not bad; it can be fulfilling and enriching, but one-sided dependence can result in exploitation and disrespect. In Maneesha's relationship, her boyfriend made every decision, including when to telephone or message each other, when to meet, when to go out and when to have sex. She didn't like this, but she never spoke up. Instead she protected him by not telling anyone that he had become a dictator in the relationship. And she instinctively isolated herself from her friends to ensure that they never knew.

When girls are trained to depend on men and any attempt to be independent is declared bad, it is difficult for women to suddenly change. Anoushka, 25, says, 'I was overprotected by my dad and by my brother. And now my father suddenly wants me to be self-dependent. I have a habit of dependence on him, how can it be possible that I do everything by myself now, even though I am married?'

Women feel lonely and afraid when they are alone. Women have a complex relationship with being alone. Their systematic training in dependence cuts them off from themselves so they never really develop a healthy ability to be alone. In addition, dependence is encouraged by teaching women to be afraid of being alone. Being alone is made unsafe. Pinky, 31, says, 'I find it hard to enjoy solitude. Every time I am alone, I start feeling lonely. Feeling lonely is a fear. But Sherry, 60, describes her marriage as 'bone-numbing loneliness'. Lonely when living with others and afraid to be living alone. For Sakshi, 25, the biggest fear is 'being alone, social isolation'.

Be loyal, don't share your problems with others

Across cultures, the powerful bind themselves to the powerless, particularly through marketing the idea of loyalty. Loyalty is an allegiance, an attachment which gives meaning, a sense of belonging, a promise of protection, and hence an escape from feeling alone. Loyalty binds the powerless to the more powerful, even when it is not in their best interest, as in the case of Naaz. Papiya, 25, works as a domestic maid in a Gurgaon household. Her husband loves her very much but he also uses loyalty to stop her from discussing the family with anyone and he effectively isolates her from other women. 'He told me not to share my problems with others, *ghar ka mamla, ghar pe hi rakho*, matters of the house, keep in the house.' Don't air your dirty laundry. When asked about friends, Papiya says, 'My husband says, what is the need to have friends? He has seven brothers and their families. He tells me why do you want to have friends when our family is so big.' Obediently she lets go of her social interactions with neighbours and rationalizes her aloneness saying, 'I don't have time left after work anyway.'

Papiya has no intimate friends. Papiya is not friends with the other women in her husband's family even though they do things together, nor does she have any women friends outside of the family. She proves her loyalty and protects her husband by keeping her hurts, fears and problems to herself. 'I don't say much, I just keep it inside my heart.' Even though her husband treats her with respect, some part of Papiya is always on alert. She knows that if her husband changes his mind, she can be thrown out with nothing, which she sees happen to other women. She says, 'I can't trust men. My husband, he is so good to me right now, but in the future you can't say.' Dependent on a man she loves but cannot trust completely, loyal but isolated, Papiya knows that if there is trouble at home, she is alone, without a support network.

There is another hugely negative consequence to loyalty. Loyalty demands not sharing problems and therefore not asking others for help. Asking for help becomes wrong and provokes great anxiety. This too keeps women trapped. No matter what the problem, women said with great pride, 'I can handle it alone.' In fact, women have been trained to confuse independence with not asking for help. Cultural pride in being good isolates and traps women even when they seemingly belong to a community.

Don't let the women unite

Women internalize negative attitudes towards other women by growing up within systems that breathe out poisonous fumes about women without understanding this as a cultural strategy to keep them divided from each other, powerless despite their intellectual beliefs and desire to support each other.

Women often judge other women as 'treacherous, unreliable, unpredictable, small-hearted, manipulative, hypocritical, lying, competitive, jealous and attention-seeking betrayers'. It would of course be wise to stay far away from such unsavoury people. Such is the brilliance of a cultural strategy that turns powerless people against each other. The more powerful group, in this case men, does not need to be on guard to protect its superior power. Women do their dirty work. When women distrust and dislike each other, there is no danger of unity even with education and wealth.

Don't trust other women

Trust is the firm belief that someone or something is reliable, predictable and will not harm you. When you trust, you feel safe; the world is safe. Without trust, the world could not function. We would drown in rules. Trust makes exchange and trade possible – it makes collective action possible. Women who are trained in childhood not to trust others are therefore at a great disadvantage. It is like living permanently stalled at a red traffic light. Living in a world with women you do not trust is frightening; it cheats you of a sense of belonging and makes any collective action or resistance to unfairness, exploitation or disrespect almost impossible. Women start to hate themselves and other women; it comes with the territory of belonging to a group that is so marginal that it is not supposed to exist. For the larger culture this is perfect because it limits any possibility of fundamental change on a large scale. It preserves the status quo despite advances through legislation.

Jyoti, 36, is stylish, with a shaved head, and is raising two young daughters. Jyoti says, 'Trust means faith in someone for your own peace of mind. The biggest reason I trust easily is because it brings me peace to imagine that the world is good, that I am in no immediate or long-term threat from anyone. Having doubts destroys my peace so I choose to be at peace by trusting.' She listens well to other women and displays what researchers call both cognitive and emotional empathy.

Further conversation reveals, however, that in reality, Jyoti does not trust anyone including her own mother. She says, 'My ability to trust is ambiguous and paradoxical. On the one hand, I trust strangers easily. But I keep distance even in my closest relationships, keeping my innermost thoughts absolutely to myself. I am socially and emotionally self-sufficient.' In other words, she does not need or trust anybody. But she is proud that she is trustworthy to others which to her means an 'absence of judgement followed by the ability to listen and understand others'.

In fact, most women we interviewed categorize only themselves as trustworthy, the exception to the rule, but they categorize all other women as untrustworthy. These women see themselves as good but judge other women as 'not so good'. Devika, 25, with a degree in economics, says, 'Such a suspicious girl I am. I don't trust anyone. I believe women are a little loose with secrets. I keep my secrets with me. I don't trust telling them, it is like putting a loudspeaker on the rooftop.' Many women said, 'Why trust anyone?'

I interviewed several mother and grown-up-daughter pairs in the USA and in India. None of the mothers or daughters was willing to talk in front of the other even though they love each other. And they all said that they did not trust women, not even within the family. Like many women, Saloni, 25, who is an HR officer, said, 'As far as women in the family are concerned, I don't feel comfortable being open with them. They have never gained that trust for me to talk with them without suspecting their intentions.'

Destroy the competition

Some women hesitate but others openly say that women are jealous and constantly compete with each other. 'In front of you they appreciate you but when you are not in front of them they say negative things about you. Women are hypocrites, men are not like that, girls deceive you easily, they will say things sweetly, but in their hearts they are bad. Women backbite more than men,' says Indira, 60, from a well-off family. Muskan, 15, a science student, has reached the same conclusion. 'There is a lot of backbiting among women, so I tell my mother just not to meet other women.'

The most institutionalized form of competition and meanness is evident in the *saas–bahu* soap dramas, a response to a structured system in which women derive their power from competing and fighting for control over the same powerful man, the son/husband. The well-being of the mother-in-law in the long run depends on her son's loyalty to her, and the well-being of the new wife depends on her control over the same man, her husband. Even though marriage is essential to continue the lineage, for the mother-in-law the daughter-in-law – the new, young, sexual being – embodies the notion of romantic love, making the *jodi*, the couple, the most dominant threat to her son's loyalty to her. Educated, older, salaried daughters-in-law are even more of a threat than 18-year-olds who are easier to control. No wonder that in many households position, rank and power are clarified even today on day one, sometimes crudely, across social classes. Sunita, 35, from the lower-income group, says, 'When I got married and came to their house, she gave me *boras* [jute sacks] to sleep on. Such a bitch, she used to tell my husband to beat me up, I am happy she died.' Lekha, 27, from the educated middle-income group, says, 'On the first day my mother-in-law told me she didn't like me and had never liked me and my parents were cheap, my father useless.' Her husband stood by silently. Anu, 50, from the upper-income group, says, 'If there's one person I detest it's my mom-in-law. I would shoot her point-blank if I had a chance, but I won't since we have a common link, my husband . . . She is cruel.' Sometimes the struggle for power is more indirect, through silences and pretending the other does not exist. Sonia, 31, complains, 'No matter how much I do for her, she only asks after her son, she never asks how I am doing.' For her mother-in-law she does not exist.

In addition to backbiting, women speak about gossip, another 'weapon of the weak', which also has a social and evolutionary function. It spreads information and it reinforces norms, but it also isolates women from each other.

Sireesha, 25, has developed a strategy to cope with her need for close girlfriends and the possibility that secrets will become weapons used against her if a friendship ends. She diversifies her secret portfolio among her friends to manage risk. 'Women cannot keep things inside, it's a big noooo. So, I consider one friend, one secret at a time only. Example, none of my friends knows all my secrets. I share my secrets based on their intellectual capacity.' If the friendship ends, the damage is limited.

The worst and most common forms of betrayal are around boyfriends. Siri, 30, says, 'Yes, my roommate, who was a close friend in college, slept with my boyfriend and

I get to know about this after eight years; [she smiles] can you beat this? She used to talk to me and ask me about my relationship, showed so much concern and she screwed up my relationship.' Sona, 24, and much younger girls spoke about theft of boyfriends too. 'Yes, lots of betrayals with girlfriends. She was my closest friend in college. She started dating my boyfriend behind my back, while I was still with him. When I used to go meet Varun, now my ex, I sometimes used to take her with me. She met him a few times with me, then *dheere dheere*, slowly, they started meeting without me. I started getting suspicious and one day, *pata nahin kyun*, I don't know why, I just followed her and I saw that she was sitting with Varun. So I caught them. Eventually I broke up with that guy.' Sona, who works at Citibank, says, 'I am very cautious now, especially when it comes to making a close girlfriend. I have not introduced my boyfriend to anyone. I am scared, I can't completely trust anyone now.' Sona concludes that 'Men are more open and straightforward, more honest with me than my female friends who sugarcoat, so that is why I can trust them more. Men support more.'

As young women's contact with young men has increased, over and over again I heard that men were superior moral beings and so make better friends. Ameesha, 25, a tester of engineering devices, says, 'Men don't care what you say, they have the chill factor. They will not think, *arrey*, what have you told them! So they will not tell anyone, it doesn't matter to them.' Men are described as good friends, cool, easy-going and not as complicated as women. Ruby, 17, who interacts with boys during tuition classes, says, 'I like their company. They make you have more *masti*, fun. *Hasi mazaak*, joking and laughing, they do more, so it feels nice.' Ironically men emerge once more as heroes. Research also establishes that over time girls' solidarity and friendships with each other are more fragile. Women direct their negative behaviour to other women, their competitors for male attention and resources. Men as the power holders are outside this circle of competition and uninterested and so emerge smelling of roses. Navneet, 19, says with a grimace, 'Girls cannot keep secrets, every time they have to tell someone else. Now I have more guy friends, with them I can share my trouble.' Such is the brilliance of cultural design that women despise other women and choose men as the decent human beings.

Friendships that score high on self-validation, help, intimacy, reliability, companionship and emotional security contribute enormously to happiness. And it is not the number but quality of friendships that makes a difference. There are many popular films about deep male friendship, but few celebrating women's friendship. Men win again. Women do have girlfriends, but as many women say, 'only for fun and nice chats, nothing more'. This behaviour will change only when women are willing to own their power and do not see men as the only channel for obtaining power.

Don't build a community of women

When women judge each other as untrustworthy, mean-spirited, jealous, gossipy and unsupportive, it makes sense that they do not want to associate with each other, let alone organize themselves into groups, networks or their own political parties. Men have more extensive and influential networks than women. The absence of women's groups, alliances and networks in the middle and upper classes is not accidental. It too is guaranteed not to happen, an outcome of a system that keeps women divided from each other. Divide and conquer is a proven strategy that always works.

Despite the famed women's self-help groups in rural India, almost none of the women living in cities with whom I spoke belong to a women's group. In fact, just about all of them are anti-women-in-groups. Most women laugh at the very idea of a women's group. Suwbha, 31, an outspoken woman who teaches at Miranda House, a premier women's college in Delhi, says, 'No . . . ha ha, this is funny, I never had such an idea in my life. If I join any group, it will be the ideology of the group that will take over me as a person, which I never want to happen. I don't want to be part of groups, they kill individuality and I am determined to live on my own.'

When asked if they belong to any groups, many women said they do not indulge in gossip, assuming that when women come together gossip is all they do. In addition to judgemental negative attitudes, most women just do not see the point of women getting together. Aditi, 44, says, 'No, I never felt the need and never had the time.' Similarly, Ridhi, 25, says, 'I don't mind but I have no specific desire to join one. I have never even thought of one.' Powerless people often do not see the point of getting together with other powerless people.

'Kitty parties' are a well-established middle-class tradition. My mother belonged to a kitty party in which a group of her friends would get together once a month to save money and take turns receiving the 'kitty', the funds.

My mother loved such parties. But in our interviews, I met only four women who belong to such groups. Dolly, 26, from the middle class, says, 'I hate kitty parties, I detest them – I hate gossip, dislike anything that wastes my time, it is not meaningful and hurts others. I do not like to be attached to a group that tells me where to go, when to go.' Manushree, 54, who lives in a farmhouse, used to belong to two kitties that included wives of leading jewellers in Delhi. She dropped out after her 'kitty friends' withheld information from her that could have helped her daughter avoid going through the trauma of getting engaged to a man who turned out to be gay. She said, 'They knew, later they said "of course he is gay", but if they knew, why didn't they tell me? Clearly, they were not friends.' Kitty parties are not dead; they are taking new forms, from cultural clubs, to travelling clubs, to entertainment clubs, still primarily for women, and so still have the potential of bringing women together in a forum that is culturally sanctioned.

While city women do not belong to women's groups, they do sometimes join protests. It is primarily the anger of women supported by large numbers of men that fuelled the protests and marches to India Gate that woke up the nation after the Nirbhaya rape. Several younger women in our group had participated in this protest; fewer men reported doing so, even though they supported the outcry. Women also join or create NGOs. There are over 2 million registered NGOs in India, or one NGO per 600 people, compared to one police officer per 943 people.

Many women are involved in occasional charity, and this is good and important. Women help women 'out there', those defined as less fortunate than them. Women help women cope but not to resist or change the system. Despite working on women's issues, the women we spoke to just do not see other women as a possible source of strength. The mindset of fighting for limited resources is so deeply learned that heads of the Ford Foundation and Oxfam in India, both funding a range of organizations, said to me independently of each other, 'It is almost impossible to get women's organizations to collaborate with one another.'

Be prejudiced against women

It is difficult to get away from the conclusion that women are prejudiced against women. Ruchi, 30, an assistant professor at Delhi University, is an example of the incongruous phenomenon of women who fight for women while also being deeply prejudiced against women. Ruchi grew up with educated parents who encouraged her to be independent. 'My parents never brought me up as a female. I have a very gender-neutral mindset. I am not a woman, I am a person.' As a young, married woman, Ruchi has a husband who supports her aspirations and a mother-in-law who runs the household, freeing Ruchi to pursue a profession outside the home. Ruchi works on several women's causes through NGOs, including Breakthrough, an NGO that works to stop violence against women.

But despite her intellectual commitment and her actions on behalf of women she does not know personally, she embodies many prejudices against women and has not been able to connect the professional, personal and the political. In describing her professional life, Ruchi says, 'I work in an all-women's institution. I see women bitching about other women like crazy . . . They do backbiting, step on each other's work, take credit.' She has nothing good to say about women in her circles.

In her personal life too, Ruchi does not trust women. She says, 'Yes, I do have good relations with all the women in my family. They are good but I don't trust them. I like to maintain my distance.' This lack of trust extends to her friends as well. 'There are only two friends I trust but only up to a limit. If something good happens, even your friends sometimes, their attitude turns different. They say they are very happy and all but their face shows that they are jealous.' Ruchi concludes that women are nasty to each other. 'Yes, they are jealous. If there is something nice about you, then they won't share that with others but if there is some mistake you have made they will tell everybody.' At a personal level Ruchi is a feminist with bad habits. She is anti-women but she thinks of herself as 'gender-neutral', a ninja fighting for women's rights. And she is a ninja for poor women. It is almost as if educated women can fight for women's rights and causes only if the problems are far away from them rather than when they acquire flesh and bones close to home.

Close to home, without other ninjas, it becomes deeply threatening to disturb the power balance. It is intensely political and personal for a lone woman to challenge the very system on which her life and safety depend. It is particularly unsafe because, when a lone woman upsets an existing power balance, the system fights back with all its might and the cost of challenging the system falls on a single woman, a difficult price to bear alone. Women know this intuitively.

While women may be aware of the deep power inequality with men, they have not yet made the connection between power inequality and women's negativity towards other women or their conclusion that men are better than women. They just perpetuate the negativity without realizing that this is the most brilliant part of the cultural strategy to keep women powerless, alone and afraid.

When women judge women as a group negatively, the systems that devalue women win. When women feel alone, the systems that thrive on women's aloneness win. And it is precisely because women are diminished collectively as a group that the personal becomes a collective problem and requires collective solutions.

Female bosses are mean

Women's learned, collective distrust of women does not bode well for female bosses. Although the phenomenon of female bosses at senior levels is still not widespread, at lower levels, women bosses are already labelled as mean. It is obviously not the case that women cannot make good bosses, but it is hardly surprising that women who are brought up isolated, insecure, fear-driven and low in trust do not make good bosses. Neither would men raised in this way. When asked if they would prefer a male boss or a female boss, or either, only three women said they prefer women bosses. They explained that women will not molest you and women are likely to understand women better, particularly when they have their period. A large majority, even women who generally trust women, do not want to work with female bosses. The rest, one-fifth, were indifferent; they said, a boss is a boss.

Kanti, 24, a self-proclaimed pro-woman woman, recently moved to Mumbai to work. Her female friends are her lifeline. 'I love them, I can discuss any issue with them, be it about a guy, a job or family issues. Even about my sex life. That is the extent of my comfort level.' She is completely gender-neutral about trustworthiness, but when asked about women bosses she spits venom. 'Women are very judgemental about other women, men don't judge you . . . they are very easy. In my job interview the male boss was much more considerate. And the female boss did everything to make it bad for me and ultimately she made sure that I was not selected.' She has no intention of working for a female boss. 'No way. Women bosses are maniacs. They somehow are much more difficult to handle.' Anuradha, 31, who has worked under a woman boss, is even more scathing. 'Women bosses suck, I have one right now and she is a bitch. She treats everyone like shit.'

Others say women bosses are 'stricter, less flexible, less creative, uptight, jealous, more likely to scold and more afraid; they cannot make bold decisions, will pull you down, *do pangebaaz*, create difficulties for you, breathe down your neck, give you fewer opportunities, will not give promotions, will compete with you, will not appreciate you, talk too much, are always complaining, point out *chhoti chhoti*, small small, faults and are judgemental.'

Women seem to have no mental models of an admirable woman. In fact, when we asked both schoolgirls and women to name their female role models, over 90 per cent drew a blank. Mothers got the most mention, followed by a couple of skinny film stars. Our cultural systems, by design, do not grow women who champion other women. When women start to champion other women en masse, and when men lead, sponsor and join women-led groups, the entire structure of male–female inequality will start to collapse rather than merely go underground. Till then, we will stay in a dehumanizing mess.

Naaz Disrupts the Cultural Design

Since women's biases against women are due to cultural design, they can be broken down more easily collectively rather than individually, although every woman who changes individually matters. The cultural design can shift through women's participation in groups to achieve specific goals.

Naaz, who was totally isolated, did walk out of her abusive marriage after 17 years. Her life changed only after she broke her isolation from other women, when she stopped thinking only of herself and her son and started supporting other women in distress. This in turn led her to a new set of open-minded middle-class women friends who were also engaged outside their homes. For Naaz, this process started with meeting poor, riot-affected Muslim women living in tatters in a burial ground in Ahmedabad after one Muslim man showed up in her locality looking for help. She hesitatingly gathered some food for them. It grew from there. 'Every day we used to go and people would come, narrate what happened to them . . . something started happening to me . . . slowly I became their friend, they would phone me.' Naaz's experience of working with poor, uneducated, young, extremely vulnerable women who had lost everything but still had the courage to demand justice moved her out of her middle-class passivity and sense of helplessness. 'That thing was rekindled in me, I began valuing myself and valuing the fact that I was alive. I began feeling ashamed of myself – that if *these* women who have lost everything are so alive, I have no excuses to waste mine or my child's life with the excuse that this man [her husband] is a monster, what can I do? I felt ashamed. It became unbearable for me.' It was by connecting with other women and by seeing other examples that Naaz could re-evaluate her own life. Empathy and compassion for others shook her out of her own numbness, depression and shame. Psychologist Brené Brown demonstrates that the surest way out of shame is empathy and compassion for others.

Naaz started questioning her acquiescence with abuse in her own life. 'It helps to link your work, the personal and the political *jo bolte hain na*, you know what they say – it was happening at the subconscious level but slowly that clarity was emerging, *kyun maar khayein*? Why should we get beaten? *Galat kyun sahein, jab kuch galat kiya nahin hai*? Why should we put up with wrong-doing when we have done nothing wrong? Someone lent me a copy of *Pedagogy of the Oppressed* and I realized when I read it – oh my God, I am a sample subject. One sentence really struck me – hegemony is built on consent – and I realized I had consented to being beaten, pushed aside, misbehaved [with], shouted at, abused. Why am I consenting?' Slowly Naaz developed a new mental model. 'I understood this new world view, what it is to be poor, what it is to be a woman, what it is to be a minority and what it is to be a Dalit, what is patriarchy – all these bigger questions – what is human rights and how they get violated inside and outside the home and in a so-called democratic structure.' When she told her new friends working with NGOs about her troubles at home, they stood by her firmly when she finally walked out. Her new mental model was this: there is power in women working together, and in the collective intelligence that comes when groups work well together to solve a problem. She started living the power of community.

She intuitively understood the bonds that tie women together. 'So today working for women's rights, hearing all those stories in slums from poor women, I feel like I am one of them. So what if I have money, degrees? So what if I am fair-skinned, tall? I am fundamentally like them, the same in fact . . . some are even more assertive than I am. See, my experiences, my feeling is that even being from a high economic class does not guarantee that you will not be oppressed. You will be oppressed if you are not aware of your being and rights; to that extent it is common . . . Beyond that it differs when women are uneducated and already live in poverty,' she said. She became aware of her rights because she was no longer isolated from the world.

Naaz has since won many awards for her work and is now married to a man who is proud of her strengths and praises her at home and to his friends. She laughs as she says, 'He doesn't have the rhetoric of gender and patriarchy but he has a common sense understanding that you have to be considerate. See, I travel fifteen days a month – I am not home to do anything. And yet, he is fine with that. We have no rules, you know – we can eat at home, eat out, order in; no compulsion on me, no orders. No, you have to cook, clean. The stereotypical role expectations are not there.' She no longer needs permission to act.

Policy shifts and laws signal values that are considered good by society. Women's organizations that base their work on the assumption of power inequalities between women and men and strong feminist activism play critical roles in changing policies to reduce violence against women. A study across 70 countries found the presence of such organizations to be more important in this process than left-wing parties, the number of women legislators or even the national wealth of a country.

Rural women's membership-based self-help groups in villages in Andhra Pradesh and Uttar Pradesh are based on the power of women when they come together. The scaling-up of many of these self-movements was initiated by men. These poor women's groups have now successfully challenged bank management practices, police treatment, access to justice and punishment for domestic violence, through leveraging the power of numbers, which now run into millions. While it is easy to ignore one woman, it is not easy to ignore hundreds of organized women who show up at the house of an abused woman, the police station, the district magistrate's office or the local bank and often just sit and wait and do not go away till their concerns are addressed. These groups are not dismissed as feminist groups, gossip groups, party groups or political groups. They are dignity action groups. Well organized, the collective action of millions of women is gently nudging powerful systems to adjust to them. Innovation is now leading to new cultural approaches to access justice, counselling, training and investment money in some districts in Andhra Pradesh. Women can and do unlearn their prejudices against women.

We will know that the cultural design has cracked when women's behaviours are no longer dismissed as personal and private flaws but are subject to serious study, and public policies change to stop women's isolation and increase women's access to power.

Reflections

We train girls in fear and then we dismiss them. We need to move from fear-training for girls to training girls into the habits of freedom and in physical *Dangal*-type strength. Girls who are physically strong and know how to defend themselves physically are not afraid of going out into the world. Fathers, as power holders, need to set the context of freedom for girls – freedom to explore, learn, laugh and love the world, instead of fearing the world. As Sukanya, 24, said, 'Fathers can build their daughters' confidence by letting them make mistakes. If I were to visualize it, it is the process of slowly letting go of the hold of a rope that has been held so tight.' Radical realignment is only possible when both fathers and mothers model new behaviours.

Women are not women's worst enemies. Women are taught to become women's enemies to keep men safe and to protect the existing cultural system of privilege of men. I was not taught to champion women. It never occurred to me. Except later in my teenage years when I read books and I changed intellectually, but the visceral, gut-level change took much longer. I now consciously champion at least one woman in my intimate circles intensely over years and one outside till I am no longer needed. And if every woman and every middle- and upper-class man does this, almost 300 million of us, it will multiply quickly and it will tip the cultural design to establish a new normal for good women and men.

Behavioural change starts simply. Create or join women's groups. Work with other women in teams. Agree to group norms and listen to each other deeply. Don't bury emotions but work through differences. Don't just walk away. Instead of boycotting the beautiful, the confident, the smart and those who speak up, support them, praise them, join them and learn from them. Build community, within the family and outside, belong to something outside the family, do something for others with others, build circles of support and friendships with women like you and women unlike you. And if conversations slip into negativity, interrupt and press the buzz button. Don't shame those who slip.

We need strong female models to inspire young girls to be strong. Find 'women of daring' who inspire you. They may be near you. Naaz found her women of daring living in a burial ground, and as she engaged with them her mental model of womanhood changed and with that her entire world changed. Every woman has to find her own 'women of daring'. I have had a few women as my 'women of daring' over the years. Now, one of them is my mother, of whom I have been critical during some phases in my life, silently of course. But one year when she was 71 she visited me, and my mother, who is a little round and has always worn a sari, took off her sari, stripped down to her petticoat and blouse, got harnessed and went up alone in the sky, parasailing off a boat in the ocean. When my 80-year-old father objected fiercely on grounds of safety and then added in panic that she would have a heart attack, my mother, who does have a heart problem, said, '*Abhi jeene toh do, kya hoga, khali marenge na*, let me live now, what does it matter, I will die only, it's all right.'

7

Identity

The Clash between Duty and Desire

Pooja, 25, is a computer scientist who grew up in Mumbai and left home at 21. Pooja seems modern on the outside.

'I have a very neutralized opinion of women. A woman is expected to be everything and yet not have a say in it. Coming from a family where I have only seen women act like housemaids, they are only there to take care of the kids, cook and fulfil their husbands' needs regardless of how smart and independent they are, so I strive to be a rebel at every step. Women are supposed to have long hair; I cut mine short. Women are supposed to get married in saris; whereas I don't want to get married, but if I do, I will wear hot shorts. Women are supposed to feel shy; well, I don't want to feel that . . . So I constantly rebel against the rules for women.

'My Nani and Dadi were not treated right. My mom had a bad marriage. I have only seen women suffer, probably not physically but emotionally.' Pooja is more comfortable suffering like her mother. A Sita in shorts. Happiness fills her with guilt. She said, 'I punish myself, I don't deserve to be happy. If I am not living to fulfil my duty, I don't deserve to be happy. I literally cut myself off from things I like. So these days I shut myself off from enjoying my friends.' She kills her own desire.

Away from family control, Pooja is free, but she considers her desires wrong. She says, 'Freedom, um, I don't know. I get tense thinking about it. I am not free, I can't make decisions.' She makes herself invisible. 'I hide my thinking and I can't say no to anyone.' But she is on a quest. 'I want to be less fake, I am afraid, I am lost. I have lost my way inside my world and find it difficult in the real world . . . I feel every emotion . . . I love, I hurt, I accept, I let go, I hold on, I miss, I lose . . . I am digging and digging . . . Have I made the right choice?'

Disconnected from her desires, Pooja doesn't know what she wants, so she cannot take action, enjoy her freedom or be happy. She goes round in circles.

* * *

A woman who is trained to make herself invisible, as if she does not exist, cannot have a self and therefore a distinct identity. She is trained to have no desire, to be a shape-shifter, a pleaser, a blender, to fit into the landscape of familial relationships. She is trained to put family and marriage at the core of her being; it becomes her sacred duty. Outside these relationships, there is no such thing as a woman. Priya, 23, who lives in Rohini, Delhi, says simply, 'A woman is taboo.' When a woman is taboo, she can only exist as a permanent apology.

But when M.L. Sharma, the defence lawyer for one of the accused in Nirbhaya's gang rape, said this aloud on film and then repeated it to journalists, 'In our culture, there is no place for a woman', it evoked an outpouring of anger. In reality, the defence lawyer had merely echoed a deeply held cultural belief that women do not exist outside of family relationships, a fact reflected in popular films, TV serials and decades of research by scholars in the social sciences. India's most respected and prolific cultural psychologist, Sudhir Kakar, says the same thing.

'There is no such thing as a woman in India. A woman is not an Indian category at all.' All speak an uncomfortable truth, some crudely and some with great erudition after years of research on Indian cultural practices, psyche and scriptures. Women exist only in relationships. As daughters, wives and mothers. As mothers, women's importance has been immortalized in the one line from the film *Deewar* still current after 40 years: '*Mere paas Maa hai*', I have my mother. Outside these relationships, women are culturally illegitimate. They can be picked off by snipers.

I met Neera, 32, still in her pyjamas, on a wintry Sunday morning in Delhi's South Extension, Part II. She said, 'My mother taught me there are three important occasions in a woman's life. When she is born, when she gets married and when she becomes a mother. Every time, you make sacrifices willingly. Whether I was born this way or brought up this way, I do not know but I am always ready to make sacrifices.' She follows dharma, does her duty. Duty is morality. Morality is duty. Desire has no place in a good woman's life. It interferes with the performance of her duty in life.

For women, selfless is a good word.

The Early Training: Girls Must Be Bound by Duty

> *A good girl is disciplined, self-respecting, kind, gentle, polite, loving, caring, truthful, obedient, respects elders, helping everyone unconditionally, focuses her aim on studies and is good to others – fulfilling duty.* Muskan, 15

> *Yes, in my childhood times, my parents taught me that a woman's life is full of sacrifices. We sacrifice our* tan-man-dhan, *body, mind, wealth, to see others happy.* Ranu, 17

People constantly tell me that modern, educated young women are not like their mothers; they are totally free, they follow their own desires and they don't listen to anyone. Just look at the young women going to work in their smart clothes or walking around in shopping malls. But talking to young women in coffee shops in the same malls reveals that clothes are just a cover-up for what has not changed on the inside. There are thousands of variations of Pooja, twenty-first century on the outside and nineteenth century on the inside.

Raising good Indian girls is still all about crushing any sense of self, so they can please and serve others and feel guilty if they think of themselves. Any leftover desire of the self is channelled into desire for fulfilling dharma towards others. Duty is wrapped up in morality. Morality is wrapped up in religious myths and stories. It is even more difficult to challenge religion and morality than it is to challenge a cultural practice, which is just a way of doing something, a cultural habit. It is this framing of a woman's life as moral duty and her desires as immoral that makes any questioning by a girl an issue of moral character.

Dutiful good girls must be strong in values and ethics

India is changing so fast, even as we sleep, that we assume that the next generation is already different. In some ways they are different. But these girls are being raised by duty-bound, self-sacrificing mothers. The earliest lessons about sacrifice are around food and these are so pervasive that they are not considered a sacrifice. Keya, 19, says, 'If snacks were scarce, my mother wouldn't eat, but never did she say it is a sacrifice.' Ruchi, 30, says, 'If food is about to be finished, my mother always says I don't feel like eating, I am not hungry.' Since every woman sacrifices, it becomes 'natural'. Srija, 23, argues that not eating when there is not enough is not a sacrifice for a woman. 'You have to make it a point that everyone has eaten first and then only hog on it [food]. It's more like basic courtesy, not something related to being a lady, just being considerate. I saw my mom doing that.' It always starts small and with everyday things. Slowly self-sacrifice spreads and becomes an essential, natural, even though sometimes painful, goal. Harleen, 14, who describes her mother as 'stylish, bold and employed', says, 'I always live with a feeling of killing one's own wants and wishes and loving and working for others, sacrificing one's wants. Not doing what I or she, Mummy, wants to do but we do things according to others' convenience.' Good girls don't ask for themselves. Men sacrifice too. But sacrifice becomes a girl's defining virtue.

Girls as young as 13 use the language of duty, sounding precociously old. Princess, 13, says, 'A good girl should do her duty and not abuse and hurt others.' In many different ways, girls talk about being pure, with a soft heart. Himani, 13, says, 'Our hearts and our feelings must be pure.' This idea of purity and selfless, saint-like behaviour is a core part of the moral code of good girls.

The training in all the other habits helps girls to live a life filled with duty. Girls are trained to emanate a scent of perpetual sweetness, to become ego-less little Buddhas without worldly desires so they can do their duty to serve others. But they are not taught any tools to manage their minds. Just suppression. Girls learn early to cope with disappointment, hurt and pain simply by repressing themselves. Anushka, 13, defines a good girl as having no emotionality at all. She says, 'My point of view is that girls should not be emotionally sensitive. They should be defiant, full of attitude, no emotions . . . Emotions make women weak, they get easily hurt . . . Mom is emotional and I am also. This hurts me a lot. This is my weakness. Whenever some of my friends say something to me, I get emotional. Nah, I am an emotional fool.' Girls discount their own hurts and desires, to refocus on the mountains of desires of others.

An angry girl is not sweet. She deviates from her duty and can blow up the whole sham. So it is important to make an angry girl a bad, immoral girl. Twinkle, 14, like many other girls, focuses completely on eliminating anger; good girls don't get angry. She says, 'I hate being angry, I learned this from my mother. Being angry makes me lose my self-confidence.' Parents scold, beat and shout angrily at their girls for getting angry. Keep calm and carry on. Only one girl, Neha, 15, said she is allowed to express her 'f***ing anger'. For the rest, anger is given an early burial.

Sweet girls also nicely perform two types of activities at home as part of their everyday moral duty: cooking and cleaning the house. This too becomes a core part of a girl's identity. Learning to cook is the most often cited household activity of girls in training to be good and moral. The kitchen, is the woman's domain. *Sita-ki-rasoi*, Sita's kitchen, is a holy site in Ayodhya, visited by many. It was Sita's kingdom. My Naniji had special status when she sat in her *rasoi* and cooked for us. We couldn't touch her, our touch would pollute her, she was the kitchen queen. If it weren't for some ritualized cultural appreciation, she probably would have revolted against the slavery of cooking over an open fire every day for hours several times a day for four decades for a family of fifteen. Traditionally the kitchen is the only source of a woman's power. Many power struggles between *saas* and *bahus* still centre on how food is cooked, how it is served, how much is served, when and to whom. Decades later when my Naniji was quite elderly she told us girls, 'I would rather smoke all day than sit near a smoky chullah and cook all day.' Most young girls said they do not like to cook, nor is it a source of joy for them.

It is in learning to cook, serving food to others and cleaning the house that the differences between girls and boys creep in even in households that say they practise equality between the sexes. Eksha, 14, says, 'Whenever there is some household work to do it always comes to me even though I have a 12-year-old brother. He will not do anything. When I complain, my father says, "*Beta, yeh toh pagal hai*, darling, he is mad, you are intelligent." This hurts me.' Her father cleverly dismisses the protected, privileged son as mad and equates obedience and household work with intelligence. But Eksha knows that her father is merely protecting her brother from tedious jobs. She knows that 'boys are loved more because they are boys' while mindless, dreary jobs packaged as 'moral duty' are the lot of intelligent girls.

In training to be self-sacrificing and sweet, girls somehow learn that happiness is not a desirable goal for them. When I looked closely at the words girls aged 11 to 17, who go to some of the best schools in Delhi, use to describe themselves, 'happy' did not feature once nor did any other similar word. These young girls use words such as 'self-respect, dignity, honesty, selfless, unselfish, knowing the difference between right and wrong, able to face difficulties, respectful, non-judgemental, non-critical, polite, obedient, responsible and patient'. They are strong ethicists. But happiness is missing from their expectations.

Every other habit is preparation to fulfil duty. These girls are ready to become the next generation of dutiful women. A woman is her duty.

Consequences: Duty without Desire Deadens Women

> *A woman is not an individual but a set of adjectives. I have to fall in a bracket, follow rules, which I do not want. Mostly sacrifice is demanded of us and we are willing to give in to those demands.* Shradha, 36

Duty is the core identity of a woman. It is her moral compass, her protection and her *dharma*. The word *dharma* has a long history in Hindu thought and religion. In Sanskrit it derives from the root *dhr*, which means to hold, to maintain what is established and hence law. It is difficult to translate *dharma* the into one English word. Its meaning has varied since the times of the Rig Veda depending on the context. But even as a child of 11, I knew from a year of reading the Ramayana as a family for half an hour every morning at 6 a.m. that it was important and serious to be dharmic, to be considered good. I wanted to impress my grandfather. I was in awe of him. His first name was Dharma, and he explained the Ramayana to us.

Today the word is not heard often in everyday language, but the idea is deeply embedded in Indian homes and consciousness. It means law, order, duty, custom, steadfastness, justice, righteousness, virtue, morality, ethics, religious merit, good work, nature, character and all behaviour considered appropriate, correct or morally upright – the right way of living.

The dharma of a bee is to make honey. The dharma of a river is to flow. The dharma of a scorpion is to sting. The dharma of a woman is to be a good mother, wife and daughter. This dharma can clash with a woman's other desires, within or outside these roles. It is to prevent this clash that the training of girls has evolved as a way to iron out and flatten any sense of self. The only self that is left can then be filled by an overriding sense of duty, to be good, to do good, to serve others and exist for others. This becomes a woman's purpose. It makes sense. It simply makes following dharma easier.

The narrowly prescribed moral purpose defined for women keeps women non-existing, even when they are highly educated, earn their own money or live on their own.

The biggest threat to a woman's moral goodness is her own desire – longing, craving, wishes, wants, pleasure and passion that distract her from her duty; it is anything that makes her think of herself. Thinking of the self is bad. It is immoral. The presence of desire-less women, who say *kuch bhi*, anything goes, trumpets the success of cultural ironing and disciplining. But it also deadens women. And women who have any leftover desire are killed off by guilt.

A good woman is duty minus desire.

What does it mean to be a woman in India today?

> *Too many expectations on women, everybody thinks she is superwoman, she will do all the work, carrying all the expectations, this is the worst part of being a woman. Piled up with all these expectations, she gets confused about her identity.* Swetha, 23

The question '*What does it mean to be a woman in India today?*' was the driving force for my inquiry, and I started conversations by asking women between the ages of 17 and 85 to define what it means to be a woman to them. I also asked them, 'What are the three words that come to your mind when you think of being a woman?'

Overwhelmingly, what emerges is the burden of duty; women feel burdened by the 'shoulds', the expectations of duty imposed on them. Ujala, 23, a final year BEd student, says, 'A woman is a never-ending list where it literally means, whatever comes your way you should just render your service and voilà, you are a good woman.' Ujala also objects to the very use of the word 'woman'. But then she goes on to define herself primarily through the duties of being a good mother, a good wife, a good daughter-in-law and through other household responsibilities. Her three words are multi-tasker, patience and coping. She says, 'A woman has to be a multi-tasker to do so many things that no one can ever imagine or express.' She says patience is needed to survive womanhood. 'She should be able to bear all the difficulties and adjust with in-laws and adjust with every new change patiently.' Of coping she says, 'Women in India are trained to cope with every situation in their life, especially tackling things after marriage – cope with new family members and extend her service to satisfy their needs irrespective of her own timings, capabilities and comfort zone.'

Even women like Shradha, 36, an artist who seems a free spirit and protests loudly at the restrictions put on women, puts duty as the core of womanhood. The three words she uses to describe herself are marriage, mother and sacrifice. In fact most words chosen by women describe the emotional qualities and strengths needed to cope with the duties of being a daughter, wife and mother, in other words, meeting everyone else's needs selflessly. Like the lists given by young girls, women's list of the top three words include: 'nurturing, loving, caring, sensitive, compassion, affectionate, lovable, responsible, good, patient, tolerant, loyal, depth, courage, emotionally strong, social intelligence, emotional, organized, flexible, hard worker, wisher, beautiful at heart, epitome of love, supporting, giving, gentle, the selfless lover'.

Women as defined by women embody caregiving; it is assumed to be a biological quality. Ifrah, 25, says, 'Care is an inherent quality. It is part of every woman's nature. We care for everyone and everything – our close ones, our friends, our families, our acquaintances, our work, our pets and anyone we see on the road, park. We are caring human beings.' It is caring without worrying about returns. For Neeti, 25, this means that women have to be selfless lovers. 'She gives love with few expectations of getting much back.' Selfless is not enough, it should extend to horrible people. Swetha, 23, says, 'Nobody else but a woman can love and care for a person even if she hates them.'

Many words chosen by women focused on the physical – beauty, grace, elegance, fashion and the colour they bring into the world of men. But the other words used by these women were negative. The focus on the physical and the freedom to play with colour and clothes seem like a consolation prize for being a woman. Vidhya, 18, a student, says, 'Whenever you see a woman, she is more beautiful than a guy.' Many like Nona, 25, say, 'Women are the most beautiful creation of God, not just physically, but because of all the important parts they play in a man's life as wife or girlfriend. Actually it will be boring without women; they bring fashion, they add glamour.'

But when human resources departments reduce women's empowerment to choosing colours for the women's restroom, we have a problem.

Women's potential is unimportant

The clash between duty and desire may be the problem that has no name for women today. Women feel torn between the moral highs of fulfilling duty and sinking low into the immoral depths of desire, particularly the desire for freedom. When desire for freedom is made immoral, it is difficult to choose freely, even when it is so close you can almost taste it. As it is for rebellious Pooja, in the opening story, who left home at 21 to be free.

The biggest driver for choosing duty is moral behaviour as defined by society. Simran, 25, a research associate, says, 'The term I have heard the most in my home is be socially acceptable. Be the one that society wants you to be. Don't involve yourself in situations that are sin or illegal as judged by society. Like talking with a boy.' *Log kya kahenge?* What will people say?

But living a life based on other people's definitions of morality pushes women into a life of pretence and camouflage. The first word Sonya, 40, chooses to describe herself is 'hidden'. She says, 'We all wear masks, every day. All the time, I am being untrue to myself, saying the opposite of what I want to say because it is more convenient . . . Women play so many roles. That's where the masks come – masks as sister, daughter, mother, wife . . . enticing him and doing things when you don't want to sometimes . . . blackmailer with your husband, faking illness . . . It is difficult to connect with who you are. Women have potential, but it is unrealized. They study, become engineers and suddenly whoosh . . . they are married and everything comes crashing down.' Many women said that to be a woman is 'potential unrealized'.

Maya, 29, a high-achieving lawyer, says, 'It takes a lot of courage to give up your aspirations, to be somebody you don't want to be, but what somebody else wants to see you as. And do it with a smile. If you ask a guy to make even a 5 per cent change in his lifestyle, he will do it under protest, be unhappy about it, *sunate rahenge*, they will always remind you about it, and not be ready to change the rest of the 95 per cent.' Women, on the other hand, become masters of compromise. 'I am expected to compromise all the time. One example, when my mom's chemotherapy started, it was as a matter of right that my dad asked me to stop my job for two months so I could take her to the hospital and back and take care of her, my brother went for even longer hours to his job on those days. I could never have done that, and even if I had been defiant, it would have been nipped in the bud, they would not have let me go, very simple. If I come late from work, tired, at 10 p.m., everyone is upset; my brother, even if he comes at midnight, he is welcomed and everyone is happy.' She earns much more than her brother. She says firmly, 'You have to fight for years before you get even a little of what you want.'

Women use the words courage and strength frequently to describe themselves, but these words hide more than they reveal. Strength in this context mostly means the strength to cope with the ugliness of what it means to be a woman. Sheila, 38, says, 'You take a lot of shit from everyone around and you cannot break down ever. A woman needs to be stronger than a man. How will you otherwise support people – children, husband's family, your own family, relatives?'

In reviewing the words women use to describe themselves I found they choose many more 'negative' words to describe their lives than neutral or hopeful words. The negative words include: 'sacrifice, disadvantageous situations, defenceless, vulnerable, heartache, constant pain, struggle, difficult, unfair, not independent, judged, careful, rape, bound, fight, compromise and adjust'. Men do not use these words to define themselves as men.

Only one young woman did not use any negative words. For Tirtha, 28, the three words are 'pretty, colourful and red'. Her words could be judged as strikingly superficial, or a learned trivialization of women, who, like colourful birds, exist only to make others happy. Or she is deliberately evasive, and plays very safe. Either way, Tirtha is defining herself and her life.

One word that is striking by its absence is leadership. Even smart, competent women who are fighting for women's rights or running companies or NGOs do not define themselves as leaders. That would be terribly immodest and it is clearly not yet a part of women's core identity. A couple of years ago I attended an intimate dinner for a few heads of financial companies and NGOs. I suggested we introduce ourselves with an adjective matching the first letter of our name instead of giving our bios. One of our two hosts, a former Goldman Sachs employee and now head of a large company, introduced herself as Nagging Niharika. She put herself down in public. In fact, all the high-achieving women leaders between the ages of 35 and 55, managing crores of rupees, chose very safe, boring or negative adjectives for themselves. For women to be successful, they have to appear bland and non-threatening to men. But men do not have this problem.

In fact, when men are asked what three words come to their mind when they think of themselves as men, the words they choose, across social classes, are strikingly bolder and positive. Tarun, 21, openly claims, 'I am God's favourite child.' The words men used most frequently include 'bold, visionary, leader, adventurous, fun, lively, sports enthusiast, personality, trustworthy, determined, responsible, intelligent, risk-taker, independence and power'. When men use the term power, they mean the power to decide, to act and to take leadership so others may follow. Women rarely mention power. Of only five women who did, four feel powerless. For them, power is an aspirational goal. All four have salaried jobs but that did not seem to make any difference to their personal sense of power.

When the cultural framing is so singular and strong that women exist only in one of the three sanctioned relationships, everything associated with a woman gets redefined and changed to fit into this frame. So it is with jobs. Jobs are not framed as sources of respect, power, freedom, knowledge and ambition for women; in fact the personal desire for any of these outcomes is made bad. Women are warned that they will be ruined if they have dreams or if they become 'too career-oriented', meaning ambitious.

Except in motivational speeches, ambition in women and ambitious women are viewed as troublesome and 'dirty', because such women do not always put the family first and start thinking of other things, including themselves. No woman used the word ambitious to describe herself; it is still a dirty word even for women who have taken a strong intellectual stance on equality. There are many ways of defanging work outside the home. Working is made safe by framing it as 'time pass', till a girl gets married or has a child. Many young women described it as a temporary phase to bring in additional money. It is also safe if it is a practical strategy to attract a higher-earning husband. Women who earn money are good as long as they do not change in any other way. They should continue to live and work under the cultural tyranny of the *garam phulka*, hot roti, made by them every night. Men's expectations, too, often remain unchanged. They simply add the vocabulary of equality to their cultural framing of non-existing women. They are not to blame, they too are cultural products, but they need to wake up to the unequal world they prop up while telling themselves that everything is equal.

Nipun, 25, is completing his MBA and by his own definition is a 'cool guy', a liberal who believes 'there should be no gender discrimination and women should know that they are equal'. He sees no contradiction between his belief in equality and his expectations of his future wife. This is what his 'equal' looks like. He says, 'My cousin Pooja lives with her in-laws. She gets up at six a.m., cooks for her children, sends them to school, packs lunch for herself and her husband; she then cooks food for her in-laws, then she reaches her garment shop at eleven, she deals with clients; by two-thirty she goes back home when her children come back from school, she cooks food for them and helps them with homework; by four-thirty she goes back to her showroom, starts her work, leaves by 8–8.30 p.m. to come home, then she cooks food for the entire family, then she takes some rest. She even does the dusting of the whole house and mostly buys the vegetables and fruits. She carries the duty of both work and home for the past twelve years without speaking a word, no complaints. So I want my wife to learn to manage everything . . . to fulfil both duties at the same time, it is not impossible.' Nipun wants an all-rounder wife. Like many progressive men, he perpetuates a system that keeps women as partial humans. It is hard to see privilege and power when you swim in it and when nobody speaks up.

Rati, 23, sums up women's dread of double-duty expectations in their lives with no room for desire, when she says, 'To be a woman is to just exist and do what your mother has done and now in addition do everything in balance, even work.'

Suffering is morally good for women

If the goal of a 23-year-old, educated, smartly dressed woman is to just exist, there may be no difference, below the surface, between these educated young women and my mother's generation. One winter morning, I interview my mother, who is 85. First she hesitates, and then after breakfast she appears in my bedroom wrapped in her brown embroidered shawl, slides under the *razai* on my bed and says, '*Poocho*, ask. What do you want to know?' I ask her, 'What does it mean to you to be a woman?' Her face contracts. She says, switching from Hindi to English, 'A woman must crush every desire and forget everything she wants. She must serve others.'

My mother grew up in Varanasi. She was the eldest child and adored by her father, who, within the restrictive rules of those times, stood by her as she studied for advanced degrees at Banaras Hindu University. When she got married, her life changed dramatically. From being the adored daughter who went out of the house every day to study, she was suddenly restricted to her husband's home in Kanpur, cooking and serving a large extended family she did not know. By the third week, she developed a high fever that had no name and she became delirious, asking repeatedly for Babuji, her father. Her father, who was deeply attached to her, had taken the unusual step of sending a telegram to find out if everything was all right. When he was informed that she was ill, he jumped on a train to visit her. As he sat by her bedside, he asked her what was wrong. She said, '*Yahan jaan ghut rahi hai*, here my life is being strangled, I can't breathe, I haven't seen the sky.' As a result, my father, who was extremely shy and proper, started taking my mother out with him when he went for an evening walk. My mother 'adjusted' to her marriage.

A woman becomes residue. Her spirit is slowly drained from her, so she fits in and does her duty. Yet it is never enough, she feels guilty, so she denies joy and suffers some more, silently. When suffering is made morally superior and is no longer a source of societal concern, it makes no sense to seek escape. In a sick way suffering somehow becomes good, and things that bring pleasure, joy or happiness become bad. Eventually women find meaning in suffering. The final payoff is that silent sufferers don't have to test themselves by taking any action, speaking up, confronting others or asking for help. It is easier and safer to stay in morally superior silence. And the system continues undisturbed, in equilibrium.

Women should deny desire

To be good is to suffer. To suffer is to be good. This lie keeps women confused, trapped, powerless and in limbo, despite education, jobs and wealth. Duty is narrowly defined, strict and joyless. Desire is denied. Women become so alienated from themselves that they become afraid of their own desire. Some women become so afraid of asking for what they want, they fake illness or perhaps, given the mind–body connection, they make themselves ill to get their way. Shilpa, 42, says, 'My mother would fake illnesses to get things done. She used that ace of illness so much, now we don't know when she is really ill. She has forgotten how to be non-ill. I subconsciously do that with my kids.'

Women use a wonderfully safe phrase for not owning desire directly and say, 'I don't mind.' The phrase is a cultural adaptation that allows women to express desire indirectly. In effect what women are saying is, 'If you want to do something for me, with me or to me that may bring me pleasure, you please go ahead, but I am not taking any responsibility for this behaviour and this is not about me.' It allows women to deflect attention from themselves and their desires. Many women use the phrase, even when discussing sexual desire before marriage: Shonali, 24, says, 'I would not mind.'

To control women, desire in women is made immoral. Even though our creation myth is based on desire, as I learned from a conversation with Gurcharan Das, author of the wonderfully rich book *The Difficulty of Being Good*. But it is male desire. The *Brhadaranyaka Upanishad* (seventh century BC) and many philosophers also locate desire as the source of all action, determination and deeds. Desire fuels the mind, imagination and action. *Kama* desire, which includes pleasure and mental happiness, is one of the three essential goals of a healthy human life when pursued in balance with the other two goals, *dharma* and *artha* or material prosperity. Keeping all these in balance leads eventually to *moksha*, liberation from life. Although *kama* in our times has become almost exclusively associated with sexual desire, the term is much broader. It is the pleasure experienced through one or more senses: hearing, seeing, smelling, tasting and feeling in harmony with one's soul and mind. Being inspired by nature or shopping and feeling alive in all one's senses is *kama*. As a human being, a desire-less life without looking forward to anything is a barren life.

To discourage desire and make it wrong, women are taught that happiness in the universe is limited, it is a finite good, which means if you get more, I get less, or if you are happy, others must be unhappy. This feeds women's habit of denying or hiding happiness. But happiness is not a zero-sum game. It does not run out. In the language of economics, happiness is a public good, anyone can claim it, and you can have as much as you want. Happiness spreads. The Dalai Lama, an apostle of caring for others, writes in *The Art of Happiness*, 'I believe that the very purpose of our life is to seek happiness. That is clear, whether one believes in religion or not, whether one believes in this religion or that religion, we all are seeking something better in life. So, I think, the very motion of our life is towards happiness . . .' It is a human right to be happy. It is possible to be happy and be good. Happiness actually leads to more good deeds. Research establishes that our attitudes towards happiness affect our well-being and social relations.

But in women's everyday lives there is cultural space for negativity but not for happiness. Sukriti, 25, says, 'Of course girls should be happy but I feel we are taught that duties come before happiness. Example if I wanted to marry Kamal, I can't because my family status does not match, so my family will not accept him. Even though I know my happiness is with him, I will sacrifice it for my parents.' Burdened with low expectations of happiness, even when women are happy they often don't want to show it, they feel uneasy. Akshara, 32, says, 'I think my mother is scared to be happy, she doesn't like to talk about the good things fearing they will go away.' This is a limp cultural explanation to camouflage the harder cultural truth that women are not meant to be happy, and because this is never directly stated anywhere, it hangs around like a ghost poking at women without their conscious knowledge.

Women's duty is to stay in marriages no matter what

No girl wakes up in the morning dreaming about a horrible marriage. Every girl dreams of romance, love, family and a safe haven. As they grow older, all too often this dream becomes a nightmare. Girls learn that marriage is a compulsory gamble and they approach it with high excitement and low expectations. Sunetra, 27, from a wealthy family, married the son of a family friend in the USA, with these words of advice from her mother: 'A woman is required to be everything for her husband – be a sister, mom, an *apsara* or whatever, a good housewife; be there for him for everything, be everything for him. The only focus is *his* happiness.' Sunetra was severely abused and came close to killing herself but never said a word till her stepfather rescued her and then surrounded her with 'a fortress of love' at home. As in the movie *Queen*, she found her zest for life after travelling on her own across the USA. She still hopes to get remarried but for now she is happy and runs her own business.

Marriage, girls learn, is a core moral duty, the goal of life. Natasha, 26, a corporate lawyer, says, 'when I got engaged I was ready to give up everything.' Marriage becomes equated with living a life of duty minus desire. Not surprisingly, educated girls have pushed back to delay this future. Iksha, 23, who has just got an MTech degree, says, '*Wohi shaadi ka scene ho jata hai*, the marriage scene comes into play. There is so much pressure to marry by 25 or 26.' In many families, 'working' girls manage to delay marriage till 29. By age 30, mothers are in total panic and become non-stop 'hinting-and-wailing' dispensers offering soap to lighten skins, gym memberships and 'super foods' to slim them down, almost pimping their girls and offering them dates with screened suitable boys. And by 32 they give up on their daughters, who sometimes surprise them by marrying later a partner of their choice.

Not all marriages are unhappy, of course. Some women find freedom after their marriage, they blossom with the support of loving husbands, whether staying at home raising kids or working outside the home, or both. But there are many more bad marriages than we want to acknowledge. It would cut into our dreams and the image of us as 'good' people and as a 'good' society, revealing the existence of shadowy, miserable women.

Fifty per cent more women than men are depressed and the average age of onset of major depressive episodes is 31, just as women have babies. Not one young woman received any mental health help for depression. Googling and finding information on the Internet saved two women's lives. 'Housewives' have the highest suicide rates. Depressed dutiful women stay in dead or abusive marriages even when they have exit options. Khusbu, 32, a fashion designer with an MBA, says she only found out that something 'nasty' had been going on in her sister's home after five years, when her sister ended up in the hospital with a punched face and broken nose. And, contrary to people's assumptions, it was a love marriage. 'I was furious and I almost killed him with my words. My sister always tells me, "Don't say anything, *chup raho aur bardasht kar lo*, shut up and suffer, tolerate it."' But even Khusbu admires her sister who continues to do her duty and suffer silently. She said, 'She is so pure.' Despite her MBA Khusbu too lives the culture that glorifies women who suffer as virtuous and pure.

Earning money through employment and wealth are not an insurance against abuse or violence in the home. Naaz, 49, who was abused for years, and found employment in the second half of her seventeen years of marriage, says, 'You won't believe this, I am not exaggerating. All my earnings were only transfer entries from my account straight to the joint account. I never withdrew a rupee for me or my son, ever. *Poori kahani feminists ki*, the whole story of women and money, your money is not your money. I am an example of that. I could not even see *Lagaan*, you know the Aamir Khan movie, imagine.' Earning money and abuse run on parallel tracks.

Many younger women agree with Naaz. Tiya, 29, who works in a large firm and is very well paid, says, 'Financial independence cannot get a woman out of this powerlessness. It's all a lie. When I started working, I wanted to see if financial independence would liberate me. I wanted to find out. The only liberation I got is at times you can buy what you want if the man allows, and next time he will say we need your money for something else. She can never be free. It does not give her independence, you still have to be how he wants you to be.' National-level statistics unfortunately show that involvement in decision-making as it is currently measured, a favourite indicator of empowerment, does not reduce violence against women.

Overall 37 per cent of women in the country between the ages of 15 and 49 have suffered physical violence, mostly from spouses. The numbers go up to 66 per cent for women who are divorced, separated or deserted by their husbands – women without umbrellas. Even in highly literate Kerala, touted for its human development exceptionalism, high literacy and education rates, women get beaten up in their homes. Women in 'love marriages', as we have seen from Naaz and Khusbu's sister, are not exempt from violence.

This does not mean that earning money has no value. It is important. A man hesitates when a woman has options, especially large assets such as land and houses. The effects of employment depend particularly on men's sense of masculinity. It can increase violence against women in the initial stages if men's sense of masculinity is hurt. When masculinity means control, it leads women to tiptoe around men's egos to avoid male violence. The fear of male aggression lurks in women's psyches. It leads even highly educated Bhumi, 27, to say, 'I let him believe he has the power in the relationship.' Culture has the power to bend economic theorizing.

Women absorb the anti-women culture so deeply that they blame themselves for everything, even miscarriages. In this there is generational continuity. The government National Family and Health Survey done once every decade shows that 55 per cent of women, a higher percentage than men at 51 per cent, still believe that women's transgressions, from not having food ready to denying sex, justify a beating by their husbands. And this belief does not vary much between young and older women. Education of women matters, but 21 per cent of women with higher education justify beating women. Wealth has an effect but the middle-classes think like the poor: 62 per cent of women in poverty believe that women deserve beatings, but so do 61 per cent of the middle-wealth group and 54 per cent in the next higher wealth level, dropping only in the wealthiest (top 20 per cent of the population) to 37 per cent. But one-third of the wealthiest women is still a huge number. The majority of women across wealth levels, except the top levels of wealth, believe in their own disposability, even more so than the men. This is true success of cultural indoctrination.

Women should desire only family not freedom

Women are very clear about the importance of family in their lives. Ahimsa, 25, who works at the State Bank of India, says, 'Only family can give you a sense of belonging and identity. Only family members can guide you best as to what is wrong and what is right.' When we asked women about their biggest fear, it is invariably about loss of family and safety of family members, it is hardly ever about the self. This too makes sense.

Most women are searching for freedom within families, not freedom from families. They want to find the 'I' within the 'We' as they navigate the world inside and outside their homes. Freedom is the hotbed of choice, decision-making and desire. A young woman making a decision is therefore engaging in a dangerous political act. That is why *khap panchayats*, local-level, all-male decision-making bodies in Haryana punish girls over noodles, jeans or telephones – it doesn't matter what it is, it is the fact that a girl has made an independent decision that is dangerous. It signals moving away from the 'We', the family and community, to the 'I'.

A woman's 'self' is the sacrifice to the family, polity, economy and society. Since we have not seen or acknowledged this cultural sacrifice clearly, women blame themselves. They become the only self-blaming and self-hating species. This too keeps women in their place.

There are some shifts. Women are delaying getting married. When women are supposed to exist only in relationships, there is no single force more threatening than the single woman who delays marriage, is financially independent, lives on her own and has high earning power. She is part of the 71 million single women, altogether 21 per cent of India's 353 million adult women, that includes large numbers of widows, and abandoned and divorced women. This statistic was noticed first by marketers, who sell cars, life insurance and travel. But despite their numbers, the world has not adjusted and single women remain an awkward social phenomenon who are not desirable role models in the imagination of young girls or other women. They cause nervousness. Their mere presence shatters the fundamental cultural assumption that 'there is no such thing as a woman outside of mother, wife, daughter relations'. Single women are dangerous by definition.

If a single woman is a threat to society, a single mother successfully raising a child outside a marriage shatters completely the story of women not existing outside relationships with men. A few women are forging new paths to an independent self and defining their own mix of duty and desire. But it isn't easy. Ritika, 44, arrived at my house in a blue summer dress with her partner and daughter, 14, in tow. She married at 23 and divorced after ten years when her husband wanted to marry someone else, and she decided she would raise her baby girl even though she had very little money. She went to work in an MNC, starting at the bottom. For a decade she did nothing but work and raise her daughter. It was tough. She says, 'Even in a cosmopolitan city like Bengaluru the social structure around a single woman breaks down, it's not that people want to actively make you uncomfortable, but conversations stall, people don't know what to say to you. For many years there was very little social interaction. As a single woman, everything is easily misconstrued in society. So you draw a circle of caution around you. But you need people, you need support; I surrounded myself with women, at home to cope with the house, maids, crèches and at work my entire team is female. Women school principals were the most cruel. They blamed me for everything. My most dominant feeling was guilt, all the time. I was away from Isha a lot, I had to travel for work. I was always tired.' Today Ritika is a CEO, wealthy, and has a live-in relationship with a committed man, a former boss. She is happy.

In the quest for family and freedom a few young women are negotiating new forms of joint-ness. Gayatri, 35, is a brilliant engineer. She is warm and soft-spoken. She delayed marriage till 34, when she says she 'grew up'. She was confronted with the problem of Chetan Bhagat's *Two States* – she is from the South and he is from the

North. She was totally clear that she would not live with his very conservative mother, but she confronted the issue upfront *before* marriage rather than avoid it and face the *saas–bahu* drama after marriage. It took a couple of years before they could convince his mother that Gayatri was not a witch stealing her son away from her. They met his mother separately and together multiple times. The tide turned when Gayatri said to Dilip's mother, 'I can't live with you, but I will always come to your assistance when you need me, and I promise you that I will take care of you and in your old age when you are sick, I will live with you, but till then I need to have my own house.' Once Dilip's mother realized she may lose her son, she struck a deal that has kept everyone happy. Dilip's mother, who runs a medical clinic, cooks his lunch every day and sends it to the office where Dilip and Gayatri work as partners running a large company. Gayatri's lunch is included but there are often special treats for him but not for her! Gayatri laughs it off as a mother's love. Gayatri has negotiated her own balance between duty and desire that will keep changing with time.

Reclaim a strong Sita as woman and goddess

When the ideal of a good woman is coded in mythic stories and religious traditions, the weave becomes very tight and cannot be easily undone. When these mythic stories are told and retold they seep deep into the heart, mind and soul. They become the instinctual measure against which behaviour is judged. Rationality has no place in the deep psyche. Smart women make unconscious, negative, moral judgements about themselves when they don't measure up, wanting to be free, yet afraid of their own inner moral code.

India scores very high on religiosity, 81 per cent in global surveys. Religious traditions are considered so obvious that most women say things like, 'You pray a lot, you go to the temple (church, mosque, gurdwara), you are good, kind and think of others before yourself. You believe that whatever happens there is a reason.' But every major religion, from Hinduism to Christianity to Buddhism to Islam, ignores women, puts women down or brackets them as sources of temptation and evil.

Sita came into my being as a little girl, pre-dating any cognition, any intellectual analyses. My mother was Sita incarnate. Even at 5.30 a.m. she never looked as though she had just woken up. She would wake up even earlier, bathe, get dressed in a fresh sari, do her puja and then wake us up to get us ready for school. Our family puja room had lots of images and little statues. The central picture was of Ram, Lakshman and Sita. The Sita we grew to love was the Sita of Tulsidas's *Ramcharitmanas*, the common Ramayana in northern India. Sita was beautiful, loving, gentle, kind and followed her husband everywhere. She suffered silently; she never screamed or yelled. She was saintly. She was never the central actor; she was an accompaniment. She accompanied. When I was little, I just absorbed it all, accepted that this is how it is.

Matters of faith imprinted in early childhood are hard to crack by intellectual argumentation alone. Many women, including the great Indian dancers Sonal Mansingh and Mallika Sarabhai, have done powerful reinterpretations of stories in the Ramayana and the Mahabharata through women's eyes. Many scholars argue that Sita shows exemplary agency, the capacity to decide and act, when she chooses to submit herself to the *agni pareeksha*, the fire test, to prove her virtue after her captivity with Ravana, or when she asks mother earth to take her back instead of being tested again after being abandoned to raise her twin sons as a single mother in the forest. It is true, she chooses. But it would be nice if women's perceived choices went beyond self-annihilation.

Four years ago, I was reminded that there are many more Ramayanas, at a breakfast meeting with Amish Tripathi in Ubud, Bali. As we chatted, Amish, the author of the bestselling Shiva Trilogy, happened to mention one Ramayana in which it is Sita who kills Ravana. He said it so casually over eggs that I did not pursue it. It also seemed so ridiculous, so outlandish, that my mind automatically bypassed it. But as I left, I asked him again for the name of the Ramayana.

A few months later, I travelled through Uttar Pradesh from Lucknow to Varanasi visiting poor women's self-help groups in villages. It was a couple of weeks before Diwali, and in every town and village the Ramayana was being recited over loudspeakers in local temples. Dussehra was over, Rama had already killed Ravana, the demon who had kidnapped his wife, and was returning victorious with her to his kingdom, Ayodhya. When I told some of them the story I had heard of Sita killing Ravana, they laughed.

I got to Varanasi the day before Diwali, and on a whim I decided to go searching for the *Adbhuta Ramayana*, with little hope of finding it. *Adbhuta* means fantastic, surreal, strange, marvellous, amazing, wonderful or extraordinary. I walked to the Chowk area of Varanasi, where the street is so crowded that you don't have to walk, the crowd carries you. I noticed a bookshop close to my grandfather's once-upon-a-time sari shop. Stepping out of the crowd and standing in front of the bookshop, I felt subversive, as if I was doing something wrong. My mouth dry, I asked in a loud whisper in Hindi, as if I was buying dope, '*Aap ke paas* Adbhuta Ramayan *hai*? Do you have the *Adbhuta Ramayana*?' The man, wearing a white kurta pyjama, just said, '*Haan, andar aayiye*, yes, come in.' He acted so normal. I bought five copies for security and to share with others. It was as if the more copies I had, the more real it would become.

Valmiki, the great poet-saint, wrote the Valmiki Ramayana which is considered the original Ramayana, and much later Valmiki wrote the *Adbhuta Ramayana* because he felt remorse and unease at making Sita 'always at the receiving end of sorrows and miseries, appearing to be weak, humble and meek, cowering and weeping at the mercy of others' to fit into the culture of those times. Valmiki wanted to correct it. Therefore in the *Adbhuta Ramayana*, Valmiki summarizes the main story of the Ramayana till Rama's return from Lanka, and then in the second half he expands the story of Sita, with a strong Sita as the central actor.

Anticipating the difficulty people would have in accepting this new version of a strong Sita, Valmiki concludes the *Adbhuta Ramayana*, Canto 27, with some forceful advocacy. He writes that the *Adbhuta Ramayana* is more powerful than reading 25,000 other versions of the Ramayana and indeed more powerful than the four Vedas put together: 'When Brahma weighed this Ramayana against the weight of the four Vedas he found greater glory, prestige, honour, power, impact, stateliness, significance and authority in this Ramayana.' He continues in other verses, 'Those people who hear one or more *shlokas* [verses] get emancipation and salvation which is similar to the one achieved by an ascetic who does severe meditation . . . One doesn't have to enter the womb of a mother again after hearing this Ramayana.' That is, one gains freedom from rebirth, the ultimate salvation. Even all those centuries ago, Valmiki knew that men and women would have difficulty believing in an equal and strong Sita. The almost total eclipse of the *Adbhuta Ramayana* probably happened because it breaks the main North Indian cultural story about the right relationship between men and women.

The second half of the *Adbhuta Ramayana* begins with the gods all gathered in the royal court to sing Rama's praise after his victorious return from Lanka. Sita, uncharacteristically, reprimands the royal court and the collected gods for praising him too much, telling them about Ravana's older brother, a thousand-headed demon who had done so much penance that he was practically indestructible. She says that Rama will be really worthy of praise if he kills this Ravana. Challenged, Rama, with his brothers and army, rushes to a fierce battle. But Rama loses the battle. Ravana pierces Rama's heart with a sword and Rama falls 'mortally wounded' at Sita's feet; till this point Sita has stayed out of the battle, calm, with a smile on her face. Finally angered, Sita assumes the form of Mahakali, the goddess of death, 'ferocious, formidable, raging, ruthless, vengeful, merciless', and is surrounded by female spirits and ogres of all forms and shapes as she effortlessly kills the thousand-headed Ravana and his entire army of demons. But in her rage that Rama is 'dead' she continues the dance of destruction till the gods, sages and seers led by Brahma, the creator, plead with her to stop. Afraid that the world will be destroyed, they start to sing her praises to placate her. Brahma calls her the source of all energy, Shakti, that animates the world and creation; Jnana Shakti, the strength of knowledge and wisdom; Kriya Shakti, strength to perform action and deeds; and Prana Shakti, the supreme strength of *prana*, the vital wind force that creates life. Sita refuses to be manipulated and says to Brahma, 'How do you expect me to spare the world when Rama lies in this pitiful condition?' Brahma then touches Rama, who starts to regain consciousness.

When Rama awakens, he assumes it is he who has killed Ravana. Brahma has to tell Rama that it was not he but Sita who destroyed Ravana and when Rama looks up at Sita he faints again at the sight of the fierce Sita as Mahakali. Brahma revives and reassures Rama, and shows him that Sita is Shakti, both fierce and radiant like a thousand moons. Rama bows down at Sita's feet and sings hymns of 1008 praises to honour Sita in her Mahakali form and a little later in her calm, auspicious form. Pleased, Sita blesses Rama and they make preparations together to return home to Ayodhya where Rama repeats the whole story of his defeat and Sita's glory in full court, after which all the gods and subjects depart in peace, and Rama helped by Sita frees the earth from evil.

Isn't it time to integrate this Sita of the *Adbhuta Ramayana*, who is praised, honoured and worshipped by Rama, a Sita who is Shakti, who is complex, who challenges, who is a formidable warrior, a leader, a negotiator, angry, loving and docile, into our psyches, our hearts and our society? So women can be free to be strong. So we no longer have to hear women say, 'It is difficult to find a man who can live with a strong woman.' If men and women have absorbed the docile Sita, women and men have also absorbed the Rama of the Tulsidas Ramayana, the perfect man, who has supreme authority over his wife. It is time for men too to be liberated from the constrained Rama of the perfect man, willing to sacrifice his wife to public opinion, and embrace a Rama who is strong but can also lose, be afraid but still adore, honour, praise and thank his wife for saving him and recount with great pride in public the story of his wife's strength, greater than his own, and then with his wife jointly take care of the world.

Will Indian society be different if India absorbs this story of Sita as part of the Ramayana, if this story is also told in a television serial that every family watches on Sunday morning, making their televisions their shrine, as Rama praises Sita for her strength, as they did for Ramanand Sagar's great television serial from 1986 to 1988?

Reflections

Identity is nothing but the story society and women tell about themselves to make sense of their lives over time. It gives meaning and continuity. We have to collectively change the story so that in the rest of the twenty-first century we no longer hear generation after generation of educated girls and women defining themselves as 'taboo', 'pretenders', 'fake', 'defenceless', 'afraid', 'raped' or 'potential unrealized'. We need a new societal story to give deep meaning to women's lives.

We face three big challenges. To change women's stories and choices, first we need to broaden the definition of moral duty of a good woman and therefore also of a good man. Or as Tamasya, 26, says, 'Give a woman some elasticity.' We need to repurpose duty. We should replace the heavy word 'duty' with the word 'purpose', or two words, 'moral purpose'. Moral purpose, like duty, provides direction and meaning to life. Unlike duty, a sense of purpose does not deaden; rather, it ignites. A long-term purpose provides the ethics and fire to overcome obstacles, fuelled by passionate interest and curiosity to continue to learn over decades. An overriding sense of purpose, researchers find, is sustained by a deep moral commitment to making a difference in other people's lives.

This is what duty can be about if women are allowed to freely define and choose their duty or purpose instead of society pushing them to fulfil a predetermined duty over which women have no control.

We know that women are trained to be gritty, they have huge perseverance, huge ability to overcome obstacles, to sacrifice, to persist. But when women feel trapped in endless, joyless duty, what dies is passion – not passion as infatuation or sexuality, but passion as a life purpose. When this is missing, women become half-dead even when they dress up to sparkle for family functions.

Second, like the Sita who engaged in battle and defeated the thousand-headed Ravana and then co-governed the world with Rama in the *Adbhuta Ramayana*, like the Sita as warrior in Amish's new book, we need to broaden the cultural interpretation of a woman's moral duty or purpose being only to her family, to be a mother, wife and daughter. This narrow definition of moral duty does not fulfil women's huge potential and eventually the fire dims and burns out even among the smartest, most creative and most sacrificing women. What is left are clutching fingers, dysfunctional grit to stay on in dead or abusive relationships peddling duty without love. Women's love without any power becomes anaemic and men's power without love becomes abusive.

And third, the biggest cultural challenge is to get the 'We–I' or the 'I–We' balance right and make the well-being of children and women within families an issue of public policy. The autonomous, independent individual is a myth. In the USA and in India. The utopian community in which everyone is equal and happy is equally a myth. 'I' and 'We' are two ends of a continuum and India must shift a little from the 'We' end of the continuum towards the 'I' end. India's biggest political and democratic challenge is to reimagine the family as the smallest unit of democracy, in which parents do not rule based solely on authority, obedience and intimidation but ensure that each person in the family has a vote, a voice and a thinking mind. In which each person is taught to question, discuss, argue, listen, give and take, and in which everyone sacrifices sometimes for the collective to survive.

We need a new collective story. A new narrative about women and men.

8

Closing Reflections

Redefine Power and Morality

I started this book with Meera; I want to close this book with her. Meera's life is inspiring because she found a way out of fear and powerlessness to build a moral and fulfilling life for herself. Along the way she found support. When she moved to Chennai, she would not have survived without the initial backing of a community of women sex workers who accepted her without reservation, and later an older woman who shared her large home with her. Men used their powerful resource networks to connect her to funds to launch new programmes. But as she got involved in intimate relationships with other men, she was also beaten up when she refused to have sex or get married to them. They wanted total control over her. She walked away.

After her studies in Chennai and Bengaluru, Meera returned to Delhi to work and then left to study in the USA. Her happiness, her full life and her work with poor children eventually inspired her mother to change. One day in Delhi, when Meera went to meet her mother for tea, her mother didn't show up. Her mother, a trained medical doctor who was never allowed to practise, had run away from home. For three days there was no news, her father was frantic and Meera's grandmother started a *havan*, prayers, in the house. Meera finally connected over the telephone with her mother, who was hiding in Vrindavan. Her mother said she was fed up with life in a family where she felt caged and 'choked', where she couldn't breathe, where she couldn't sing. People said running away had become a family habit. Her mother, at 60, returned only after negotiating a new living arrangement for herself. With her husband's agreement, but without telling her relatives, she set up her own house and slowly her husband and younger daughter moved in with her. Now she no longer needs permission to sing, to practise her *sangeet*.

Reflecting on Meera's and her mother's lives, as well as the lives of the hundreds of educated girls, women and men that I was privileged to meet over the past few years, I came to one clear conclusion. Women are well trained to not exist. They live constrained, cut off, crushed, truncated, discounted and diminished lives. If you are not supposed to be alive, you don't need power, nor are you worthy of power; you are then grateful for any power at all, even when you are drenched in fear. Fear about survival. Fear about safety, physical and psychological. Fear of men. Fear of power. Desire for power itself becomes wrapped in fear. Any desire for power, any desire to exist, to be seen and heard, to speak up, to challenge, to be someone, to simply have a name, becomes morally wrong, hence shameful and guilt-ridden. This is why character assassination is the first tool used to silence women who dare to step out and challenge even in the smallest way.

In an unfair and unequal system, in which only men can be powerful, one ingrained cultural assumption is that men are the protectors. Actually it is power that provides protection. Power is the great protector. And when the distribution of cultural power shifts because of moral outrage, men too fall from their elevated perch, whether it is Harvey Weinstein, the Hollywood mogul who has been exposed as a serial molester of aspiring actresses, or the public outrage after the violent rape of Nirbhaya that led to the quick arrest of her male violators and change in rape laws. It is the violation of morality combined with the power of numbers and public conversation that cracks the power system of dominance or abuse by men.

So in these final reflections, I want to talk about power and morality. Our culture bestows power on men and morality on women. This is a stark reality. But we have to recognize this fundamental fact, without assuming that all men are bad and all women are good, or that all men are equally powerful and all women are equally powerless. That many girls and women from the middle and upper classes say 'I wish I were a boy', or 'I want to be a boy', or 'God, make me a man', is emblematic of the deep power differences they experience even today. Women are buried in moral expectations. Not a single boy or man said, 'God, make me a woman.' In fact, one seven-year-old boy, after watching his mother's life said, 'In my next life, I never want to be a woman.'

Powerless women are not attractive models. Women have raged at and sometimes denied, buried or looked away from this societal decision of unbalanced power. I believe that unless we understand power in new ways and see how *power is imbued with morality*, our strategies for change will not engage our hearts, minds and souls; they will not engage women and men to move from fear and anger to love, connection and hope. Individual change is good, but we need collective change in order to change cultural and social systems. For this we need to go beyond talking about human rights and understand power.

First, because power is unequally distributed, women's issues are not just issues about women. Women's issues are issues about cultural systems just as this book is primarily about cultural systems. The focus happens to be on women, their training, their behaviours and their habits. The same cultural systems that train and create women not to exist also train and create men, so both fit together to keep the cultural story alive. Our lives are intertwined. So if we understand half the world, that is, womanhood and the habits that discount women and make them feel powerless, we start to see how they also support a particular version of manhood, the powerful man or the man who must always appear powerful even when he is not. The coupling or complementarity between women and men means that if one changes the other has to change. Otherwise there is conflict, separation or death. Most violence in families is against women and it is by their male intimate partners.

Women's issues are therefore also men's issues. Any change must involve men as well as women. When the imagination of power holders changes, countries and their economic, political and social systems change almost overnight. My research shows, for example, that when fathers, as power holders, get involved and raise daughters more like boys, as people who have the right to be alive, free and powerful, girls grow up with a greater sense of confidence, competence, strength and a sense of self. India's most famous example is Rani Lakshmibai, Jhansi ki Rani, the Queen of Jhansi. She was only four when her mother died, so she was raised by her father under the protection of Peshwa Bajirao and taught all the skills of a warrior that would have been taught to a boy. She went down in history as the warrior queen who played a key role in 1857, India's first war of independence from the British Raj.

Second, bias against a less powerful group is always widespread, and this shows up as a general bias, which of course loops back to justify the system of unequal power. Women and men said, 'Of course women should stay at home when the children come; of course men are the leaders, look at the world; of course the best education should be given to boys, they earn the money; of course girls should learn to cook.' Not surprisingly, then, we find that almost everyone is biased against women. Girls learn these biases early and parents and society perpetuate them.

Even in the USA, hundreds of high-profile cases from Google to Uber to President Trump's pre-election statements show that bias against women still runs deep across society including in the field of medicine. Research indicates, for example, that highly trained American doctors, totally unaware of their own gender bias, are less likely to refer women for knee replacement for knee pain compared to men with the same condition. Two other examples establish the deep cultural core of this bias despite surface equality. Research again in the USA shows that by age six, girls conclude that they are not as brilliant as boys even though they agree that girls get better grades. And parents google the question 'Is my son a genius?' more than twice as often as they google 'Is my daughter a genius?' How do we change this?

Since just about everyone is biased, we must reframe gender bias. We must assume that every organization is gender-biased. We must assume the presence of gender bias from the prime minister or president's office down to the local school, irrespective of whether the organization is headed by a woman or a man. We should approach it as a fact like the mundane fact that all homes, offices and streets have to be cleaned and if the cleaning services break down there is dirt. Bias is cultural dirt. Accumulated dirt becomes filth. It kills. We need to spot the biases. And then we need to redesign organizations.

We read so much about men's biases and prejudices against women, and these are fiercely damaging and need to be interrupted, that we start to think that only men are prejudiced against women. But women too are prejudiced against women. It is part of the training. And this cuts across class. We in the middle and upper classes have tricked ourselves into believing that we are so educated that we are automatically more enlightened and gender-equal. When a culture is so anti-women, when it is in the very air we breathe, how can we escape it completely?

The first time I took the Implicit Gender Bias test available online, I was stunned. I discovered that I was biased against women. I took the test several times, but the results did not change. This means of course that I am biased against myself. My cultural habits went deeper than my intellectual awareness, my work and my commitment to equality. But four years of delving into women's lives and my own life, week after week, loosened my deep biases and associations and my scores did change. It is possible to change. I have changed.

When women are biased against each other, the system that presses them down is the winner. Most women compete rather than light each other's torches and rejoice for one another. This prevents them from uniting to become a force for change. It is absolutely true that not all women are the same, and women's problems vary depending on the intersection of many markers: caste, tribe, location, occupation and income, to name a few. But like the divide-and-rule strategy of the British Raj, the danger of intersectionality is that the more we divide women into smaller and smaller identity groups, the more we lose the commonality, the ties that bind, and the force of solidarity to solve each other's priority problems through collective action, through standing as one. Organization is the key ingredient to bring about collective change but without core commonality there is no basis for it.

Organizing brings the power of numbers and strategic allies to mobilize ideas, strategies, symbols and other resources for transformative change. Pinjra Tod is just one powerful example of a small group of organized university students forcing the government to systematically examine the discriminatory rules at women's hostels.

But we in the wealthier classes do not really believe in collective action by women. We don't stand together. We continue to perpetuate the individual hero's journey, the woman who has to be superhuman just to claim her life. We perpetuate this dangerous myth because this is what we have learned, but this is also what serves a punishing culture that does not want women to be visible or shine.

Most recent books about successful women are stories told of lone heroes. Everyone wants to become the exceptional one, the one who escaped. The successful escapees then look back at the mass of women who are still stuck and say, 'If we did it on our own, so can you', instead of seeing and questioning the prison itself. The mantra for success becomes one of rugged individualism: work hard, overcome challenges, dare, be humble and marry well.

When women buy into their own hero's journey they become blind to the unfair systems that squash less resilient women and those who have not learned how to navigate a tightly guarded male world. They don't identify with other women, nor do they help them. Otherwise we would see strong links between women bosses or CEOs and women doing well in an organization. In a man's world women who escape are afraid of being labelled a woman or playing 'the women's card' in case they get marginalized again.

If the cultural context was equal, we would see millions of female heroes; it would become the new normal, alongside male heroes. Double standards would disappear. And we would not see such wrenching differences in the three words women and men choose to describe their essence.

Bias is a difficult area. Of course we need rules, laws and tough enforcement against explicit bias. But we also need to uncover and transform our implicit bias in our everyday lives. We need to really listen to each other; go within ourselves and pause, rather than pounce on each other for using the wrong language, which just pushes bias undercover without change. We need to question, we need to be curious, we need to explore and we need compassion for each other as we engage in difficult conversations about ourselves.

Finally, we have to explore the meaning of power. We have misunderstood power. Power has become a dirty word. Power in our imagination only means one thing: control through force. It is associated with power over others and the power to make others do what you want them to do. So as decent people we keep away from claiming power. But power is also persuasion, inspiration, motivation, creativity and collaboration with others to achieve one's dreams. In relationships between men and women this vision of power has been forgotten. For men, power has been misunderstood only as absolute control over women and children. In fact, controlling men are violent men. When parents look for bridegrooms for their daughters, smart parents would do well to screen for controlling men rather than for caste and wealth. A single slogan on marriage sites like shaadi.com and dating sites could wake up girls and their families.

Women have been trained and conditioned so well to live without power that they have become afraid of power. The training to focus on serving others and to put themselves last trains women to accept unequal distribution of power. It becomes morally good not to desire or want power. Women disown or suppress their own power. It becomes a habit. Such a good woman may eventually yearn for more power, but it is one step forward and one step back. Approaches that seek to 'empower' women need to tackle women's learned fear of power and the morality that makes power wrong for women. This fear of power is usually not conscious and does not automatically go away with education. It makes even highly successful women from the head of the International Monetary Fund, Christine Lagarde, to the COO of Facebook, Sheryl Sandberg, feel like imposters or frauds. Women are hesitant, afraid of claiming their power; it still feels a little morally wrong; they feel that they don't deserve to be powerful, to be seen and heard. They are uncomfortable with power.

Perhaps the biggest misunderstanding about power is that if I am powerful, you have to be powerless. If women become powerful, men will become powerless. This is just not true. Power is not a zero-sum game. It expands. When more people are educated, it does not mean education is being taken away from others. It means more people have awakened. When Meera started an NGO many years ago that still functions, she created new power in the world without taking away from anyone else's power. And when Meera's father moved from power as control to power as love and support, he enabled his daughter to achieve her dreams, and he in turn was both more respected and loved by her.

And there is another way to look at Meera, her mother and her father. We need to ask why it was necessary for Meera to risk her life by running away before she could speak up or before she was heard. Why did change take so long and necessitate so much drama, when all three people involved are highly educated, highly intelligent, have enough money and love each other?

Each person's desires clashed with their inner notions of goodness that they had internalized deeply as their moral compass whether as a good daughter, a good wife, a good mother, a good father, a good son or a good husband. Morality or moral codes do not change easily; otherwise they would not serve as our inner moral compass. Morality is not just intellectual, it is cemented by passion, by our emotions and we are willing to die for our moral beliefs, our sense of right and wrong.

As Meera was growing up, she often gave up what she wanted when each little decision in her life clashed with what her father unthinkingly wanted for her. She was good, even when it slowly started killing her. Goodness for her was obeying her father. When she was forced to give up playing cricket at puberty because she was a girl, she put on 20 kilos and went into depression. When she focused on biology in school, she became even more lethargic and put on another 10 kilos. But she obeyed, she could not lie and she could not violate her inner moral code. Goodness was respecting and not questioning her father. She became a morose observer until she thought she would suffocate and die. But she still had enough life in her to run away rather than die slowly over the rest of her life.

Meera's mother was caught in her own moral code of inner goodness, fulfilling her role as the silent, obedient, suffering, dutiful daughter-in-law serving both her mother-in-law and her husband. She upheld culture. She could neither speak up about her own desires nor speak up about her daughter's desires and dreams because these violated her inner moral code. Despite being a medical doctor, she could not claim any power for herself. It felt morally wrong. She became a silent ghost in her own life. She was 60 years old before she could take a stand for herself, when her moral code shifted enough for her to realize that she wasn't a bad woman if she stepped out of suffering and claimed her right to sing for herself after a lifetime of gracious service without meanness. But she was still governed by *log kya kahenge*, what will people say, and she wanted to avoid conflict, so she chose to set up a new household in secrecy with her husband's support.

Meera's father played out his moral duty as provider and controller of his household. He was a good provider. He was never abusive, just dominant; expecting obedience and exerting control as his way of being. His privilege. He wasn't particularly happy trying to cater to a demanding mother whom as a good son he had to obey. As a result the entire house descended into silence. He did not know another way of being till the actions of his daughter, and later his wife, slowly forced a change. He had to change his moral vision and definition of a good daughter. It took him longer to change his vision for his wife. He also had to change his definition of a good husband. He found some peace and happiness going between his wife's house and his old house that became his mother's home. This moral *jugaad* worked for him.

If changing behaviour were only about intellectual understanding, there would be little divergence between what we believe and how we behave. We have to wake up and question the moral conditioning and our habits around our definitions of a good woman and a good man, and align them with our broader moral claims to goodness, decency, equality, compassion, generosity and giving.

It doesn't have to be war between women and men. Seeing power only as control pits women and men against each other; it wastes both women's and men's lives, and it shuts down decency, generosity and democracy. We need to question what we have been taught about men and women and reclaim our inner fountains of moral goodness. We need to listen deeply with empathy. As human beings, we are stronger together. Only then can we collectively create a moral culture that allows both women and men to flourish in families, in communities and at work. We need to stop outsourcing this cultural creation to others.

We are the culture. We create the code. We can create new cultural codes. New compassionate moral codes for women and for men. So we can flourish together.

Acknowledgements

It is always a joy and a relief to get to the stage when everything else is done and an author can look back and think of all those who have been part of the process. I want to thank Kevin at the Planning Forum at St Stephen's College, Delhi, for his invitation in 2013 that spurred my curiosity about how young women and men think about themselves and each other.

My daughter Priya and son-in-law Anand were both intrigued and enthusiastic when I shared this first encounter over dinner at a neighbourhood restaurant in Brooklyn. That lively conversation unfolded over time into a research project.

There were many turning points. One was when I met Manju in New Delhi. She asked me to mentor her and I ended up asking her to become my research coordinator. She not only brought some order to my research life but was instrumental in coordinating the young women interested in working on the research project as well as the outreach to colleges and schools. Nishtha, Navneet, Shashi, Anisha, Priyanka, Arpita, Ila and Akansha all helped enormously in conducting interviews, analyses or secondary research. I want to also thank Malushree in New York, Nandita in Delhi and Bharathi and Suchetha in Bengaluru who so kindly gave me access to both companies and NGOs. And in Mumbai to friends at Magic Bus, Mathew and Monica, where I felt enriched by conversations with both young people and staff.

This book would not have been possible without the women, men, girls and boys who shared with us their lives, thoughts, hopes and fears so freely, so openly. Even though I could not write about each one of you, each conversation helped me understand and sift through patterns of behaviour. It was humbling just to listen to you.

My mother, Saraswati, was always curious and consistently more confident than I that I would write something useful. Thank you for your unquestioning support.

I was fortunate enough to be supported by family and friends, including Kavita, who encouraged me from very early on not to stop. They also provided incisive comments on various chapters. These include Priya, Pratima, Peggy, Anisha, Nisha, Manju, Suchetha and John.

There is fine academic writing on women by both women and men whose work has inspired me over the years. The classics include those by the Nobel laureate Amartya Sen, Bina Agarwal, Rita Banerji, Kamala Bhasin, Urvashi Butalia, Devaki Jain, Sudhir Kakar, Vina Mazumdar and Nivedita Menon. I admire the work of activists in bureaucracies and on the streets, who take huge risks so our world can be a better place for all. The work of novelists including Chitra Banerjee Divakaruni and Meena Kandasamy, film-makers, actors, poets and musicians continues to be critical in changing our imagination, our hearts and our actions.

I owe my many editors a big vote of thanks. My earliest helper in framing chapters was Vrinda. When I look back, I marvel at her unquestioning support of my first drafts! Priya's early support at Juggernaut was invaluable. Kaveri, Hannah and Jaishree helped make the book shorter and better. And thanks to Chiki who is always fearless in coaxing the best out of you and then standing by you.

My anchor has been my husband, John, who knew before I did that I was getting into a big multi-year project. He has stood with me intellectually, emotionally and editorially through these years of interviewing, researching, delving, writing, editing and starting all over again.

I of course take full responsibility for everything in the book. I hope reading about women's lives makes you question more deeply. We need to stay in dialogue, until girls and their mothers are free to fly. I would love to hear from you. Do email me at chupread@gmail.com

Notes and References

Chapter 1. Introduction

1. page 6. **It was a small news item in the *Times of India*.** Dhananjay Mahapatra, 'SC Awards Death for Killing "Male Child"', *Times of India*, 5 February 2013, New Delhi. http://timesofindia.indiatimes.com/india/SC-awards-death-for-killing-male-child/articleshow/18357214.cms

2. page 7. **fewer women in technology and leadership positions**. Women account for only 5% of the senior-level employees in India. The global average is about 20%. Almost 48% women in India drop out of the workforce in their late 30s and early 40s. The Asia regional average is 29%. The Sheroes Report, *Women at Work*. India. 2014. www.sheroes.in. See also Rohini Pande and Charity Troyer Moore, 'Why Aren't India's Women Working?' *New York Times*, 23 August 2015, New York. http://www.nytimes.com/2015/08/24/opinion/why-arent-indias-women-working.html?smprod=nytcore-iphone&smid=nytcore-iphone-share&_r=0

3. page 7. **Women's fears keep society stable. It serves society but it costs women**. 95% of women feel unsafe in Delhi in broad daylight. The survey was conducted jointly by the NGO Jagori and the International Center for Research on Women (ICRW). Nearly 75% of women and girls surveyed said they had faced sexual violence in their own neighbourhoods. Nine out of ten

reported experiencing sexual aggression or violence – from obscene comments to being groped, stalked or sexually assaulted – in a public space in their lifetime. Gillian Gaynair, 'ICRW Survey: 95 Percent Women and Girls Consider Delhi Unsafe', International Center for Research on Women, 2 April 2013, New Delhi. http://www.icrw.org/media/news/icrw-survey-95-percent-women-and-girls-consider-new-delhi-unsafe. More recent National Crime Records Bureau (NCRB) data reveals that Delhi remains the rape capital of India, with 1996 rape cases recorded in 2016, followed by 712 in Mumbai. Neeraj Chauhan, '2016 Saw 106 Rapes a Day, Delhi the Capital Here Too', *Times of India*, 12 January 2017, New Delhi. https://timesofindia.indiatimes.com/india/2016-saw-106-rapes-a-day-delhi-the-capital-here-too/articleshow/61872073.cms

A 2014 study revealed that 64% of working women in Delhi said that incidents of violence against women affect their work hours. Women feel that they cannot work long hours or late shifts and 44% say they are unable to be efficient in their workplace due to these fears. Almost half responded that they are looking for employment outside of Delhi and are willing to take on a salary reduction due to safety concerns. A 2015–16 study found that for single women living in Delhi commuting was the most dangerous daily concern. Delhi remains the fourth least safe city in the world. 'Safe Cities for Women and Girls: Recent Developments', Jagori, May 2016, New Delhi. http://www.jagori.org/sites/default/files/publication/SAFE_CITIES_FOR_WOMEN_AND_GIRLS_0.pdf

4. page 7. **The statistics on acceptability of wife beating have not changed dramatically.** National Family Health

Survey-4, 2015–16, India Fact Sheet, International Institute of Population Studies, Government of India.

5. page 7. **Even in Kerala, the state with the highest literacy rate in India**. N.R. Nithya, 'High Literacy and Mounting Violence: A Case of Women in Kerala, India', *International Journal of Scientific and Research Publications* 3(9), September 2013. http://www.ijsrp.org/research-paper-0913/ijsrp-p2115.pdf

Sexual violence against women may be higher in Kerala than in New Delhi. Using data from the NCRB and the National Family Health Surveys, Aashish Gupta estimates that less than 1% of sexual violence against women committed by husbands is reported, violence that is 40 times higher than by other men. The rate of sexual violence in Kerala is 3390/100,000 women and in Delhi it is 1330, despite higher reporting rates in Delhi, 6.15, compared to 0.56 in Kerala. Aashish Gupta, 'Reporting and Incidence of Violence against Women in India', 25 September 2014. http://riceinstitute.org/wordpress/wp-content/uploads/downloads/2014/10/Reporting-and-incidence-of-violence-against-women-in-India-working-paper-final.pdf

6. page 8. **The World Health Organization (WHO) estimates that one in three women in the world experiences violence**. WHO: '1 in 3 Women Experience Physical or Sexual Violence', CNN, 20 June 2013. www.cnn.com/2013/06/20/health/global-violence-women/index.html

7. page 8. **West including the USA, the UK and Sweden as evidenced in the #MeToo movement**. Deepa Narayan, 'Four Reasons Why Even Gender Equality Does Not Prevent Sexual Harassment', Scroll.in, 23 December 2017.

https://scroll.in/article/862413/four-reasons-why-even-gender-equality-does-not-prevent-sexual-harassment

8. page 8. **One way of ensuring that women do not exist is to kill them**. In 1990, Amartya Sen coined the term 'Missing Women' to highlight a demographic fact: a skewed sex ratio meant that as many as 100 million women were missing. According to the 2011 Census, India had 37.25 million fewer women than men. Some villages in Punjab report as few as 300 women to every 1000 men. They have either been aborted before birth, killed once born, died of neglect because they were girls or perhaps murdered by their husband's family for not paying enough dowry at marriage. Amartya Sen, 'More Than 100 Million Women Are Missing', *New York Review of Books*, 20 December 1990. http://www.nybooks.com/articles/1990/12/20/more-than-100-million-women-are-missing/. Sunny Hundal, 'India's 60 Million Women that Never Were', Al Jazeera, 8 August 2013. http://www.aljazeera.com/indepth/opinion/2013/07/201372814110570679.html

According to the 2011 Census the child sex ratio, the ratio of girls to boys aged 0–6, is the lowest or worst since Independence, meaning fewer girls survive in these years.

The ratio of girls surviving is worst among Sikhs (828), Jains (889) and Hindus (913) compared to Christians (958) and Muslims (943) per 1000 boys. The child sex ratio of total population in the country was 918 girls against 1000 boys. In general it is worst in the large northern states. 'Census 2011: Sikhs, Jains Have the Worst Sex Ratio', http://www.dnaindia.com/india/report-census-2011-sikhs-jains-have-the-worst-sex-ratio-2161061.

In Delhi it is the worst in the richer neighbourhoods, Chanakyapuri and Connaught Place, then in Lutyens' Delhi and in affluent South Delhi and best in the Central district. http://www.dnaindia.com/india/report-delhi-s-sex-ratio-skewed-in-high-end-areas-1685769

Chapter 2. Body

1. page 17. **After this initial burst of nudity at birth, the body is covered by silence**. I want to acknowledge the presence of transgender people and the fact of gender fluidity. A girl may have a girl's body but 'know' she is a boy and vice versa.

2. page 18. **boys tease, after all, that is their nature**. Some women too including actor Jaya Bachchan called the new rape bill anti-men as it would punish men found stalking women. Sandip Roy, 'Anti-Rape Bill Is Anti-Male', Firstpost, 22 March 2013. http://www.firstpost.com/politics/sharad-yadav-itis-did-jaya-bachchan-catch-it-on-anti-rape-bill-671277.html. See also *Times of India*, 22 March 2013. http://timesofindia.indiatimes.com/india/Anti-rape-bill-is-anti-male-Jaya-Bachchan/articleshow/19118622.cms

3. page 18. **boys will be boys**. This is literally what Mulayam Singh, who has been chief minister of Uttar Pradesh many times, said during an election campaign in 2013, when he spoke out against the more punitive new rape laws passed in India. He said that girls *tempt* boys and later when the boys lose interest, the girls scream rape. If the new molestation laws were passed, he said, the Indian prisons would not be able to hold all the men as most men would have to be put behind bars. Mohammed

Faisal Fareed, 'Mulayam's Shocker: Boys Will Be Boys, They Make Mistakes… Will You Hang Them for Rape?', *Indian Express*, 11 April 2014. http://indianexpress.com/article/india/politics/mulayam-singh-yadav-questions-death-penalty-for-rape-says-boys-make-mistakes/#sthash.SsveIdqM.dpuf. See also Preetika Rana, 'Indian Politicians: Forgive Men for Rape; Hang Women', *Wall Street Journal*, India Real Time WSJ, 11 April 2014. http://blogs.wsj.com/indiarealtime/2014/04/11/indian-politicians-forgive-men-for-rape-hang-women

4. page 19. **Psychologists call this 'learned helplessness'**. The term was coined and first linked to depression by Marty Seligman, considered the father of positive psychology. Christopher Peterson, Steven F. Maier and Martin E.P. Seligman, *Learned Helplessness: A Theory for the Age of Personal Control*, Oxford University Press, 1993. See also Rashmi Nemade, Natalie Staats Reiss and Mark Dombeck, 'Cognitive Theories of Major Depression – Seligman', Mentalhelp.net,19 September 2007.https://www.mentalhelp.net/articles/cognitive-theories-of-major-depression-seligman/

5. page 24. **half the children in India are exposed to some form of sexual abuse**. P.B. Behere, T.S. Sathyanarayana Rao and A.N. Mulmule, 'Sexual Abuse in Women with Special Reference to Children: Barriers, Boundaries and Beyond', *Indian Journal of Psychiatry* 55(4):316–19, October 2013. See also Mannat Mohanjeet Singh, Shradha S. Parsekar and Sreekumaran N. Nair, 'An Epidemiological Overview of Child Sexual Abuse', *Journal of Family Medicine and Primary Care* 3(4): 430–35, October–December 2014. http://www.ncbi.nlm.nih.gov/pmc/articles/PMC4311357/

6. page 24. **girls have gone through sexual trauma before the end of their teenage years**. Aparajita Ray, '42% of Indian Girls Are Sexually Abused before 19: UNICEF', *Times of India*, 12 September 2014. http://timesofindia.indiatimes.com/india/42-of-Indian-girls-are-sexually-abused-before-19-Unicef/articleshow/42306348.cms

7. page 24. **This is part of life, office politics – go for a better option. I left my job**. Women are sexually harassed in some offices and most do not complain. A new study conducted by the Indian National Bar Association (INBA) found that 37.8% of participants in several metro cities reported having been sexually harassed at their workplace; 69% of the victims did not complain. Mariyam Alavi, 'Most Women Still Don't Report Sexual Harassment at Work: Study', *Hindustan Times*, 4 January 2017, New Delhi. http://www.hindustantimes.com/delhi/most-women-still-don-t-report-sexual-harassment-at-work-study/story-8Efvy12aScvKBsAkoAxy2I.html

8. page 25. **she will be a *zinda laash*, living corpse, for the rest of her life**. Sushma Swaraj makes an impassioned plea for the government to act against rape and impose capital punishment on the perpetrators in the gang rape of Nirbhaya in a speech in Parliament. ABP News, 'Sushma Swaraj Demands Capital Punishment over Delhi Gangrape Case', 18 December 2012. See also T.K. Arun, 'Not a Zinda Lash: Don't Stigmatise Rape Victims', *Economic Times*, ET Bureau, 22 December 2012. http://articles.economictimes.indiatimes.com/2012-12-22/news/35969301_1_victim-of-sexual-assault-indian-culture-female-sexuality

9. page 29. **Amy Cuddy, a professor at Harvard University and researcher**. Amy J.C. Cuddy, Caroline

A. Wilmuth and Dana R. Carney, 'The Benefit of Power Posing before a High-Stakes Social Evaluation', Harvard Business School Working Paper, No. 13, 27 September 2012. http://nrs.harvard.edu/urn-3:HUL.InstRepos:9547823. https://dash.harvard.edu/bitstream/handle/1/9547823/13-027.pdf?sequence=1. See also Amy Cuddy, *Presence: Bringing Your Boldest Self to Your Biggest Challenges*. Little, Brown and Company, New York, 2015.

10. page 29. **And with their bodies, so do their voices**. Based on learning from the SERP in Andhra Pradesh, the self-help women groups movement and further experimentation, 1.6 million poor women have been networked into over 1.5 lakh self-help groups, 8600 village organizations and 241 block organizations across 49 districts in Uttar Pradesh over the last 15 years. See https://rgmvp.org/download-centre/

11. page 35. **initiating other actions that can change one's life**. Charles Duhigg, *The Power of Habit: Why We Do What We Do in Life and Business*, Random House, New York, 2012.

12. page 35. **Sports awaken power in the self**. Participation in sports gives girls confidence, they develop a stronger sense of self and belief in self and as a result they depend less on relationships with boys to build their self-esteem. S. Pedersen and E. Seidman, 'Team Sports Achievement and Self-Esteem Development among Urban Adolescent Girls', Society for the Psychology of Women, 2004.

13. page 35. **breaks all cultural taboos about what girls are allowed to do**. While the middle classes are in many ways more culturally conservative, several NGOs

use football and rugby to change the lives of young girls living in poverty in cities and in villages. These include the NGO Magic Bus (http://www.magicbus.org/), which now has offices in every state in India, Dream a Dream (http://dreamadream.org) in Bangalore and YUWA (http://www.yuwa-india.org/) in Jharkand, whose girls' football team won the international championship for teens in Spain. In Delhi while Jamia Milia Islamia University does not allow girls to play football, an NGO CEQUIN (http://www.cssg.info/) runs the only football club for girls in a Muslim neighbourhood. The girls beat the American team in 2014.

14. page 35. **Participation in vigorous sports**. It is almost as if it prepares girls for success in life. Girls who play sports have better health, fewer illnesses, reduced risk of obesity, better body image, better self-esteem, are more likely to remain virgins, have fewer sex partners, adopt greater contraceptive use and are less likely to get pregnant. The incidence of smoking, drugs, depression and suicide is less among them. Women's Sports Foundation, 'Go out and Play', 2008, New York. See also D. Sabo, K.E. Miller, M.J. Melnick and L. Heywood, 'Her Life Depends on It: Sport, Physical Activity and the Health and Well-Being of American Girls', Women's Sports Foundation, 2004. For leadership see Ernst & Young, 'Female Executives Say Participation in Sport Helps Accelerate Leadership and Career Potential', PR Newswire, 9 October 2014. https://www.prnewswire.com/news-releases/female-executives-say-participation-in-sport-helps-accelerate-leadership-and-career-potential-278614041.html

15. page 37. **Therefore, the logic goes, a good girl or woman cannot get raped**. A 6-year-old girl who was

raped in Ranchi was asked by the principal not to come to school any more, a charge denied when the case got media coverage. Prashant Pandey, '6-year-old Girl a Rape Victim, Ranchi School Asks Parents to "Pull Her Out"', *Indian Express*, 24 February 2016, Mumbai. http://indianexpress.com/article/india/india-news-india/6-year-old-girl-a-rape-victim-ranchi-school-asks-parents-to-pull-her-out/

16. page 38. **Society dumps an undeclared war on women's bodies**. Amartya Sen highlighted the demographic fact that as many as 100 million women worldwide were missing due to lack of attention and care provided to women. Amartya Sen, 'More Than 100 Million Women Are Missing', *New York Review of Books*, 20 December 1990, New York. http://www.nybooks.com/articles/1990/12/20/more-than-100-million-women-are-missing/

Siwan Anderson and Debraj Ray document that the bias against surviving girls and women in India does not end at birth. The authors estimate that roughly 12% of missing women are found at birth, 25% die in childhood and 18% at reproductive ages and 45% at older ages. They estimate that 225,000 excess female deaths are a result of 'injuries', and each year 100,000 women are killed by 'fire', likely to be dowry-related deaths. And there is huge regional variation, with fewer adult missing women in the three southern states of Tamil Nadu, Kerala and Andhra Pradesh. Debraj Ray and Siwan Anderson, 'The Age Distribution of Missing Women in India', *Economic & Political Weekly* 47(47–48), 1 December 2012. http://www.epw.in/journal/2012/47-48/special-articles/age-distribution-missing-women-india.html#sthash.YQYtqMEg.dpuf. See also Siwan Anderson and Debraj Ray, 'India's Missing Women by Age and State', Ideas for India, 11 January 2013. www.ideasforindia.in/article.aspx?article_id=93.

17. page 40. **Verma Committee to reform the rape laws in 2013**. Leila Seth, *Talking of Justice: People's Rights in Modern India*, Aleph Books, Delhi, 2014.

18. page 42. **86% of rapists were close family members**. National Crime Records Bureau, 'Crime against Women', Chapter 5, 15 November 2016. Out of 34,651 rape cases, in 33,098 cases the offenders were knows to the victim. 54.5% of total incest rape victims were children below 18 years: 306 out of 561 reported. victims.http://ncrb.gov.in/StatPublications/CII/CII2015/chapters/Chapter%20 5-15.11.16.pdf

19. pages 42–43. **13 per cent involved fathers, uncles, cousins, brothers, stepfathers and in-laws**. Kanti Bajpai, 'Safe in Public: Women Are More Susceptible to Sexual Assaults from Those They Trust', *Times of India*, 6 December 2014. http://blogs.timesofindia.indiatimes.com/toi-edit-page/safe-in-public-women-are-more-susceptible-to-sexual-assaults-from-those-they-trust/

20. page 43. **This is only for reported crime**. But even so Delhi reported experiencing sexual harassment or assault. HT-C fore Survey reported that rape cases have increased almost four times from 572 in 2011 to 1985 in November 2014 while reported sexual harassment has increased six-fold. Karn Pratap Singh, 'Sorry, Delhi Braveheart: Sex Crimes in City Grow Unfettered', *Hindustan Times*, 18 December 2014, New Delhi. http://www.hindustantimes.com/delhi/sorry-delhi-braveheart-sex-crimes-in-city-grow-unfettered/story-YhACca8Vqx7rb2tjyOZEMM.html

21. page 46. **Only 12 per cent feel safe in public transportation**. Shivani Satija and Amrita Datta, 'Crime against Women and Children in Delhi: Analysis of Secondary and Empirical Data', *Economic & Political Weekly* 50(9), 28 February 2015. http://www.ihdindia.org/hdidelhi/pdf/Crime_against_Women_and_Children_in_Delhi.pdf

22. page 46. **safety apps have been developed**. These include Sentinel, Fightback, Circle of 6, SOS Whistle, Life 360, ICE and TellTail. Actor Nandita Das and Mary Kom both launched phone apps for women's safety. The Delhi Police department released Pukaar, based on GPS, and Himmat – it is unclear how well these are working or if they are monitored regularly.

23. page 47. **Girls cannot leave hostels in the evenings to even go to the library that stays open till midnight**. Pinjra Tod, '"Your Parents Want the Curfew" – Is This University's Reasoning for "Caging" Women Students', YouthKiAwaaz, 23 October 2015. http://www.youthkiawaaz.com/2015/10/pinjra-tod-womens-hostel-curfews/

24. page 48. **have to stop acting like a transit between fathers and husbands**. *Pinjra Tod* filed a complaint with the Delhi Commission for Women which in turn issued notice to all 23 registered universities in Delhi asking for explanations on the biased treatment of women in their hostels. Many colleges of Delhi University lock women up in the hostel by 7 p.m. or 10 p.m., women are not allowed even in the college grounds, but no such restriction is imposed on men. Jahnavi Sen, 'The Pinjra Tod Movement: DCW Issues Notice to Universities on Gender Biased Hostel Rules', The Wire, 9 May 2016.

https://thewire.in/34782/the-pinjra-tod-movement-dcw-issues-notice-to-universities-on-gender-biased-hostel-rules/

25. page 48. **The proposed ban was revoked after a public outcry**. Tanushree Roy Chowdhary, 'Don't Work after 8pm, Gurgaon Tells Women', *Times of India*, 14 March 2012. http://timesofindia.indiatimes.com/city/gurgaon/Dont-work-after-8pm-Gurgaon-tells-women/articleshow/12254740.cms

26. page 48. **made by former Haryana chief minister Om Prakash Chautala**. 'Girls Should Marry Early to Prevent Rising Number of Rapes', *India Today*, 10 October 2012. http://indiatoday.intoday.in/story/haryana-former-chief-minister-om-prakash-chautala-girls-should-get-married-early/1/224182.html

27. page 49. **The 'generous rapist' has extended his protection to the victim whom nobody will now want to marry**. Arun Janardhanan, '"One Day, I'll Tell My Girl Her Father Was a Rapist." Unwed mother of 6-year-old says she will never agree to mediation suggested by Madras High Court judge', *Indian Express*, 28 June 2015. http://indianexpress.com/article/india/india-others/one-day-ill-tell-my-girl-her-father-was-a-rapist/

28. page 49. **Majority of the men took absolutely no responsibility for their behaviour**. Nandita Bhatla, Pranita Achyut, Sancheeta Ghosh, Abhishek Gautam and Ravi Verma, 'Safe Cities Free from Violence against Women and Girls: UN Women, New York', ICRW, 2013, Washington, DC. http://www.icrw.org/publications/safe-cities-free-from-violence-against-women-and-girls-baseline-finding-from-the-safe-cities-delhi-programme/

29. page 49. **16 per cent said they were afraid of the police**. Karn Pratap Singh, 'Sorry, Delhi Braveheart: Sex Crimes in City Grow Unfettered', *Hindustan Times*, 18 December 2014. http://www.hindustantimes.com/delhi/sorry-delhi-braveheart-sex-crimes-in-city-grow-unfettered/story-YhACca8Vqx7rb2tjyOZEMM.html

Chapter 3: Voice

1. page 56. **As a result have a greater vocabulary at 16 months**. Language comprehension and speaking start as early as around 12 months for most girls as compared to the 13–14 months for boys, and girls continue to talk more throughout the toddler years. While girls produce as many as 100 words by 16 months, boys produce only around 30 words at the same age. Anita Sethi, 'The Real Difference between Boys and Girls'. http://www.parenting.com/article/real-difference-between-boys-and-girls. See also Laura E. Berk. *Child Development*, PHI Learning Pvt. Ltd, 2011.

2. page 59. **Schools may teach girls to read and write but not to speak their minds**. This may be a part of the inheritance of the colonial education systems adopted in India. In a survey of 2000 women in the UK more than half the women said their insecurities about themselves started in school. Kate Winter, 'Are Women Creating Their Own Glass Ceiling?' Mail Online UK, 20 August 2013. http://www.dailymail.co.uk/femail/article-2397808/Are-women-creating-OWN-glass-ceiling-Survey-finds-lack-confidence-holds-48-cent-workplace.html

3. pages 60–61. **Having an opinion is egoistic**. Most opinion columnists in India are male. Dustin Harp found

that 20% of all female-authored opinion columns were about 'hard hitting news' such as business, economics and politics; the rest were relegated to writing about traditionally feminine topics such as health and parenting. Bridget Lewis, 'UT Arlington Researcher Examines Lack of Female Opinion Columnists in the U.S.', University of Texas, News Center, 23 June 2014. https://www.uta.edu/news/releases/2014/06/dharp-female-columnists.php

4. page 64. **Arguing still definitely not considered a desirable female virtue**. Amartya Sen won the Nobel Prize in Economics in 1998 and has written extensively on development, development as freedom and the importance of democracy. He makes a case for the Indian tradition of reasoned argumentation. Amartya Sen, *The Argumentative Indian: Writings on Culture, History and Identity*, Penguin Books, New Delhi. 2005.

5. page 68. **but snowballs into something ugly . . . I'll self-destruct**. Keeping quiet out of fear should not be confused with being quiet as a temperament. Susan Cain, in her book *Quiet: The Power of Introverts in a World that Can't Stop Talking* (Crown Books, USA, 2012), makes an important distinction between introverts and extroverts. Introverts prefer to be quiet and need to process information quietly and don't have the same need to speak as extroverts, the life of the party. It is a temperamental choice, not driven by fear.

6. page 71. **It's good karma. It will come back**. 'Karma Remark on Women Dogs CEO Satya Nadella', *Times of India*, 10 October 2014. http://timesofindia.indiatimes.com/tech/tech-news/Karma-remark-on-women-dogs-Microsoft-CEO-Satya-Nadella/articleshow/44769633.cms

7. page 71. **Women should ask for a raise when they feel they deserve it**. However, Nadella did not state that Microsoft would take the lead in equalizing pay between men and women for equal work. In the USA, despite passage of equal pay for equal work, even today a woman makes 78 cents to a man's dollar for the same work. Only 29% of Microsoft's employees are female. Ariane Hegewisch and Heidi Hartmann, 'The Gender Wage Gap: 2014 Report', Institute for Women's Policy Research, September 2015.

8. page 71. **Women systematically ask for less**. Linda Babcock and Sara Laschever, *Women Don't Ask: Negotiation and the Gender Divide*, Princeton University Press, Princeton, 2009.

9. page 72. **Only when biases are made undesirable do they disappear**. In one experiment when a circular was sent to all managers in an organization about widespread bias against women, there was no change in behaviour but later when the sentence 'vast majority of people try to overcome their stereotypic preconceptions' was added managers were 28% more interested in working with female candidates who negotiated salaries assertively and judged her as 25% more likeable. Without that sentence such women were not considered likeable. Adam Grant and Sheryl Sandberg, 'When Talking about Bias Backfires', *New York Times*, Sunday Review, 6 December 2014. Based on research by Michelle Duguid, Washington University, and Melissa Thomas-Hunt, University of Virginia.

10. page 72. **While the ratings for male CEOs increases by 10%**. Ibid.

11. page 73. **She remained a stranger**. Over time,

with coaching, mentoring and accountability, I did get to know her and she did change somewhat.

12. page 73. **Frozen women terribly afraid of failure**. Bob Sullivan and Hugh Thompson, *Getting Unstuck: Break Free of the Plateau Effect*, Penguin Publishing, New York, 2013.

13. pages 73–74. **COO of Facebook, in her book by the same name**. Sheryl Sandberg, *Lean In: Women, Work and the Will to Lead*, Random House Ebury Publishing, New York, 2013. See also Sheryl Sandberg, 'Why We Have Too Few Women Leaders', TED Women, Filmed December 2010. http://www.ted.com/talks/sheryl_sandberg_why_we_have_too_few_women_leaders?language=en

14. page 74. **raised till the mostly male professors called on them to speak**. Jodi Kantor, 'Harvard Business School Case Study: Gender Equity', *New York Times*, 7 September 2013. http://www.nytimes.com/2013/09/08/education/harvard-case-study-gender-equity.html?pagewanted=all

15. page 74. **this deference later transfers to other authority figures, politicians, bosses, husbands**. Sudhir Kakar, *The Inner World: A Psychoanalytic Study of Childhood and Society in India*, Oxford University Press, Delhi, 1978.

16. page 75. **men interrupt women much more frequently than they interrupt other men**. In one study men not only interrupted twice as often as women but were nearly three times as likely to interrupt women as they were to interrupt other men. Alice Robb, 'Why Men Are Prone to Interrupting Women', Women in the World, 19 March 2015. http://nytlive.nytimes.com/womenintheworld/2015/03/19/google-chief-blasted-for-repeatedly-interrupting-female-government-official/

17. page 77. **They find it difficult to speak up**. Researchers conducted a review of 7000 survey and feedback evaluations of 1100 female executives at the VP level or higher, from big companies like JP Morgan Chase, eBay and McDonald's. They found that more than half of the executives found meetings to be a 'significant issue'. Men felt that women were not loud enough, allowed others to interrupt, apologized often and failed to back up their opinion on evidence. Women on the other hand felt outnumbered, had difficulty reading the room, felt uncomfortable with conflict and felt they had difficulty articulating their opinions because of time constraints. Kathryn Heath, Jill Flynn and Mary Davis Holt, 'Women, Find Your Voice', *Harvard Business Review*, 2014. https://hbr.org/2014/06/women-find-your-voice

18. page 78. **My mom calls me *Jhansi ki Rani***. Rani of Jhansi has been immortalized in several novels, a ballad and a TV serial produced and aired by Zee TV from 2009 to 2011. Her mother died when she was four and she was raised by her father who made sure she was taught all the skills of war, just like a boy. Kedar A. Kulkarni, 'The Historical and Literary Rani', *Economic & Political Weekly* 50(22), 30 May 2015.

19. page 79. **Research also indicates that to succeed confidence matters more than competence**. See Katty Kay and Claire Shipman, *The Confidence Code: The Science and Art of Self-Assurance – What Women Should Know*, HarperCollins, New York, 2014. Men apply for jobs when they have 60% of the qualifications and women only when they have 100% of the qualifications because women want to avoid failure more than men. See Tara

Sophia Mohr, 'Why Women Won't Apply for Jobs Unless They're 100% Qualified', *Harvard Business Review*, 25 August 2014, Cambridge.

20. pages 80–81. **Women ruminate and personalize small things and conclude something is wrong with them**. Daniel P. Johnson and Mark A. Whisman, 'Gender Differences in Rumination: A Meta-Analysis', *Personal Individual Difference* 55(4): 367–74, PubMed Central, 2013 Aug. https://www.ncbi.nlm.nih.gov/pmc/articles/PMC3786159/

Researcher Itziar Etxebarria found that women displayed more feelings of guilt and shame and the tendency to brood over even the slightest mistakes, turning that anger at themselves, while men appeared to be more self-centred and their feelings of guilt were mostly towards overeating or excessive drinking rather than how their behaviour affects others. Women are the caregivers while men concentrate on their own wants and needs. The researchers conclude that while social roles may be changing, the feelings associated with them haven't changed. Itziar Etxebarria's research reviewed by Wayne, P.L.L.C., 'Why Women Feel Guilty & Men Don't Care', Apex Behavioral Health Western, 28 January 2010. http://www.apexwesternwayne.com/why-women-feel-guilty-and-men-dont-care/

21. page 85. **Interrupt when they see bad behaviour or bias, and make it uncool**. Adam Grant and Sheryl Sandberg, 'When Talking about Bias Backfires', *New York Times*, Sunday Review, 6 December 2014. Based on research by Michelle Duguid, Washington University, and Melissa Thomas-Hunt, University of Virginia. http://mwr.nytimes.com/images/100000003273254/2014/12/07/

opinion/sunday/adam-grant-and-sheryl-sandberg-on-discrimination-at-work.html

Chapter 4. Pleasing

1. page 91. **In marriage it is reflected in dowries and at work in lower salaries**. In a study at Manchester Business School in the UK, when graduating business school students were asked what they deserved to earn, women gave themselves salaries that were 20% lower than men's salaries. Marilyn J. Davidson and Ronald J.Burke, *Women in Management Worldwide*, Ashgate, Aldershot, UK, 2004.

2. page 92. **Compulsive people pleaser particularly among women**. In psychology, the concept of sociotropy, i.e., people pleasing comes straight out of the research literature on depression. Julie J. Exline, 'People Pleasing Sounds So Nice, but Here's How This Strategy Can Backfire', *Psychology Today*, 27 September 2014. https://www.psychologytoday.com/blog/light-and-shadow/201409/people-pleasing-short-term-benefits-and-long-term-costs

3. page 99. **Reward centre of the brain; laughter is a joyous high**. Gina Mireault, 'Five-Month Babies Know What's Funny', AEON, 20 January 2017.

4. page 103. **Women, the supposed emotional experts, become emotionally illiterate**. See Daniel Goleman who popularized the idea of emotional intelligence and later social intelligence. Daniel Goleman, *Emotional Intelligence: Why It Can Matter More Than IQ*, Bantam Books, New York, 1995.

5. page 104. **The power of emotions and the strong mind–body connection**. Daniel G. Amen, *Change Your*

Brain, Change Your Body: Use Your Brain to Get and Keep the Body You Have Always Wanted, Harmony Press, 2010. See also Bessel van der Kolk, M.D., *The Body Keeps the Score: Brain, Mind, and Body in the Healing of Trauma*, PenguinRandomHouse, 2015. Also, V. Brower, 'Mind–Body Research Moves towards the Mainstream'. EMBO Reports, 7(4): 358–61. http://doi.org/10.1038/sj.embor.7400671

6. page 104. **Depression rates are 50 per cent higher for women than for men in India**. Neena Bohra, Shruti Srivastava and M.S. Bhatia, 'Depression in Women in Indian Context', *Indian Journal of Psychiatry* 57(Suppl 2): S239–S245, July 2015. https://www.ncbi.nlm.nih.gov/pmc/articles/PMC4539868/

7. page 107. **It becomes harder to make subsequent decisions**. Women often score low in tests that involve spatial and temporal decisions, for example, because they don't even try. When encouraged to try, their scores improve dramatically and there are no differences between women and men. Z. Estes and S. Felker, 'Confidence Mediates the Sex Difference in Mental Rotation Performance', *Archives of Sexual Behavior*, 41: 557–70. doi: 10.1007/s10508-011-9875-5. 2012.

8. page 111. **The perceived dark cloud and conflict associated with power**. Francesca Gino and Alison Wood Brooks, 'Explaining Gender Differences at the Top', *Harvard Business Review*, 23 September 2015. https://hbr.org/2015/09/explaining-gender-differences-at-the-top. http://www.pnas.org/content/112/40/12354.full

9. page 112. **Equal numbers of men and women enter the IT field at the college level**. NASSCOM has launched a 10,000 start-up initiative to provide

an ecosystem of support to new entrepreneurs and has initiatives to encourage women. Saritha Rai, 'Women-Led Startups in India Signals Progress for Gender Diversity in Tech', TechRepublic, 1 April 2015. http://www.techrepublic.com/article/women-led-startups-in-india-signals-progress-for-gender-diversity-in-tech/

10. page 112. **Remain primarily at lower- or mid-managerial levels**. Arunima Shekhar, 'Why Are Women in India Still Not at the Forefront of Technology?' 5 March 2014. http://www.thealternative.in/society/why-are-women-still-not-at-the-leading-forefront-in-technology/

11. pages 112–13. **retail business rather than capital-intensive manufacturing or knowledge-intensive businesses**. Catherine Clifford, 'Lack of Confidence, Fear of Failure Hold Women back from Being Entrepreneurs', The Global Entrepreneurship Monitor (GEM) study, Survey of 2012 (198,000 people in 67 countries), 31 July 2013. http://www.entrepreneur.com/article/227631.

12. page 119. **influencing and selling ideas to others**. It is how a person carries herself that matters – confident people achieve greater social status, respect and are more liked. Cameron Anderson, Sebastien Brion, Don. A. Moore and Jessica A. Kennedy, 'A Status-Enhancement Account of Over-Confidence', *Journal of Personality and Social Psychology*, American Psychological Association, 2014. http://haas.berkeley.edu/faculty/papers/anderson/status%20enhancement%20account%20of%20overconfidence.pdf. See also Katty Kay and Claire Shipman, *The Confidence Code: The Science and Art of Self-assurance – What Women Should Know*, Harper Business, New York, 2014.

13. page 119. **It is risky and immodest to shine or want to shine**. Researchers identify four patterns of behaviours common among women that stunt their career growth: being overly modest, not asking, blending in and remaining silent. Jill Flynn, Kathryn Heath and Mary Davis Holt, 'Four Ways Women Stunt Their Careers Unintentionally', *Harvard Business Review*, 19 October 2011. https://hbr.org/2011/10/four-ways-women-stunt-their-careers

14. page 122. **It takes a strong woman, and usually a male sponsor**. Research by the organization Catalyst indicates that women have more mentors than men, but women's sponsors are not as senior or as powerful as men's mentors. A sponsor is someone with clout who actively advocates on your behalf at the decision-making table, putting your name forward for promotions and highly visible opportunities. Herminia Ibarra, Nancy M. Carter, Christine Silva, 'Why Men Still Get More Promotions Than Women', *Harvard Business Review*, September 2010. https://hbr.org/2010/09/why-men-still-get-more-promotions-than-women. Heather Foust-Cummings, Sarah Dinolfo and Jennifer Kohler, 'Sponsoring Women to Success', Catalyst. http://www.catalyst.org/system/files/sponsoring_women_to_success.pdf

Chapter 5. Sexuality

1. page 129. **In the temple of Pundurai, in present-day Tamil Nadu**. Vidya Dehejia, *The Body Adorned: Dissolving Boundaries between Sacred and Profane in India's Art*, Mapin Publishing, Ahmedabad and Columbia University Press, 2009.

2. page 130. **Followed by 82 more shocks to protect their 'purity and integrity'**. The motivation to develop the breast armour is described as follows: 'Studying in a convent girls school, we were taught to be good to everyone around and bear a cheerful smile. After stepping into the real and cruel world we realized that our smile could not last for long as the threat to our *purity* and integrity always lingered on. Since the law makers take ages to come up with just laws and even after that, women are unsafe.' Kharunya Paramaguru, 'Indian Students Develop Rape-Prevention Underwear', 5 April 2013. http://newsfeed.time.com/2013/04/05/indian-students-develop-rape-prevention-underwear/

3. page 139. **are exposed to some form of sexual abuse, and 20 per cent to extreme forms**. P.B. Behere, T.S. Sathyanarayana Rao, A.N. Mulmule, 'Sexual Abuse in Women with Special Reference to Children: Barriers, Boundaries and Beyond', *Indian Journal of Psychiatry* 55(4):316–19, October 2013. See also Mannat Mohanjeet Singh, Shradha S. Parsekar and Sreekumaran N. Nair. 'An Epidemiological Overview of Child Sexual Abuse', *Journal of Family Medicine and Primary Care* 3(4): 430–35, October–December 2014. http://www.ncbi.nlm.nih.gov/pmc/articles/PMC4311357/

4. page 139. **They will become sexually active**. See Ira Trivedi, *India in Love: Marriage and Sexuality in the 21st Century*, Aleph, New Delhi, 2014.

5. page 139. **As well as greater use of contraceptives**. See *Sexuality Education Q and A. Sexuality Information and Education Council of the United States* (SIECUS). http://www.siecus.org/index.cfm?fuseaction=page.viewpage&pageid=521

6. page 142. **Taboos around women's menstrual blood are particularly strong**. Diksha Madhok, 'The Full Extent of What Urban India Believes about Menstruation Is Extraordinary', Quartz, August 2014. http://qz.com/252419/the-full-extent-of-what-urban-india-believes-about-menstruation-is-extraordinary/

7. page 144. **tourism losses due to poor sanitation and hygiene**. Julie Mollins, 'Menstruation Taboo Puts 300 Million Women in India at Risk', AlterNet, 11 February 2013. https://www.globalpolicy.org/social-and-economic-policy/the-millenium-development-goals/52263-menstruation-taboo-puts-300-mln-women-in-india-at-risk-experts.html?itemid=id

Women need something other than unwashed, shared, dirty rags, newspaper, leaves or ash to manage their periods. Sanitary pads do not mean plastic wrapped 'whisper' pads advertised on TV but clean home-made or locally made pads by local entrepreneurs and women's self-help groups that can be disposed of properly or reusable menstrual cups, where there is enough water to keep them clean.

8. page 146. **30 per cent of class 10 students in some metro cities are not virgins**. http://indiatoday.intoday.in/sex-survey-2014/

9. page 146. **What is new is that 30 per cent of women watch porn**. http://timesofindia.indiatimes.com/life-style/relationships/love-sex/More-women-watching-online-porn-in-India/articleshow/48294410.cms

10. page 147. **including Tinder, make casual sex a right swipe away**. 'TrulyMadly Makes Casual Sex a Swipe Away'. http://tech.economictimes.indiatimes.com/news/startups/dating-apps-like-tinder-trulymadly-and-woo-are-the-new-arrows-for-cupid/51836179

11. page 147. **official WHO position and should not be used or quoted as such**. WHO (2006) working definition of sexuality is '…a central aspect of being human throughout life encompasses sex, gender identities and roles, sexual orientation, eroticism, pleasure, intimacy and reproduction. Sexuality is experienced and expressed in thoughts, fantasies, desires, beliefs, attitudes, values, behaviours, practices, roles and relationships. While sexuality can include all of these dimensions, not all of them are always experienced or expressed. Sexuality is influenced by the interaction of biological, psychological, social, economic, political, cultural, legal, historical, religious and spiritual factors.' http://www.who.int/reproductivehealth/topics/sexual_health/sh_definitions/en/

12. page 147. **healthy sexuality, intimacy and sexual closeness**. 'What Is Healthy Sex?' HealthySex.com. http://healthysex.com/healthy-sexuality/part-one-understanding/what-is-healthy-sex/

13. page 148. **healthy sex requires five basic conditions: consent, equality, respect, trust and safety**. The CERTS Model for Healthy Sex is still being used to help people understand healthy sex. Wendy Maltz and Beverly Holman, *Incest and Sexuality: A Guide to Understanding and Healing*, Lexington Books, 1987, Lexington, USA.

14. page 149. **28 per cent of women said that they were not virgins before marriage**. 'Sex Survey 2016: All Sexed Up. Middle Class India is having wilder sex and loving it', *India Today*, 8 February 2016, New Delhi.

15. page 149. **determined to lose her virginity before her thirtieth birthday**. Madhuri Banerjee, *Losing My Virginity and Other Dumb Ideas,* Penguin, Delhi, 2012.

16. page 153. **to be virgins, and in Delhi that number is even higher, 67 per cent**. 'Broad Minded or Bored?' Youth Survey 2014, *Hindustan Times*, 11 August 2014, Mumbai. http://www.marspvt.net/Marsproj/HTMaRS-YouthSurvey-Aug2014.pdf

17. page 155. **human body, fluidity of gender and sexuality in its many forms**. The simplest objection to Section 377 is keeping the law out of love decisions between consenting adults, the decision of who-should-love-who. A judgement of the High Court of Delhi repealed Section 377 and decriminalized sex between consenting adults in July 2009. This was overturned by the Supreme Court of India in December 2013, with the court holding that the decision should be made by Parliament and not by the judiciary. In early 2016, the Supreme Court appointed a special five-member constitutional bench of the Supreme Court to review the petition submitted by Naz Foundation.

18. page 156. **16 million men using condoms, a five to one ratio**. Paromita Vohra, 'Who's Afraid of Virginity Wolf?' India Today Sex Survey 2016, *India Today*, pp. 64–67, 8 February 2016.

19. page 156. **more entitled to sex with their wives without consent and they punish resistance**. ICRW and Instituto Promundo, 'Evolving Men: Initial Results from the International Men and Gender Equality Survey' (IMAGES), January 2011, Washington, DC and Rio de Janeiro. See also Sreeparna Ghosh, 'Violence against Married Women in India: Can the Data Tell Us Anything?', Idea for India, 11 Febraury 2013. She uses NFHS-3 and police data. At a national level, 8% of married women report experiencing sexual violence,

including rape. http://www.ideasforindia.in/article.aspx?article_id=105#sthash.EgWmB2Jw.dpuf

See also Priya Nanda, Abhishek Gautam, Ravi Verma, Sanjay Kumar and Dhanashri Brahme, 'Masculinity, Son Preference and Intimate Partner Violence', ICRW and UNFPA, November 2013, New Delhi. Ellen Weiss, 'Unmasking Masculinity in India', 2013. http://www.icrw.org/news/unmasking-masculinity-in-india/

https://www.icrw.org/wp-content/uploads/2016/10/Domestic-Violence-in-India-4-Men-Masculinity-and-Domestic-Violence-in-India.pdf

20. page 157. **Aashish Gupta estimates that less than 1 per cent of sexual violence**. Aashish Gupta, 'Reporting and Incidence of Violence against Women in India', 25 September 2014. http://riceinstitute.org/wordpress/wp-content/uploads/downloads/2014/10/Reporting-and-incidence-of-violence-against-women-in-India-working-paper-final.pdf

21. page 158. **through celebrating the inevitable changes in girls' bodies**. In some colleges and private schools I did more in-depth work involving art and movement. Young women started with a sense of apprehension about their bodies. Once some fear had been removed through writing and artistic expression, young women quickly took to celebrating their bodies in great excitement. For them, simply talking openly about their bodies and breasts in a safe, non-judgemental atmosphere of women in a group made a big difference. Art and movement release stored emotion, energize and empower. See H.L. Stuckey and J. Nobel, 'The Connection between Art, Healing, and Public Health: A Review of Current Literature', *American*

Journal of Public Health 100(2):254–63. doi:10.2105/AJPH.2008.156497.

Chapter 6: Isolation

1. page 166. **Women's employment has been decreasing even with increasing education and a growing economy**. As India's economy grew at 7% between 2004 and 2011, the female participation in the paid labour market dropped by 7%, from 31% to 24%. Yet one-third of the women engaged primarily in housework want to work. The ILO ranks India 11th from the bottom in the world on female labour force participation. See Rohini Pande and Charity Troyer Moore, 'Why Aren't India's Women Working?' *New York Times*, 23 August 2015, New York. http://nyti.ms/1EdD5c9.

2. page 166. **Living alone increases it by 32 per cent, numbers as high as other better-known health risk factors**. Julianne Holt-Lunstad, Timothy B. Smith, Mark Baker, Tyler Harris and David Stephenson, 'Loneliness and Social Isolation as Risk Factors for Mortality: A Meta Analytic Review', *Perspectives on Psychological Science* 10(2): 227–37, March 2015.

3. page 166. **a term popularized by political scientist Robert Putnam**. Robert Putnam, *Making Democracy Work*, Princeton University Press, USA, 1993. Social capital captures the richness of social life; it is the networks, trust and reciprocity that make it easier for people to undertake collective action. Bonding social capital involves people who are like each other coming together and bridging involves people who are unlike each other. It's easy to get together with three school friends who

tend to be people like you, but a different world opens up if you can connect to a professor or employer who belongs to a different social group. See Deepa Narayan, 'Bonds and Bridges: Social Capital and Poverty', World Bank, Policy Research Working Paper; No. WPS 2167, 1999, Washington, DC. http://documents.worldbank.org/curated/en/989601468766526606/Bonds-and-bridges-social-and-poverty.

4. page 167. **subjective well-being or happiness across 158 countries, both rich and poor**. Edited by John Helliwell, Richard Layard and Jeffrey Sachs, *The World Happiness Report*. The other three contributors to subjective well-being or happiness are GDP per capita, life expectancy and trust in government as measured by levels of corruption. India unhappily is at 118 in the ranking of countries, scoring particularly poorly on social support, generosity and trust in government or corruption. It is below Pakistan (81) and Bangladesh (109) and China (84). http://worldhappiness.report/wp-content/uploads/sites/2/2016/03/HR-V1_web.pdf

5. page 167. **The same parts of the brain light up**. N.I. Eisenberger, 'The Pain of Social Disconnection: Examining the Shared Neural Underpinnings of Physical and Social Pain', *Nature Reviews Neuroscience* 13(6): 421–34. https://www.ncbi.nlm.nih.gov/pubmed/22551663

6. page 168. **Fathers hold power has a big impact on their children's self-esteem**. 'Indian Kids Impacted More by Their Fathers', *Times of India*, 7 October 2015. http://timesofindia.indiatimes.com/life-style/relationships/parenting/Indian-kids-impacted-more-by-their-fathers/articleshow/49257032.cms. Naama Atzaba-Poria and Alison Pike, 'Through a Cultural Lens: Links between

Maternal Paternal Negativity and Children's Self-Esteem', *Journal of Cross-Cultural Psychology*. http://journals.sagepub.com/doi/abs/10.1177/0022022115581011

7. page 168. **Girls receive much less praise than boys**. Dr S. Anandalakshmy said praise is avoided to ward off the evil eye, or nazar, and egoism, or self-pride, ahankar, in the child. Her earlier research was conducted in rural areas. S. Anandalakshmy, 'The Girl Child and the Family: An Action Research Study', India University, ED 379 062, PS 022 603, 1994.

8. page 179. **Without trust, the world could not function**. Francis Fukuyama, *Trust: Human Nature and the Reconstitution of Social Order*, Simon & Schuster, New York, 1996. See also the links to happiness and wealth. Kirk Hamilton, John Helliwell and Michael Woolcock, 'Social Capital, Trust and Well-Being in the Evaluation of Wealth', Working Paper 22556, National Bureau of Economic Research, Cambridge, USA, August 2016. http://www.nber.org/papers/w22556

9. page 182. **Women speak about gossip another 'weapon of the weak'**. R.I.M. Dunbar, 'Gossip in Evolutionary Perspective', *Review of General Psychology* 8(2): 100–10, June 2004. http://dx.doi.org/10.1037/1089-2680.8.2.100

10. page 184. **Solidarity and friendships with each other is more fragile**. Research by J.F. Benenson and A. Christakos (2003) in the USA establishes that from elementary through high school girls had more previous friendships that had ended and that their current friendships were shorter than those of boys. Brittany Gentile, 'Gender Differences in Domain-Specific Self-Esteem: A Meta Analysis', *Review of General Psychology*

13(2009): 34–45. https://shellygrabe.sites.ucsc.edu/wp-content/uploads/sites/41/2014/10/Gentile-Grabe...-Self-esteem-Meta-RGP-2009.pdf

11. page 184. **It is not the number but quality of friendships that makes a difference**. Kirsten Weir, 'How to Deal with Frenemies', *Scientific American Mind*, 1 May 2011. https://www.scientificamerican.com/article/fickle-friends/

12. page 186. **Bringing women together in a forum that is culturally sanctioned**. Pooja Birla, 'The New, Revised Kitty Party', *Hindustan Times*, 15 October 2011. http://www.hindustantimes.com/india/the-new-revised-kitty-party/story-S6g1P3wim3Q7On0GWiymcI.html. According to some, there are over 15,000 kitty party organizers. 'All the Rage: Kitty Parties Get a Revamp', Daily Mail Online, 25 April 2014. http://www.dailymail.co.uk/indiahome/indianews/article-2613361/ALL-THE-RAGE-Kitty-parties-revamp.html

13. page 186. **One NGO per 600 people, compared to one police officer per 943 people**. The Central Bureau of Investigation conservatively estimates 20 lakh NGOs are already operating across India. Dhananjay Mahapatra, 'India Witnessing NGO Boom, There Is 1 for Every 600 People', New Delhi, 23 February 2014. http://timesofindia.indiatimes.com/india/India-witnessing-NGO-boom-there-is-1-for-every-600-people/articleshow/30871406.cms

14. page 192. **Psychologist Brené Brown demonstrates that the surest way out of shame**. Brené Brown, *Women & Shame: Reaching Out, Speaking Truths and Building Connection*, 3C Press, 2004.

15. page 192. **Somehow someone lent me a copy of *Pedagogy of the Oppressed*.** Paulo Freire, *Pedagogy of the Oppressed*, Herder and Herder, New York, 1970. *Pedagogy of the Oppressed* is one of the foundational texts that aims to help students question and challenge domination, and the beliefs and practices that dominate. Originally written in Portuguese, it is based on the conviction that every human being, no matter how 'ignorant' or submerged in the 'culture of silence', is capable of looking critically at his world.

16. page 193. **collective intelligence that comes when groups work well together**. A team of scientists found – through two studies of 699 people working together in groups of two to five – that a team's collective intelligence had nothing to do with individual intelligence of team members but was strongly correlated with 'average social sensitivity of group members, the equality in distribution of conversational turn-taking and the proportion of females in the group'. Social sensitivity is mind-reading, being able to tell how someone is feeling, and has nothing to do with personality but is a learned skill. Derek Thompson, 'The Secret to Smart Groups: Its Women', *The Atlantic*, 18 January 2015. https://www.theatlantic.com/business/archive/2015/01/the-secret-to-smart-groups-isnt-smart-people/384625/

17. page 194. **Number of women legislators or even national wealth of a country**. S. Laurel Weldon and Mala Htun, 'Feminist Mobilisation and Progressive Policy Change: Why Governments Take Action to Combat Violence against Women', *Gender & Development* 21(2): 231–47. http://dx.doi.org/10.1080/13552074.2013.802158

18. page 194. **Access to justice, and punishment for domestic violence**. I travelled extensively in Warangal district, now in Telangana, meeting women members and non-members of SHGs and attended meetings between district officials, counselors and women leaders who settled disputes about property and return of jewellery to women who have been thrown out of their homes. In UP, young girls' SHGs are preparing girls for a different future. Deininger and Yanyan found strong effects of SHG membership on female social capital, economic empowerment, political participation, protein intake and per capita consumption, but not on per capita income or assets. Klaus Deininger and Liu Yanyan, 'Economic and Social Impacts of Self-Help Groups in India', World Bank Policy Research Working Paper No. 4884, 1 March 2009. https://ssrn.com/abstract=1372961

Chapter 7: Identity

1. page 202. **It evoked an outpouring of anger**. Abhinav Garg, 'Defence Lawyers Blame Nirbhaya for Rape', *Times of India*, 4 March 2015. https://timesofindia.indiatimes.com/india/Defence-lawyers-blame-Nirbhaya-for-rape/articleshow/46451407.cms. See also Reported by Ketki Angre, Edited by Sugam Singhal, 'Outrage Over Defence Lawyers' Comments in Nirbhaya Documentary', 5 March 2015. http://www.ndtv.com/india-news/outrage-over-defence-lawyers-comments-in-nirbhaya-documentary-744572

2. page 203. **A woman is not an Indian category at all**. Author of more than 20 scholarly books, Sudhir Kakar has delved into the richness of Indian culture and

deep psyche. Interview, Goa, 5 February 2014. See also Sudhir Kakar, 'We Are Caught between Extremes of Traditional and Western Perspectives on Women', *Times of India*, 9 July 2013. http://timesofindia.indiatimes.com/edit-page/We-are-caught-between-extremes-of-traditional-and-western-perspectives-on-women/articleshowprint/17944379.cms

3. page 208. **Its meaning has varied from the times of the Rig Veda depending on the context**. 'Dharma', from Wikipedia, the free encyclopedia. https://en.wikipedia.org/wiki/Dharma. See also Gurcharan Das's beautifully written book focused on characters from the Mahabharata. *The Difficulty of Being Good: On the Subtle Art of Dharma*, Allen Lane, Penguin Books, New Delhi, 2009.

4. page 212. **The problem that has no name for women today**. This is the language used by Betty Friedan when she first articulated the problem of women of her generation in 1950s USA when women were meant to be deliriously happy doing housework and buying new household gadgets to help them clean. Betty Friedan, *The Feminine Mystique*, W.W. Norton and Co. Inc., New York, 2001.

5. page 220. **A conversation with Gurcharan Das**. 17 October 2014. See also Gurcharan Das, 'Desire or Dharma: Dilemma that Is as Old as the Vedas', *Times of India*, 8 December 2013. http://blogs.timesofindia.indiatimes.com/men-and-ideas/desire-or-dharma-dilemma-that-is-as-old-as-the-vedas/

Book 10 of the Rig Veda describes the creation of the world thus: 'Thereafter rose desire in the beginning'. The Hymns of the Rig Veda, Book X, Hymn CXXIX, Verse

4, p. 575. Ralph T.H. Griffith, translator, 1895. https://archive.org/stream/hymnsrigveda00unkngoog#page/n580/mode/2up. Kama: https://en.wikipedia.org/wiki/Kama

6. page 220. **The term is much broader**. See also Sudhir Kakar's novel which is a dialogue between a student and Vatsayana, the author of the Kamasutra: *The Ascetic of Desire: A Novel of the Kamasutra*, Overlook Press, Woodstock, New York, 2000.

7. page 221. **Happiness actually leads to more good deeds**. Lalin Anik, Lara B. Aknin, Michael I. Norton and Elizabeth W. Dunn, *Feeling Good about Giving: The Benefits (and Costs) of Self-Interested Charitable Behavior*, Harvard Business School. Working Paper, 10–12, Draft, 2009. http://www.hbs.edu/faculty/Publication%20Files/10-012.pdf

8. page 221. **Happiness affects our well-being and social relations**. Kira Newman, 'What Words Do You Associate with Happiness?' Greater Good Science Center, Berkeley, 27 February 2017. http//greatergood.berkeley.edu/article

9. page 223. **Major depressive episodes is 31, just as women have babies**. Kounteya Sinha, 'Women More Prone to Depression Than Men, Indians Worst Hit: WHO', *Times of India*, 10 October 2012. http://timesofindia.indiatimes.com/india/Women-more-prone-to-depression-than-men-Indians-worst-hit-WHO/articleshow/16746142.cms

10. page 223. **'House-wives' have the highest suicide rates**. According to the NCRB data over two decades, every fifth suicide in India is by a housewife. And though farmer suicides, in comparison, are a much smaller

fraction (5%) and have fortunately witnessed a sharp decline over the last ten years, the rates for housewives have not declined. Shamika Ravi, 'Indian Housewives: A Cry for Help', *Times of India*, 26 November 2015. https://blogs.timesofindia.indiatimes.com/shamika-ravi-blog/indian-housewives-a-cry-for-help/

11. page 225. **between the ages of 15 and 49 have suffered physical violence, mostly from spouses.** India's National Family Health Survey-3, carried out in 29 states during 2005–06, found Bihar to be the most violent, with the abuse rate against married women being as high as 59%. It was followed by Madhya Pradesh (45.8%), Rajasthan (46.3%), Manipur (43.9%), Uttar Pradesh (42.4%), Tamil Nadu (41.9%) and West Bengal (40.3%). These figures are likely to be significantly underestimated given that violence within families continues to be a taboo subject everywhere. Violence rates have gone down in Bihar. Ravneet Kaur and Suneela Garg, 'Addressing Domestic Violence against Women: An Unfinished Agenda', *Indian Journal of Community Medicine* 33(2): 73–76.

12. page 225. **Even in highly literate Kerala, touted for its human development exceptionalism.** Barbara Burton, Nata Duvvury and Nisha Varia, 'Domestic Violence in India: A Summary Report of a Multi-Site Household Survey', International Clinical Epidemiologists Network (INCLEN), International Center for Research on Women, May 2000, Washington, DC. https://www.icrw.org/publications/domestic-violence-in-india-part-3/

Thiruvananthapuram, the capital city of Kerala, ranks first among five cities in India in prevalence of domestic violence. Violence in Thiruvananthapuram is about 64% in urban non-slum areas, higher than in Delhi, Lucknow,

Chennai and Vellore. It was 71% in rural areas, higher than in Delhi, Bhopal, Lucknow, Nagpur and Vellore.

13. page 225. **Naaz and Khusbu's sister, are also not exempt from violence**. C.H. Rocca, S. Rathod, T. Falle, R.P. Pande and S. Krishnan, 'Challenging Assumptions about Women's Empowerment: Social and Economic Resources and Domestic Violence among Young Married Women in Urban South India', *International Journal of Epidemiology* 38(2009): 577–85. See also Purnima Madhivanan, MBBS, MPH, PhD, Karl Krupp, MPH, and Arthur Reingold, MD, 'Correlates of Intimate Partner Physical Violence among Young Reproductive Age Women in Mysore, India', *Asia Pacific Journal of Public Health* 26(2): 169–81.

14. page 225. **Especially large assets like land and houses**. The study does not find links to higher economic status or educational attainment of husband or wife or matrilineal inheritance. Rather the key factor is ownership of large property. Women who owned both land and a house suffered the lowest physical or psychological violence. See Pradeep Panda and Bina Agarwal, 'Marital Violence, Human Development and Women's Property Status in India', World Development Report 33(5): 823–50, 2005.

15. page 225. **In the initial stages if men's sense of masculinity is hurt**. See S. Vyas and C. Watts, 'How Does Economic Empowerment Affect Women's Risk of Intimate Partner Violence in Low and Middle Income Countries? A Systematic Review of Published Evidence', *Journal of International Development* 21(5): 577–602.

Some researchers treat women's work status and violence as simultaneously determined and find that women's engagement in paid work and ownership of property are associated with sharp reductions in marital violence. Manasi Bhattacharya, Arjun S. Bedi and Amrita Chhachhi, 'Marital Violence and Women's Employment and Property Status: Evidence from North Indian Villages', Forschungsinstitut zur Zukunft der Arbeit, Institute for the Study of Labor, IZA DP No. 4361, Bonn, Germany, August 2009. http://ftp.iza.org/dp4361.pdf

The complex relationship between local context and employment has important implications for programmes that aim to reduce violence. See Mara Bolis and Christine Hughes, 'Women's Economic Empowerment and Domestic Violence Links and Lessons for Practitioners Working with Intersectional Approaches', Oxfam Intersectionality series, 2015. https://www.oxfamamerica.org/static/media/files/Womens_Empowerment_and_Domestic_Violence_-_Boris__Hughes_hX7LscW.pdf

16. page 226. **This belief does not vary much between young and older women**. While there is a strong relationship with education, 21% of women with higher education justify wife-beating. National Family Health Survey (NFHS-3), 2005–06: India: Volume I. Mumbai: International Institute for Population Sciences and Macro International. 2007. http://pdf.usaid.gov/pdf_docs/Pnadk385.pdf. See also NFHS-III: 40% of Indian women face domestic violence. Info Change Women, 17 June2016. http://infochangeindia.org/women/news/nfhs-iii-40-of-indian-women-face-domestic-violence.html

17. page 227. **She is part of the 71 million single women**. Rachi Salve, '71 Million Single Women, 39% Rise Over a Decade', 14 November 2015. https://

thewire.in/15616/71-million-single-women-39-rise-over-a-decade/

18. page 230. **India scores very high on religiosity, 81 per cent in global surveys**. 'Win-Gallup International Global Index of Religiosity and Atheism', Press Release, 2012. http://www.wingia.com/web/files/news/14/file/14.pdf

19. page 231. **Being abandoned to raise her twin sons as a single mother in the forest**. See also the great anthology that includes women and men scholars and artists edited by Malashri Lala and Namita Gokhale: *In Search of Sita: Revisiting Mythology*, Yatra Books and Penguin Books, New Delhi, 2009; and Devdutt Pattanaik, *Sita: An Illustrated Retelling of the Ramayana*, Penguin, New Delhi, 2013.

20. page 232. **The more copies I had, the more real it would become**. It included the Sanskrit text and English commentary by Sri Ajai Kumar Chhawachharia, a Rama devotee and scholar who also translated the *Adhyatma Ramayan*, focusing on Rama, and the Upanishads in five volumes.

21. page 232. **To fit into the culture of those times**. This is from the translation of the *Adbhuta Ramayan* by Sri Ajai Kumar Chhawachharia. It includes the shlokas in Sanskrit (page 305). He lives in Ayodhya and describes himself as a humble bachelor in service to the perfect lord. *Adbhuta Ramayan*, Commentary by Sri Ajai Kumar Chhawchharia, Chaukhamba Surbharati Prakashan, Varanasi, 2010.

22. page 236. **A deep commitment to making a difference in other people's lives**. Angela Duckworth,

Grit. The Power of Passion and Perseverance, Simon & Schuster, New York, 2016.

23. page 236. **Dress up to sparkle for family functions**. This framing is taken from Angela Duckworth's excellent book *Grit*, which reflects her decades of work starting as a young graduate student looking for a theory to explain differences in student achievement.

24. page 237. **Men's power without love becomes abusive**. Inspired by Martin Luther King Jr's famous quote: 'What is needed is a realization that power without love is reckless and abusive, and love without power is sentimental and anaemic.' http://www.wisdomquotes.com/quote/martin-luther-king-jr-31.htm. See also Adam Kahane, *Power and Love: A Theory and Practice of Social Change*, Berrett-Koehler, 2010.

Chapter 8: Closing Reflections

1. page 245. **Totally unaware of their *implicit* gender bias**. Jessica Nordell, 'A Fix for Gender Bias in Health Care', *New York Times*, 11 January 2017. https://www.nytimes.com/2017/01/11/opinion/a-fix-for-gender-bias-in-health-care-check.html.

2. page 245. **Girls conclude that they are not as brilliant as boys**. Lin Bian, Sarah-Jane Leslie and Andrei Cimpian, 'Gender Stereotypes about Intellectual Ability Emerge Early and Influence Children's Interests', *Science* 355(6323): 389–91, 27 January 2017. http://science.sciencemag.org/content/355/6323/389

3. page 245. **Is my daughter a genius**. Andrei Cimpian and Sarah-Jane Leslie, 'Why Young Girls Don't Think

They Are Smart Enough', *New York Times*, 26 January 2017, New York. https://www.nytimes.com/2017/01/26/well/family/why-young-girls-dont-think-they-are-smart-enough.html

4. page 246. **Implicit Gender Bias test available online, I was stunned**. Implicit Gender Bias test. Harvard Implicit Association Test – Project Implicit, Harvard University. https://implicit.harvard.edu/implicit/india/takeatest.html. See the work of Mahzarin R. Banaji and Anthony G. Greenwald, *Blindspot: Hidden Biases of Good People*, Delacorte Press, New York, 2013.

5. page 249. **to the COO of Facebook, Sheryl Sandberg, feel like imposters or frauds**. See Katty Kay and Claire Shipman, *The Confidence Code: The Science and Art of Self-Assurance – What Women Should Know*, HarperCollins, New York, 2014.

AN EXTENSIVE LIBRARY

Fresh new original Juggernaut books from the likes of Sunny Leone, Twinkle Khanna, Rujuta Diwekar, William Dalrymple, Pankaj Mishra, Arundhati Roy and lots more. Plus, books from partner publishers and all the free classics you want.

www.juggernaut.in

Ask authors questions

Get all your answers from the horse's mouth. Juggernaut authors actually reply to every question they can.

Rate and review

Let everyone know of your favourite reads or critique the finer points of a book – you will be heard in a community of like-minded readers.

Gift books to friends

For a book-lover, there's no nicer gift than a book personally picked. You can even do it anonymously if you like.

Enjoy new book formats

Discover serials released in parts over time, picture books including comics, and story-bundles at discounted rates.

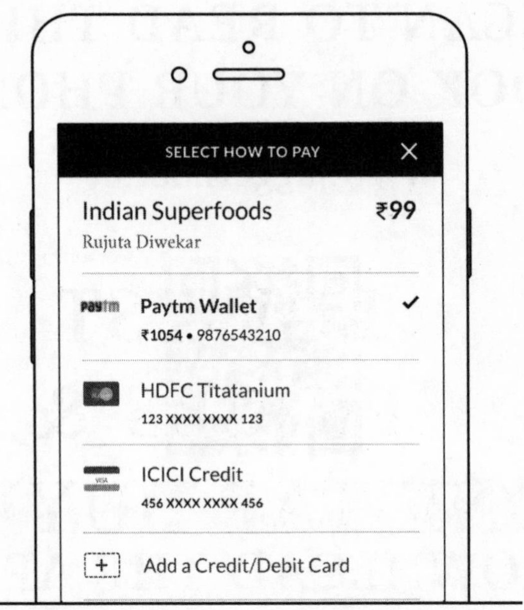

Paytm Wallet, Cards & Apple Payments

On Android, just add a Paytm Wallet once and buy any book with one tap. On iOS, pay with one tap with your iTunes-linked debit/credit card.

Click the QR Code with a QR scanner app
or type the link into the Internet browser
on your phone to download the app.

SCAN TO READ THIS BOOK ON YOUR PHONE

www.juggernaut.in

DOWNLOAD THE APP

www.juggernaut.in

For our complete catalogue, visit www.juggernaut.in
To submit your book, send a synopsis and two
sample chapters to books@juggernaut.in
For all other queries, write to contact@juggernaut.in